Stress Management For Dummies®

Cheat

P9-DNW-709

The Stress-Symptom Scale

Rate the frequency with which you've experienced each of the items listed below. Take the last two weeks as your time frame. Use this helpful rating scale:

- 0 = Never
- 1 = Sometimes
- 2 = Often
- 3 = Very often

Fatigue or tiredness	_____	Feeling helpless or hopeless	_____
Pounding heart	_____	Excessive drinking	_____
Rapid pulse	_____	Excessive smoking	_____
Increased perspiration	_____	Excessive spending	_____
Rapid breathing	_____	Excessive drug or medication use	_____
Aching neck or shoulders	_____	Feeling upset	_____
Low back pain	_____	Feeling nervous or anxious	_____
Gritting teeth or clenching jaw	_____	Increased irritability	_____
Hives or skin rash	_____	Worrisome thoughts	_____
Headaches	_____	Impatience	_____
Cold hands or feet	_____	Feelings of depression	_____
Tightness in chest	_____	Loss of sexual interest	_____
Nausea	_____	Feeling angry	_____
Diarrhea or constipation	_____	Sleep difficulties	_____
Stomach discomfort	_____	Forgetfulness	_____
Nail biting	_____	Racing or intrusive thoughts	_____
Twitches or tics	_____	Feeling restless	_____
Difficulty swallowing or dry mouth	_____	Difficulty concentrating	_____
Colds or flu	_____	Periods of crying	_____
Lack of energy	_____	Frequent absences from work	_____
Overeating	_____	**Your total Stress-Symptom Score**	_____

Your Stress Rating

Your Score	Your Comparative Rating
0 – 19	Lower than average
20 – 39	Average
40 – 49	Moderately higher than average
50 and above	Much higher than average

Use Your Imagination to Deal with Stress

If you can replace that stress-producing thought or image with one that is relaxing, chances are that you'll feel much better. Here's how:

1. **Find a place where you won't be disturbed for a few minutes, and get comfortable, either sitting in a favorite chair or lying down.**

2. **Think of an image — a place, a scene, a memory — that relaxes you.**

   Use all your senses to bring that imagined scene to life. Ask yourself: What do I see? What can I hear? What can I smell? What can I feel?

3. **Let yourself become completely immersed in your image, allowing it to relax you completely.**

Try Progressive Relaxation

The following technique is highly effective and has been proven to be a valuable tool for quickly reducing muscle tension and promoting relaxation.

1. **Lie down or sit, as comfortably as you can, and close your eyes.**

   Find a quiet, dimly lit place that gives you some privacy, at least for a while.

2. **Tense the muscles of a particular body part.**

   Begin by simply making a fist. As you clench your fist, notice the tension and strain in your hand and forearm. Without releasing that tension, bend your right arm and flex your biceps, making a muscle the way you might to impress the kids in the school-yard.

   Do not strain yourself in any of these muscle tensing maneuvers; don't overdo it. When you tense a muscle group, don't tense as hard as you can. Tense about three-quarters of what you can do. If you feel pain or soreness, ease up on the tension, and if you still hurt, defer your practice till another time.

3. **Hold the tension in the body part for about seven seconds.**

4. **Let go of the tension fairly quickly, letting the muscles go limp.**

   Notice the difference in the way your hand and arm feels. Notice the difference in feelings between the sensations of tension and those of relaxation. Let these feelings of relaxation deepen for about 30 seconds or so.

5. **Repeat Steps 1 through 4, using the same muscle group.**

6. **Move to another muscle group.**

   Simply repeat Steps 1 through 4, substituting a different muscle group each time. Continue with your left hand and arm, and then work your way through other major muscle groups.

For Dummies: Bestselling Book Series for Beginners

Stress Management

FOR

DUMMIES®

Stress Management FOR DUMMIES®

by Allen Elkin, Ph.D.

Foreword by Paul J. Rosch, M.D., F.A.C.P.

Wiley Publishing, Inc.

Stress Management For Dummies®

Published by
Wiley Publishing, Inc.
909 Third Avenue
New York, NY 10022
www.wiley.com

Copyright © 1999 by Wiley Publishing, Inc., Indianapolis, Indiana

Published simultaneously in Canada

For general information on our other products and services or to obtain technical support, please contact our Customer Care Department within the U.S. at 800-762-2974, outside the U.S. at 317-572-3993, or fax 317-572-4002.

Wiley also publishes its books in a variety of electronic formats. Some content that appears in print may not be available in electronic books.

Library of Congress Cataloging-in-Publication Data:

Library of Congress Catalog Card No.: 99-65863

ISBN: 0-7645-5144-2

Manufactured in the United States of America

10 9 8

1O/TR/QZ/QS/IN

About the Author

Allen Elkin, Ph.D., is a clinical psychologist, a certified sex therapist, and the director of The Stress Management & Counseling Center in New York City. Nationally known for his expertise in the field of stress and emotional disorders, he has appeared frequently on *Today, Good Morning America,* and *Good Day New York,* as well as programs of PBS, CNN, FNN, Fox 5, and National Public Radio. He has been quoted in *The New York Times, The Wall Street Journal, The Washington Post, Newsweek, Men's Health, Fitness, Cosmopolitan, Glamour, Redbook, Woman's Day, Self, Mademoiselle, McCall's, Parents,* and other publications. Dr. Elkin holds workshops and presentations for professional organizations and corporations, including the American Society of Contemporary Medicine and Surgery, the Drug Enforcement Agency, Morgan Stanley, IBM, PepsiCo, and the New York Stock Exchange.

His first book, *Urban Ease: Stress-Free Living in the Big City,* was published by Penguin Putnam (Plume, 1999).

When he's not talking about stress, you can probably find him at his home on the Upper West Side of Manhattan, where he lives with his wife, Beth, their two children, Josh and Katy, and their two cats, Skittles and Sophie.

Dedication

To my wife, Beth, my best friend, and our children, Josh and Katy, who bring us great joy.

Author's Acknowledgments

First, and certainly foremost, I would like to thank my wife Beth who not only tolerated all the stress and tension that came with writing this book, but also helped me edit the manuscript and kept me on track when I got lost. Her caring patience and sense of humor made writing this book much less stressful than it might have been.

And my kids, Josh and Katy, who were mildly deprived by having a father who was chained to his keyboard. Daddy can come out and play now.

Special thanks are due to Tami Booth, Executive Editor at Hungry Minds, for her warm support and constant encouragement. Thanks are due to Brian Kramer and Tim Gallan who did marvellous jobs as Project Editors. I would also like to thank the many other wonderful people at HMI for their attention and care in turning an idea into a book.

I would also like to thank all my teachers and mentors whose thoughts, ideas, and insights are blended in these pages. I owe a special debt to my patients, who daily show me that there is still much more to learn.

Workshops and Presentations

Dr. Elkin would be delighted to speak at your next business meeting, conference, or convention. For date availability, he can be reached at The Stress Management & Counseling Center, 110 East 36th Street, New York, New York, 10016.

Publisher's Acknowledgments

We're proud of this book; please send us your comments through our online registration form located at www.dummies.com/register.

Some of the people who helped bring this book to market include the following:

Acquisitions, Editorial, and Media Development

Senior Project Editor: Tim Gallan, Brian Kramer

Acquisitions Editor: Tami Booth

Copy Editors: Kathleen Dobie, Elizabeth Elizabeth Netedu Kuball, Tamara Castleman

Technical Editor: Nancy Dail, Director, Downeast School of Massage

Editorial Coordinator: Karen S. Young

Editorial Manager: Seta K. Franz

Editorial Assistant: Alison Walthall

Production

Project Coordinator: Maridee Ennis

Layout and Graphics: Amy Adrian, Angela F. Hunckler, Kate Jenkins, Barry Offringa, Jill Piscitelli, Brent Savage, Brian Torwelle, Mary Jo Weiss, Dan Whetstine

Illustrator: Pam Tanzey

Proofreaders: Vickie Broyles, Jennifer Mahern, Melissa Martin, Nancy Price, Marianne Santy, Ethel Winslow

Indexer: Johnna VanHoose

Publishing and Editorial for Consumer Dummies

Diane Graves Steele, Vice President and Publisher, Consumer Dummies
Joyce Pepple, Acquisitions Director, Consumer Dummies
Kristin A. Cocks, Product Development Director, Consumer Dummies
Michael Spring, Vice President and Publisher, Travel
Brice Gosnell, Publishing Director, Travel
Suzanne Jannetta, Editorial Director, Travel

Publishing for Technology Dummies

Richard Swadley, Vice President and Executive Group Publisher
Andy Cummings, Vice President and Publisher

Composition Services

Gerry Fahey, Vice President of Production Services
Debbie Stailey, Director of Composition Services

Contents at a Glance

Cartoons at a Glance

By Rich Tennant

page 263

page 45

page 7

page 223

page 139

Cartoon Information:
Fax: 978-546-7747
E-Mail: richtennant@the5thwave.com
World Wide Web: www.the5thwave.com

Table of Contents

Foreword

∙ ∙

*E*verybody has it, and everybody talks about it, but nobody really knows what stress is. Why? Because stress signifies different things for each of us, and also really is different for each of us. The same steep roller coaster ride that is a terrifying experience for some can be a pleasurable thrill for others, or seem to have little effect either way. Stress can be the spice of life or the kiss of death — one man's meat and another's poison.

Stress is not necessarily bad. Winning a race or election can be just as stressful as losing, or more so. A passionate kiss and contemplating what might follow is stressful, but hardly evokes the same feelings or biological responses as having the periodontist scrape your gums. Increased stress increases productivity, up to a point, after which things go rapidly downhill. But that level differs for each of us. It's very much like the tension in a violin string. Not enough produces a raspy sound, and too much causes a shrill, irritating noise, or makes it snap. However, just the right amount creates a beautiful tone. Similarly we each have to find the right amount of stress that allows us to make pleasant music in our daily lives. This book shows you how.

After five decades in the field, I can confirm that trying to define stress scientifically is like trying to nail a hunk of jelly to a tree. Stress is one of the few words that defy translation. That is why we have *le stress*, *el stress*, *der stress*, and *lo stress* in European languages, and the word "stress" sticks out in Japanese, Chinese, Russian, and Arabic publications. However, one thing that all our clinical and experimental research has taught us is that the feeling of not having any control is always distressful. Not infrequently, we create our own stress because of faulty perceptions that lead to inappropriate behaviors or erroneous conclusions. These are things you can learn to identify and correct, and this book provides the tools to help you accomplish this.

Stress is an unavoidable consequence of life. There are some stresses you can do something about, and others you can't hope to avoid or control. The trick is in learning to distinguish between the two, so that you're not constantly frustrated like Don Quixote, tilting at windmills. This book teaches you how to use your time and talents effectively so that stress can make you more productive, rather than self-destructive.

Paul J. Rosch, M.D., F.A.C.P.
President, The American Institute of Stress
Clinical Professor of Medicine and Psychiatry
New York Medical College

Introduction

••

*J*ust about everyone feels they have too much stress in their life. Daily, I hear people complaining that stress is getting to them, robbing them of many of life's pleasures, and depriving them of life's satisfactions. And that's not just from the people who walk into my office or show up at one of my stress-management workshops — stress seems to be everywhere. Just take a look at your local newsstand. You're bound to see more than a few cover stories on stress, warning you of its dangers and telling you what you can do about it. These days more and more people are signing up for stress-management workshops, taking yoga classes, and learning how to meditate, massage their bodies, and quiet their psyches.

You may have expected that by the time you hit the millennium, you'd have less stress in your life. After all, with all this new technology saving you time and effort, your life should, by now, be a piece of cake — one long stress-free vacation. Clearly, this hasn't happened — for anybody.

Your life has become more stressful, not less stressful. Your stress may take the form of work pressures, financial worries, too little time for yourself, or the demands that come with having or being a part of a family. You may have more specific stresses — illness, unemployment, a new baby, or a new mortgage. Whatever the source of your stress, having a guide would be helpful, right? Unfortunately, life doesn't come with an instruction booklet or a user's manual. You need to find your own help.

"Don't Worry, Be Happy!"

Years ago, there was a song around whose title advised us, "Don't worry, be happy." If only it were so simple. Would that a nugget of sound advice could put you on the right track and relieve your stress. Unfortunately, when it comes to stress-management, a little sound bite, however wise, may not go a long way. Being told by your doctor, spouse, or best friend, to "Relax. Take it easy," just doesn't do it. The advice may be well-meant and sound terrific, but it's still not enough.

To effectively manage the stress in your life, you need the right stress-reducing tools. In fact, you need an entire toolbox filled with a wide variety of stress-management techniques, strategies, and tactics.

Stress: Take It or Relieve It

Stress Management For Dummies is written to give you these tools. This book is your guide, helping you to navigate the often confusing array of stress-management options and choices. It gives you the skills and expertise you need to effectively manage and minimize the stress in your life. Virtually every important aspect of stress management is covered in these pages. The book helps you understand where your stress comes from, how it affects you, and most importantly, what you can do about it. It shows you how to relax your body, quiet your mind, and let go of the tension that comes with too much stress. It shows you how you can control your anger, worry less, and create a lifestyle that is stress resistant.

In these pages, I have been careful to ensure that your stress-management program does not add to the stress in your life. I tried to be practical and realistic, recognizing that you may not be able to meditate for 20 minutes twice a day and still keep your job. And, although I recognize that having a chauffeur, or owning a fabulous house in the country, or having live-in help can lower your stress level; I also realize that this may not be an option for you (or for me, either!).

No one single idea or technique can magically relieve all your stress; nor does every technique or approach work equally well for everyone. You need to put together a package of ideas and methods that you can integrate into the various aspects of your life. It extends from caring about what goes into your mouth to the kind of chair you sit in; from how much sleep you get, to how to turn off your racing mind. Effective stress management really comes down to effective lifestyle management. That's why, in these pages, you can find a variety of stress-management approaches. You fill up your stress tool-box with the techniques in this book, and then you can take out the tool you need, when you need it.

Five Good Reasons to Manage Your Stress

In case you're not quite convinced that you should read this book, look at what you can gain if you do:

1. Better health

2. Probably a longer life span

3. More fun

4. More energy

5. Something to talk about at parties

How to Use This Book

Although I wrote this book so that you can follow it sequentially, you don't have to do that. You can dip into any part that interests you. Most of the material was written to stand alone, and isn't dependent on the other chapters. Having said that, there is one exception. The chapters that show you how to relax your body and quiet your mind — Chapters 4 and 5 — are particularly important, and are central and pertinent to several other chapters. Try to read these chapters earlier on.

Don't try to master all of the material presented in one shot. Or even two shots. It takes time and practice to learn how to become comfortable with, and competent in, many of the exercises described. Don't rush yourself. After all, it took years to develop many of your stress-producing habits, so you can't expect to get rid of them in a flash. Every day, allow yourself at least some time to devote to some aspect of your stress-management program. It may only be a few minutes, but those minutes add up and can result in some impressive stress-management skills.

If you can find someone — a friend, family member, coworker — to whom you can teach your newly mastered skills, that's great. Most people learn best when they can teach someone else. If you can find someone to work with you on your stress-management program, even better. Having a stress-buddy can help keep you interested and motivated. Most importantly, see your involvement with this book as an ongoing journey that will take some time — and some effort — but that is well worth the trip. Good luck!

How This Book Is Organized

Here's how the structure of this book breaks down:

Part I: Stress Management — Without the Stress

I open the book by talking about what stress is and how it can affect you mentally, physically, and emotionally. I then discuss various techniques that you can use to get a rough measure of just how much stress you may be experiencing.

Part II: Mastering the Basics

What do I mean by "the basics"? This part presents common-sense ways for you to deal with stress. I show you how to treat the physical symptoms of stress, quiet your mind, and deal with day-to-day issues that may be causing stress: Maybe you aren't as organized as you'd like to be, or maybe your career is taking time away from your family, or maybe you're not eating right. I can help.

Part III: The Fancy Stuff

Think of this part as preventative medicine. It covers more advanced techniques that you can use to decrease the amount of stress in your life. If you make minor changes in the way you think when put in potentially stressful situations, you can actually reduce and perhaps eliminate stress.

Part IV: Managing Your Stress in Real Life

This part helps you develop day-to-day habits for home and work that will ultimately help you live a less stressful life. For example, the simple act of taking a break and doing a few stretches can really reduce the affects of stress at work. And has it occured to you that if you do more fun things in life — hang out with friends or spend time on a hobby — you'll be better able to deal with stress.

Part V: The Part of Tens

This part presents some brief top-ten lists, like the ten habits of effective stress managers, the ten most stressful jobs, and more.

Icons Used in This Book

This book has lots of little round pictures in the margins, calling your attention to various details in the text. Here's what these icons mean:

I use this icon to flag a particular good idea that you should consider.

When presenting a concept that I feel you shouldn't forget, I use this icon.

When I need to give you a word of caution, I toss this icon your way.

This icon indicates that I'm about to present a specific technique for dealing with stress.

Throughout the book, I ask you to evaluate your situation — determine your stress level, examine how you react in given situations, and so on. When I give you one of these quizzes, I use this icon.

This icon flags ancedotes and trivia that you're likely to find interesting.

Where to Go from Here

As I mentioned earlier, you don't have to read this book from cover to cover, but I think you'll benefit greatly if you do. Or you can use the Table of Contents or Index to look up topics of interest and jump to them right away. For example, if you need stress relief this very second, feel free to flip to the chapters in Part II.

Part I
Stress Management — Without the Stress

The 5th Wave   By Rich Tennant

"Okay, you were depressed because you didn't win, but couldn't you have been happy enough about finishing second to pick up the $100,000 check?"

In this part . . .

1 talk about what stress is and how it can affect you mentally, physically, and emotionally. I then discuss various techniques that you can use to get a rough measure of just how much stress you may be experiencing.

Chapter 1

Stressed-Out? Welcome to the Club!

Are you feeling more tired lately than you used to? Is your fuse a little shorter than normal? Are you worrying more? Enjoying life less? If you feel more stress in your life these days, you aren't alone. Count yourself among the ranks of the overstressed. Most people feel that too much stress is in their lives. Your stress may come from your job, your personal life, or simply from not having enough time to do everything you have to do — or *want* to do. You could use some help. Thankfully, you can eliminate or certainly minimize much of the stress in your life and manage the stress that remains. This chapter helps you get started in the right direction.

Experiencing a Stress Epidemic?

You probably can't make it through a single day without seeing or hearing the word *stress* someplace. Just glance at any magazine stand and you'll find numerous cover stories all about stress. In most larger bookstores, an entire section is devoted just to books on stress. TV and radio talk shows regularly feature stories documenting the negative effects of stress in our lives. Why all the fuss? Hasn't stress been around forever? Wasn't it stress that Adam felt when he was caught red-handed with little bits of apple stuck between his teeth? Is all of this just media hype, or are people *really* experiencing more stress today?

One good way of finding out how much stress people are experiencing is to ask them about the stress in their lives. Here are some findings from recent polls and surveys that did just that:

✔ A *U.S. News*/Bozell survey found that 7 out of 10 people felt stress at some point on a typical weekday. Within this group, 30 percent reported that they experience a lot of stress, and 40 percent said they feel some stress on weekdays.

✔ In a survey conducted by *Prevention* magazine, 54 percent of respondents felt that they had more stress in their lives than their parents did.

✔ People also reported that they lost their temper an average of 5 times a month. More than half (56 percent) reported that stress made them do something that they would later regret.

✔ About 75 percent of those asked said that stress was preventing them from enjoying their lives more.

Our lives, it seems, have indeed become far more stressful. But why? The next section provides some reasons.

Understanding Where All This Stress Is Coming From

In his popular book, *Future Shock* (originally published in 1984), Alvin Toffler observed that people experience more stress whenever they are subjected to a lot of change in a short span of time. If anything characterizes our lives these days, it is an excess of change. We are in a continual state of flux. We have less control over our lives, we live with more uncertainty, and we often feel threatened and, at times, overwhelmed. The following sections explain some of the more common sources of stress in our lives.

Getting frazzled at work

For most people, their jobs and careers are the biggest source of stress in their lives. Killer hours, a long commute, unrealistic deadlines, a boss from hell, office politics, toxic coworkers, and testy clients are just a few of the many job-related stresses people experience. Workloads are heavier today than they were in the past, leaving less and less time for family and the rest of your life. A new lexicon of work-related stresses exists: downsizing, organizational redeployment, early retirement. Whatever the word, the effect is the same: insecurity, uncertainty, and fear. People are experiencing more stress at work than ever before, as these findings illustrate:

- ✔ A Gallup poll found that 90 percent of respondents were stressed at work at least once a week. Twenty-five percent said they were stressed at work on a *daily* basis.

- ✔ The percentage of employees who indicated that their workload was "excessive" rose to 44 percent in 1995, up from 37 percent in 1988 (WSJ-International Survey Research Corporation).

- ✔ The percentage of employees who "frequently worry about being laid off" rose to 46 percent in 1995 from 25 percent in 1991 (WSJ-International Survey Research Corporation).

All of this translates into more tension headaches, sore necks and backs, and an overwhelming feeling of too much stress in our lives.

Acting like a woman, thinking like a man, and working like a dog

If you're a woman, you may experience even more stress on the job. Despite all the hoopla about women's rights and sexual equality, added pressures and limitations on women still exist in the workplace. Women are paid less and are promoted less frequently than their male counterparts, even though they may be more qualified. If a woman has children, her career may be shunted onto the "Mommy Track," a glass ceiling that limits career advancement.

STRESS TIDBIT

Think "Lucy Ricardo"

Researcher Robert Karasek and his colleagues at the University of Southern California have identified what they consider the recipe for a stressful job:

1. **Find someone with a typical job.**

2. **Add lots of pressure to perform.**

3. **Add a lack of control over the work process.**

   You're left with a very stressed-out person.

When you have too much to do and a demand that you get it done, combined with a lack of input about when and how it will happen, you have a recipe for stress. To get a picture of a worst-case, high-pressure, little-control scenario, think back on that *I Love Lucy* episode in which Lucy is madly stuffing chocolates in her mouth in a futile attempt to keep up with an unrelenting conveyer belt. Is that you at your job?

More subtle pressures come from the prevailing notions of the roles and behaviors expected from men and women. Men and women can act in similar ways that may advance their careers — competitive, aggressive, assertive — but a double standard is common. When such behavior comes from a woman, people often view the behavior negatively, as unfeminine and inappropriate. But when it comes from a man, people see it as strong and in control.

Sexual harassment for women on the job is no small source of stress. A woman may find herself in the no-win situation of either complaining openly or silently enduring the abuse. Both options can be highly stressful. Women who belong to a racial or ethnic minority may experience even more stress. Hiring and promotional practices may act in subtle and not-so-subtle discriminatory ways. Even where affirmative action policies are in place, women may experience the stress of feeling that others see any hiring or advancement as unfairly legislated rather than legitimately deserved.

Feeling frazzled at home

After you leave work, you may start to realize that the rest of your life is not exactly stress-free. These days, life at home, our relationships, and the pressure of juggling everything else that has to be done only add to our stress level.

Life at home has become more pressured and demanding. True, we now have microwaves, dust-busters, and take-out menus, but the effort and stress involved seems to be growing rather than lessening. Meals have to be prepared, the house tidied, clothing cleaned, bills paid, chores completed, shopping done, the lawn and garden tended, the car maintained and repaired, phone calls returned, homework supervised, and the kids chauffeured. And that's for starters. Did I mention the dog?

"I need two more hours in the day!"

This plea is a commonly heard lament. The stress of not having enough time to do everything that has to be done is enormous. We overwork at home and at our jobs. The result? We just don't have enough time.

- ✔ Research shows that American women work an average of 290 more hours per year than they did 30 years ago. That comes to about 7 full weeks.

- ✔ Between 1973 and 1993, the number of men working 49 hours or more had risen from 23.9 percent to 29.2 percent, according to the U.S. Bureau of Labor Statistics.

STRESS TIDBIT

Less leisure time?

In her insightful book, *The Overworked American,* economist Juliet Schor points out that, in spite of all the new innovations and contraptions that could make our lives easier, we still need about the same amount of time to do what has to be done at home. In the 1910s, a full-time housewife was spending about 52 hours a week on housework. Sixty years later, in the 1970s, the figure was about the same. Yes, some activities did become less time consuming. Food preparation fell almost 10 hours a week, but this was offset by an increase in the time spent shopping and taking care of the home and kids. Contrary to everyone's predicted expectations, we have less leisure time now than we did 50 years ago.

Ozzie and Harriet we ain't

Some of this stress comes from the ways in which families have changed over the years. Our stereotypical *Leave It to Beaver* or *Ozzie and Harriet* picture of the American family, in which Dad goes off to work while Mom stays home and takes care of the kids, is no longer even close to what really happens. More likely, both parents are now working, and, in a growing number of families, two parents aren't even in the picture. Nearly half of all marriages end in divorce. The number of single-parent households is multiplying. Families tend be more fragmented, with relatives often living great distances away. Although in certain cases, this situation can be stress-reducing, more often it promotes a greater sense of disconnectedness and alienation.

A woman's work is never done

Add on the additional stress of being a mother with a family to manage at home, and you compound the level of stress. Women may find themselves in the not-so-unusual position of having to cope with the problems of aging and ailing parents in addition to the problems of their own children. Caught in this generational divide, this "stress sandwich" can be incredibly draining, both physically and emotionally. Although men give lip service to helping with the kids and the elderly (and they do, in fact, do more than their fathers or grandfathers), the woman is still the one who most often takes primary responsibility for these care-giving roles.

A study conducted by the Family and Work Institute found that even when a working woman has a partner, she still does most of the shopping (87 percent), the cooking (81 percent), the cleaning (78 percent), and the bill-paying (63 percent). As an old adage reminds us, "Father works from sun to sun, but Mother's work is never done."

Managing the money malaise

Money may or may not be the root of all evil, but worrying about it certainly is a major source of stress in our lives. Actually, the *lack* of money is really the problem. Balancing your checkbook at the end of the month (if you bother) reminds you that living is expensive. You remember that your parents bought their house for a pittance and now realize that you couldn't afford to buy that same house if you wanted to today. The mortgage, college tuition, braces for the kids' teeth, camp, travel, taxes, savings for retirement — it all adds up. And so does the stress. Money, however, can produce stress in other ways, especially for us guys. Many men tend to tie their self-worth to their financial worth. When our financial worth is down, we're down. And society doesn't help. Other people tend to equate success with your portfolio, and if you're not measuring up to what you think you should have, you may feel depressed, anxious, or even angry.

Piling on new stresses (Hint: Grandma never wore a beeper)

Our lives have become stressful in ways we never would have imagined even a decade ago. Whoever said there is nothing new under the sun probably never surfed the Web or carried a laptop. Changes in technology have brought with them new pressures and new demands; in short, new sources of stress. Imagine this implausible scenario:

> You've been in a coma for the last dozen or so years. One day, out of the blue, you wake up and take the bus home from the hospital. You quickly notice that life has changed. Technology rules. Your trusty typewriter is now obsolete. Your record player is a joke. Your telephone has no cord, and it fits perfectly into your pocket. Just as quickly, you realize that you have no idea how to operate any of these electronic gadgets. You cannot set the clock on your VCR or change the date on your laptop. Worse, you cannot escape from this technology, at home, on the street, or in your car. You can be beeped, faxed, e-mailed, and voice-mailed, as well as irritated by some clod on the train who is talking loudly and interminably on his cell phone to his accountant. All this technology is beginning to drive you a bit crazy. You notice that your next-door neighbor, who was never in a coma, also does not know how to change the time on his VCR and is just as stressed as you are, trying to keep up with all this technological change.

The importance of hassle (Or, the little things add up)

When we think of stress, we usually think of the major stresses we may face occasionally: death, divorce, financial ruin, a serious illness. And then of course there are those so-called moderate stresses: losing our wallets, denting the car, or catching a cold. Finally, we have the even smaller stresses: the mini-stresses and micro-stresses. These stresses are what we refer to as *hassles*.

Here is just a sample of the kinds of hassles we face every day (a complete list would be endless):

- ✔ Noisy traffic
- ✔ Loud neighbors
- ✔ Rude salesclerks
- ✔ Crowds
- ✔ Public telephones that don't work
- ✔ Bicyclists from nowhere
- ✔ Deliveries made "sometime between 9 and 5"
- ✔ Long lines
- ✔ No public washrooms
- ✔ Beepers sounding in theaters
- ✔ Cell phones in restaurants and on public transportation

Yes, I realize these things are relatively small. But the small things can add up. We can deal with one, maybe two, or even three of these at once. But when the number begins to rise, so does our stress level. When you reach a high enough level of stress, you notice that you overreact to the next hassle that comes along. And that results in even more stress. Alas, life is loaded with hassle. The funny part is, we usually deal fairly well with the bigger problems. Life's major stresses — the deaths, illnesses, divorces, or financial setbacks — somehow trigger hidden resources within us. We rise to each demand, summoning up some unrecognized inner strength, and we somehow manage to cope. What gets to us are the little things. It's the small stuff — the little annoyances, petty frustrations, and minor irritations — that ultimately lead to a continuing sense of stress. Life's hassles are what becomes the real source of our stress.

(Too) great expectations

Many years ago, I remember telling my grandfather that I wasn't happy at the place where I was working. In essence, his response was, "Why do you have to like it as long as they give you a paycheck at the end of the week?" For him, job satisfaction, was nice, but it was clearly a bonus. Today, we want and expect more. We expect a high level of satisfaction in our jobs and in our relationships, and we expect a certain lifestyle to go with all of this. In short, we demand a life of personal happiness and achieved goals. We want it all — or at least most of it. And, although our expectations may be understandable, they also may be a big source of much of our stress.

Identifying the Effects of Stress

If you are experiencing stress, and you probably are, you are paying for it in some way. Take a look at some sobering statistics gathered from recent polls and surveys:

- About 50 percent of those surveyed said that stress was affecting their health.

- 21 percent said that stress was negatively affecting their friendships.

- 19 percent said that stress was hurting their marriages.

- 15 percent said that stress was affecting their performance at work.

- Job stress is estimated to cost American industry $200–$300 billion annually in absenteeism, lost productivity, accidents, and medical insurance.

Those statistics are enough to make *anyone* feel stressed!

Looking at the Signs and Symptoms of Stress

The signs and symptoms of stress range from the benign to the dramatic — from simply feeling tired at the end of the day to having a heart attack. The more serious stress-related problems come with intense and prolonged periods of stress. These disorders and diseases I save for later in this chapter. Here are some of the more benign, more commonly experienced stress signs and symptoms. Many will be all too familiar to you.

Physical signs of stress:

- Tiredness, fatigue, lethargy

- Heart palpitations, racing pulse, rapid, shallow breathing

- Muscle tension and aches

- Shakiness, tremors, tics, twitches

- Heartburn, indigestion, diarrhea, constipation, nervousness

- Dry mouth and throat

- Excessive sweating, clammy hands, cold hands and/or feet

✔ Rashes, hives, itching

✔ Nail-biting, fidgeting, hair-twirling or hair-pulling

✔ Frequent urination

✔ Lowered libido

✔ Overeating, loss of appetite

✔ Sleep difficulties

✔ Increased use of alcohol and/or drugs and medications

Psychological signs of stress:

✔ Irritability, impatience, anger, hostility

✔ Worry, anxiety, panic

✔ Moodiness, sadness, feeling upset

✔ Intrusive and/or racing thoughts

✔ Memory lapses, difficulties in concentrating, indecision

✔ Frequent absences from work, lowered productivity

✔ Feeling overwhelmed

✔ Loss of sense of humor

That's just for starters. Prolonged and/or intense stress can have more serious effects.

Understanding How Stress Can Make You Sick

Researchers estimate that 75 to 90 percent of all visits to primary care physicians are for complaints and conditions that are, in some way, stress-related. Every week, 112 million people take some form of medication for stress-related symptoms. This statistic is not surprising given the wide-ranging physiological changes that accompany a stress response. Just about every bodily system or body part is affected by stress. Just take a look at Figure 1-1. Stress can play a role in exacerbating the symptoms of a wide variety of other disorders and illnesses as well. The following sections illustrate some of the more important way stress can negatively impact your health and well being.

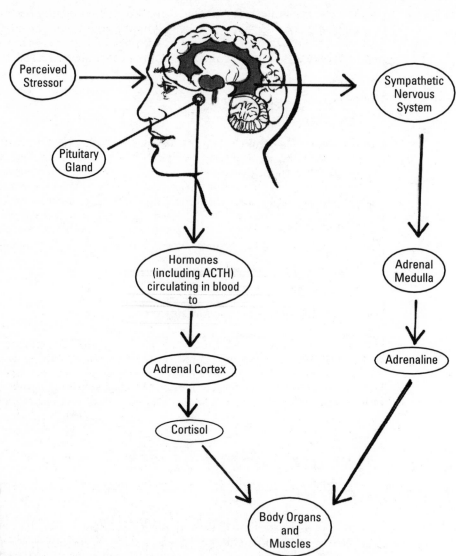

Figure 1-1:
How stress
affects us.

How stress can be a pain in the neck (and other places)

Your muscles are a prime target for stress. When you are under stress, your muscles contract and they become tense. This muscle tension can affect your nerves, blood vessels, organs, skin, and bones. Chronically tense muscles can result in a variety of conditions and disorders, including muscle spasms, cramping, facial or jaw pain, bruxism (grinding your teeth), tremors, and shakiness. Many forms of headache, chest pain, and back pain are among the more common conditions that result from stress-induced muscle tension.

Taking stress to heart

Stress can play a role in circulatory diseases such as coronary heart disease, sudden cardiac death, and strokes. This fact is not surprising because stress can increase your blood pressure, constrict your blood vessels, raise your cholesterol level, trigger arrhythmias, and speeds up the rate at which your blood clots. Stress is now considered a major risk factor in heart disease, right up there with smoking, being overweight, and a lack of exercise. All of this becomes very important when you consider that heart disease kills more men over the age of 50 and more women over the age of 65 than any other disease.

Hitting below the belt

Ever notice how your stress seems to finds its way to your stomach? Your gastrointestinal system can be a ready target for much of the stress in your life. Stress can affect the secretion of acid in your stomach and can speed up or slow down the process of peristalsis (the rhythmic contraction of the muscles in your intestines). Constipation, diarrhea, gas, bloating, and weight loss all can be stress-related. Stress can contribute to gastroesophageal reflux disease and can also play a role in exacerbating irritable bowel syndrome and colitis.

Stress can be taxing

A number of studies have shown that when you are under stress, your cholesterol level goes up. In one now classic study, researchers looked at the stress levels of accountants before and after the month of April, a notoriously busy time for tax accountants. They also looked at cholesterol levels in corporate accountants, who had stressful deadlines in both April *and* January.

The researchers found that for both groups, cholesterol levels rose significantly before the April deadline and fell after the deadline. They observed a second rise in cholesterol levels for the corporate accountants as their January deadline approached. Again, after the deadline passed, blood lipid levels fell back to normal.

What about stress and ulcers?

Once considered the poster disease for stress, ulcers have lost much of their stress-related status in recent years. Stress is no longer considered the primary cause of ulcers. It now appears that a bacterium called Helicobacter pylori, or H. pylori for short, is the culprit.

However, the final word on the relationship between stress and ulcers has yet to be written. More recent thinking has begun to question whether stress plays some role. We know that stress can affect secretions in the stomach that may exacerbate ulcers. We also know that a majority of those who do carry the H. pylori bacterium do not develop an ulcer, and many who do not carry the bacterium still develop ulcers. And of course, there is that body of research that has linked stress to ulcers. For example, the bombing of London during World War II and the earthquake in Kobe, Japan, both precipitated outbreaks of ulcer disease. Stay tuned.

Stress can affect your immune system

In the last decade or so, growing evidence has supported the theory that stress affects your immune system. In fact, researchers have even coined a name for this new field of study. They call it *psychoneuroimmunology.* Quite a mouthful! Scientists who choose to go into this field study the relationships between moods, emotional states, hormonal levels, and changes in the nervous system and the immune system. Without drowning you in detail, stress — particularly chronic stress — can compromise your immune system, rendering it less effective in resisting bacteria and viruses. Research has shown that stress may play a role in exacerbating a variety of immune system disorders such as HIV, AIDS, herpes, cancer metastasis, viral infection, rheumatoid arthritis, and certain allergies, as well as other auto-immune conditions. Some recent studies appear to confirm this.

You may want a second opinion

All of the symptoms, illnesses, and conditions I mention in this chapter can result from a number of medical conditions, not just stress. And for many of the disorders and diseases mentioned, stress may not be the *direct* cause of the condition, but stress may make these conditions worse. If you are concerned about one or more of these symptoms, be sure to consult your physician. He or she is the best person to give you advice and guidance.

The cold facts: Stress can make you sniffle

In that wonderful musical comedy *Guys and Dolls,* a lovelorn Adelaide laments that when your life is filled with stress, "a person can develop a cold." It looks like she just may be right. Recent research conducted by Dr. Sheldon Cohen, a psychologist at Carnegie Mellon University, has concluded that stress really does lower your resistance to colds. Cohen and his associates found that the higher a person's stress score, the more likely he was to come down with a cold when exposed to a cold virus. Chronic stress, lasting a month or more, was the most likely to result in catching a cold. Experiencing severe stress for more than a month but less than six months doubled a person's risk of coming down with a cold, compared with those who were experiencing only shorter-term stress. Stress lasting more than two years nearly quadrupled the risk. The study also found that being unemployed or underemployed, or having interpersonal difficulties with family or friends, had the greatest effect. The exact mechanism whereby stress weakens immune functioning is still unclear. Tissues anyone?

"Not tonight, dear. I have a (stress) headache."

A headache is just one of the many ways stress can interfere with your sex life. Stress can affect sexual performance and rob you of your libido. When you are feeling stress, feeling sexy may not be at the top of your to-do list. Disturbed sexual performance may appear in the form of premature ejaculation, erectile dysfunction, and other forms of difficulty in reaching orgasm. The irony is, sex can be a way of *relieving* stress. In fact, for some people, sexual activity *increases* when they feel stressed.

Stress Can Be Good?

Not all the news about stress is bad. As Hans Selye, the pioneer researcher in the field of stress said, "Stress is the spice of life." He termed the good kind of stress *eustress,* as opposed to *distress,* or the nasty kind of stress. (The *eu* part of *eustress* comes from the Greek, meaning "good.") Stress can be a positive force in your life. Watching a close playoff game, taking a ride at an amusement park, solving an interesting problem, falling in love — all can be stressful. Yet these are the kinds of stresses that add to the enjoyment and satisfaction of our lives. We want *more* of this kind of stress, not less.

"But I thrive on stress"

"I'm at my best when I'm under pressure — a tight deadline, a major crisis. That's when I feel most alive, most vital." A surprising number of people claim to *thrive* on stress. They like to be challenged; to have their abilities stretched and tested. For them this is a good kind of stress that can be satisfying and rewarding. Many people who claim to thrive on stress are workaholics. They get stressed when they have nothing to do. Lying on a beach, sitting in the park — now *that's* stressful for them!

Interestingly enough, some research suggests that part of the addictive quality that some people feel about stress my be more than just psychological. It may be that people can become hooked on the adrenaline secretions that occur during a stress response. Like other addictions, this adrenaline boost may be experienced by some people as pleasurable. This could explain that feeling of being "truly alive" that some people feel when they are super-stressed. Most of the rest of us, however, could live quite nicely without this boost, thank you very much.

And even many of the less pleasant uncertainties and surprises of life can be a source of challenge and even excitement and interest. Change and the pressures of modern life don't necessarily create the bad kind of stress. Rather, how you view the potential stresses in your life and how you cope with them makes all the difference. The good news is that, with a little help and the right direction, learning to manage your stress is easier than you think.

Chapter 2

Stress Explained
(In Surprisingly Few Pages)

• •

In This Chapter

▶ Understanding stress

▶ Looking at a model of stress

▶ Finding the right balance

• •

You've heard the word *stress* a thousand times. Yet, if you were pressed to explain the concept, you could find yourself a little stuck. Intuitively, you know what stress is, but explaining it isn't easy. This chapter helps you answer the question, "What exactly is stress?" So the next time you find yourself at a dinner party and someone asks, "Does anyone here know what stress is?" you will grin knowingly, raise your hand, and proceed to dazzle and delight your tablemates.

So What Is Stress Anyhow?

You would think that defining *stress* would be relatively easy. Yet those who have spent most of their professional lives studying stress still have trouble defining the term. As one stress researcher quipped, "Defining stress is like nailing Jell-O to a tree. It's hard to do!" Despite efforts over the last half-century to define the term, no satisfactory definition of stress exists. Defining *stress* is much like defining *happiness*. Everyone knows what it is, but no one can agree on a definition.

"Sorry, but I really need a definition"

Perhaps you were one of those people who always began their high-school English essays with a dictionary definition ("Webster defines *tragedy* as. . ."), and you *still* have to start with a definition. Okay, here goes:

Stress is what you experience when you believe you cannot cope effectively with a threatening situation.

What this means is that you experience stress whenever you are faced with an event or situation that you perceive as challenging to your ability to cope. If you see the event or situation as only *mildly* challenging, you will probably feel only a little stress; however, if you perceive the situation or event as *threatening* or *overwhelming* your coping abilities, you will probably feel a lot of stress. So, having to wait for a bus when you have all the time in the world triggers little stress. Waiting for that same bus when you are late for a plane that will take off without you triggers much more stress.

This difference between the demands of the situation and your perception of how well you can cope with that situation is what determines how much stress you will feel.

The other definition of stress

You may prefer the more tongue-in-cheek definition, commonly seen in business offices, usually taped to a wall in the employee washroom:

Stress is created when your mind overrides the body's basic desire to choke the living daylights out of some idiot who desperately deserves it.

Stick with the first definition.

"Oops, pardon my English!"

It was an Austrian-born endocrinologist by the name of Hans Selye who actually came up with the stress concept as it pertains to a physiological and emotional response. In the 1930s, Selye came upon the stress response while working with animals in his laboratory at McGill University in Montreal. Selye went on to publish widely in the area of stress and is today considered the "Father of Stress."

Selye later admitted that he may have misnamed what he was studying. He borrowed the term from the field of physics and engineering where the concepts of stress and strain were in common use. English was not his mother tongue. He chose the word stress but later realized the word strain would have been more appropriate. Too late. The term stuck, and it still remains.

Stress causes stress?

Part of the problem with defining stress is the word *confusion* of it. We use the word *stress* to refer to the thing or circumstance *out there* that is stressing us (stress = the bus that never comes, the deadline, the traffic jam, the sudden noise, and so on). We then use the *same* word to describe the physical and/or emotional discomfort we are feeling *about* that situation (stress = anxious, headachy, irritated, and so on). So we end up feeling stress about stress! This can be very confusing. My advice? Don't worry about it. This chapter helps you understand what stress is all about, even if you can't spout a definition.

How This Whole Stress Thing Got Started

Believe it or not, you have stress in your life for a good reason. To show you why stress can be a useful, adaptive response, you need to take a trip back in time.

Imagining you are a cave person

Picture this: You have regressed in time to a period millions of years ago when men and women lived in caves. You notice that you are roaming the jungle dressed in a loincloth and carrying a club in your hand. Your day, so far, has been routine. Nothing more than the usual cave politics and the ongoing problems with the in-laws. Nothing you can't handle. Suddenly, on your stroll, you spot a tiger. This is not your ordinary tiger; it's a saber-toothed one. You experience something called the *fight-or-flight response*. This response is aptly named because, just then, you realize that you have to make a choice. You can stay and do battle (that's the fight part) or you can run like the wind (the flight part, and probably the smarter option here). Your body, armed with this automatic stress response, prepares you to do either. You are ready for anything. You are wired.

Seeing how your body reacts

When you are in the fight-or-flight mode, your physiological system goes into high gear. The first thing you notice is that you're afraid, very afraid. You also notice that you're breathing much faster than you normally do, and your hands feel cool and more than a little moist. But that's just for starters. If you could see what's happening below the surface, you would also notice some other changes going on. Your sympathetic nervous system, one of the two branches of your autonomic nervous system, is producing changes in your body. Your *hypothalamus,* a part of your brain, is activating your *pituitary,* a small gland near the base of your brain, which releases a hormone into the bloodstream. This hormone (it's called ACTH or adrenocorticotropic hormone) reaches your adrenal glands, and they in turn produce more adrenalin (also known as epinephrine) along with other hormones called glucocorticoids (cortisol is one). This melange of biochemical changes is responsible for an array of other remarkable changes in your body. Some highlights include the following:

- Your heart rate speeds up, and your blood pressure rises (more blood is pumped to your muscles and lungs).

- You breathe more rapidly. Your nostrils flare, causing an increased supply of air.

- Your digestion slows. (Who's got time to eat?)

- Blood is directed away from your skin and internal organs and is shunted to your brain and skeletal muscles. Your muscles tense. You feel stronger. You are ready for action.

- Your blood clots faster, ready to repair any damage to your arteries.

- Your pupils dilate, so you see better.

- Your liver converts glycogen into glucose, which teams up with free fatty acids to supply you with fuel and some quick energy. (You'll probably need it.)

In short, when you are experiencing stress, your entire body undergoes a dramatic series of physiological changes that readies you for a life-threatening emergency. Clearly, stress has adaptive, survival potential. Stress, way back when, was nature's way of keeping you alive.

Stress can convict you

As pointed out in Chapter 1, one of your body's responses to a threatening situation is a dry mouth. In ancient China, this phenomenon was used as a lie detector test. Suspected criminals had their mouths filled with cooked rice and then were required to answer questions. The guilty one, it was assumed, would be under such a high level of stress that his throat would be too dry for him to swallow and talk. Got milk?

Surviving the modern jungle

You've probably noticed that you don't live in a cave. And your chances of running into a saber-toothed tiger are very slim, especially considering the fact that they're extinct. Yet this incredibly important, life-preserving stress reaction is still hard-wired into your system. And once in a while, it still can be highly adaptive. If you are picnicking on a railroad track and you see a train barreling toward you, an aggressive stress response is nice to have. You want to get out of there very quickly.

The reality is, in today's modern society, we are required to deal with very few life-threatening stresses on a normal day. Unfortunately, your body's fight-or-flight response is activated by a whole range of stressful events and situations that are *not* going to do you in. The physical dangers have been replaced by social or psychological stresses, not worthy of a full flight-or-fight stress response. Your body, however, does not know this and reacts the way it did when your ancestors were facing danger.

Panicking on the podium

Imagine the following modern-day scenario. You are standing in an auditorium in front of several hundred seated people. You are about to give a presentation that is important to your career. You suddenly realize that you have left several pages of your prepared material at home on your nightstand next to your bed. As it dawns on you that this is not just a bad dream you will laugh about later, you start to notice some physical and emotional changes occurring. Your hands are becoming cold and clammy. Your heart is beating faster, and you are breathing harder. Your throat is dry. Your muscles are tensing and you notice a slight tremor as you hopelessly look for the missing pages. Your stomach feels a little queasy, and you notice an emotion that you would definitely label as anxiety. You have read Chapter 1, so you know you are experiencing a stress reaction. You now also recognize that you are experiencing the same fight-or-flight response that your caved ancestors experienced. The difference is, you probably won't die up there on that podium, even though it feels like you will.

In today's modern jungle, giving that presentation, being stuck in traffic, confronting a disgruntled client, facing an angry spouse, or trying to meet some unrealistic deadline are what stresses you. These far less-threatening stresses now trigger that same intense stress response. It's overkill. Your body is now not just reacting; it is *overreacting*. And *that* is definitely not good.

It's like driving a car with your foot on the brake

Triggering this fight-or-flight response repeatedly can wear you down. The stress response was designed to work best in short bursts — hit and then run, or maybe just run — not the prolonged and chronic stress that we deal with on a routine basis.

I remember, as a child, riding in our car with my mother at the wheel. She had an overly-cautious habit of driving with her right foot on the gas pedal and her left foot on the brake. Besides being an incredibly jerky ride, I'm quite certain that the car had more than its share of brake adjustments. She wore them down. Stress can have a similar wear-and-tear effect on you. Too much stress, day-in and day-out, can exact a price.

Understanding Stress Is As Simple As ABC

One of best ways of understanding stress is to look at a model of emotional distress elaborated by psychologist Albert Ellis. He calls his model the ABC model, and it's as simple as it sounds:

A⇨B⇨C where

- ✔ A is the <u>A</u>ctivating event or potentially stressful situation.
- ✔ B is your <u>B</u>eliefs, thoughts, or perceptions about <u>A</u>.
- ✔ C is the emotional <u>C</u>onsequence or stress that results from holding these beliefs.

In other words,

> *A potentially stressful situation⇨your perceptions⇨your stress (or lack of stress)*

An example, please

Consider one of the more common source of stress in our lives: having to wait. This could be waiting in a supermarket checkout line, waiting in a bank line, or waiting for that bus that should have been there 15 minutes ago. The waiting is your "A" part of the equation. Now, whether you experience stress (your "C") about waiting depends upon how you look at the situation — your beliefs, attitudes, and interpretations. That is, your "C" depends on your "B."

The stress sequence looks something like this:

A⇨B⇨C

Having to wait⇨my thoughts about the waiting⇨potential stress

It's the thought that counts

What happens at "B" — your beliefs, thoughts, perceptions, and interpretations — is critical in determining just how much stress you will feel. So, in the examples in the preceding section, if you are waiting in that line and, at point "B," you are thinking: "I just can't stand this! I hate waiting! Why can't they figure out a better way of doing this? I hate lines! I hate lines! I hate lines!", chances are, you are creating more than a little stress for yourself. On the other hand, if you were thinking, "Perfect. Now I have time to read these fascinating articles on alien babies and Liz Taylor's weight in the *National Tattler*. What luck!", you would feel much less stress. Your thinking plays a larger role than you may believe in creating your stress. Whenever we perceive a situation or an event as overwhelming or beyond our control, or whenever we think we cannot cope, we experience stress.

Managing Stress: A Three-Pronged Approach

This three-pronged model of dealing with stress provides you with a useful tool to help you understand the many ways you can manage and control your stress. You have three major choices, outlined in the following sections.

You can change your "A"

Changing your "A" means modifying your environment. Spiders stress you out? Stay away from spiders. Traffic stresses you? Leave home earlier. Hate deadlines? Finish the project earlier.

Many of the stress management tools in this book are designed to help you change those situations that are triggering your stress. But what if you can't? You can't avoid spiders — you work in pest control. You can't leave home for work earlier. You can't finish the project before the deadline. You need to change *you*.

You can change your "B"

Even if you cannot significantly change those situations and events that are triggering your stress, you can change the way you perceive them. An important subset of stress management skills focuses on ways of changing the way you view your world. You will see that much, if not most, of your stress is self-induced, and you can learn to see things differently.

You can change your "C"

Even if you cannot change the situation, and cannot change the way you view that situation, you can still manage your stress by mastering other skills. You can learn how to relax your body and quiet your mind. You can learn the secrets of becoming calm and how to turn off your stress.

Tuning Your Strings: Finding the Right Balance

Stress is part of life. No one makes it through life totally stress free, and you wouldn't want to. You certainly want the good stress, and you even want some of the stress that comes with dealing with life's challenges and disappointments. What you don't want is too much stress in your life, or too little stress. Too much (or prolonged) stress can become a negative force, and can rob you of much of life's joy. Too little stress means you are missing out, taking too few risks, playing it too safe. Finding the right amount of stress in your life is like finding the right tension in a violin string. Too much tension and the string can break; too little tension and there is no music.

You want to hear the music, without breaking the strings.

Chapter 3

Getting Started

• •

In This Chapter

▶ Measuring your stress

▶ Your starting tools

▶ Avoiding roadblocks

• •

As a Chinese proverb reminds us, "A journey of a thousand miles must begin with a single step." You've taken that initial step by reading this book. So far, so good. But there's more. The proverb's author may have added that the first single step you take should be in the right direction. On any long trip, you want to have a pretty good idea of where you're going and make sure you have the right equipment to get you there. The same wisdom holds true as you begin your journey on the road to becoming your own stress manager. You want to begin with the proper gear — an accurate roadmap, a good compass, and the right attitudes (and maybe a light lunch). This chapter gives you these tools and starts you off on the right foot.

Just How Stressed Are You?

Certainly, one of the very first steps in mastering your stress is knowing just how stressed you are. You may think that measuring stress is a relatively simple matter. The fact is, measuring your stress level is a tricky business. Part of the difficulty stems from the multifaceted nature of stress. It's both a stimulus and a response. It's what's on your plate, and it's how you react to what's on your plate. Stress also appears in the form of various biochemical and physiological changes in your body. It would be nice if you could be hooked up to a machine and measure your stress level as easily as your doctor measures your blood-pressure or heart rate. Alas, this is not the case. However, measuring your stress is still possible. What follows are some relatively easy ways of finding the number that tells you just how stressed you are.

The simplest way to measure your stress

Oddly enough, one of the better ways of measuring your stress is asking yourself this simple question:

"How much stress am I currently feeling?"

In an age of high-tech, computer-driven, digitally-monitored gadgets and gear, this lowest-of-low tech ways of measuring your stress may seem like a joke. Yet it really is an incredibly useful way of assessing your stress level. This subjective measure of your stress has some advantages. It measures those aspects of your stress that you feel truly reflect *your* stress. This may take the form of anxiety, anger, muscle tension, or some other manifestation of your stress. This measure is also sensitive to the ways in which your stress level can change from day to day and even from moment to moment. All in all, it's not a bad measure to start with.

Use a stress gauge

To help you put a number on your stress level (and to give this approach the appearance of technological sophistication), I suggest that you use a simple 10-point scale that permits you to calibrate your level of stress in a more quantitative way.

10	
9	I feel extremely stressed.
8	
7	
6	I feel a moderate amount of stress.
5	
4	
3	
2	I feel only a little stress.
1	
0	I don't feel any stress.

So, right now, you may say to yourself, "I'm feeling a little 5-ish." This morning when you were stuck in major traffic you probably described your stress level as a 7.

You can get the hang of using this scale very quickly. It comes in handy in other parts of this book.

Other ways of measuring your stress

In order to get a more complete picture of your overall stress, a more objective measure of your stress level may be useful. There are times when you experience stress, but you're not aware of your stress. That's when a questionnaire measure of your stress may be appropriate. Two such measures follow, and taken together, they give you a valid and reliable measure of your stress level. If you are not in a test-taking mood right now, you can skip this section and come back to it later. But don't skip it entirely. These measures are useful in helping you understand your stress better. Also, by retaking these scales from time to time, your scores can tell you how well you're doing as you master the various stress-management techniques and strategies in later chapters.

The Stress-Symptom Scale

This index gives you a measure of your stress level by looking at the number and the severity of your stress-related symptoms and behaviors. To use this measure, simply rate the frequency with which you've experienced each of the items listed below. Take the last *two weeks* as your time frame. Use this helpful rating scale:

- ✔ 0 = Never
- ✔ 1 = Sometimes
- ✔ 2 = Often
- ✔ 3 = Very often

Fatigue or tiredness   _____

Pounding heart   _____

Rapid pulse   _____

Increased perspiration   _____

Rapid breathing   _____

Aching neck or shoulders   _____

Low back pain   _____

Gritting teeth or clenching jaw   _____

Hives or skin rash   _____

Headaches   _____

(continued)

(continued)

Cold hands or feet	_____
Tightness in chest	_____
Nausea	_____
Diarrhea or constipation	_____
Stomach discomfort	_____
Nail biting	_____
Twitches or tics	_____
Difficulty swallowing or dry mouth	_____
Colds or flu	_____
Lack of energy	_____
Over-eating	_____
Feeling helpless or hopeless	_____
Excessive drinking	_____
Excessive smoking	_____
Excessive spending	_____
Excessive drug or medication use	_____
Feeling upset	_____
Feeling nervous or anxious	_____
Increased irritability	_____
Worrisome thoughts	_____
Impatience	_____
Feelings of depression	_____
Loss of sexual interest	_____
Feeling angry	_____
Sleep difficulties	_____
Forgetfulness	_____
Racing or intrusive thoughts	_____
Feeling restless	_____
Difficulty concentrating	_____
Periods of crying	_____
Frequent absences from work	_____
Your total Stress-Symptom Score	_____

What your Stress-Symptom Scores mean

Your scores are compared with the scores of others who completed this scale. The higher your score, the more stress-symptoms you are reporting. A higher frequency and/or intensity of stress-related symptoms and behaviors is generally associated with higher levels of stress. Table 3-1 helps you determine your rating:

Table 3-1	Determining Your Stress Rating
Your Score	*Your Comparative Rating*
0 – 19	Lower than average
20 – 39	Average
40 – 49	Moderately higher than average
50 and above	Much higher than average

Many of the symptoms and behaviors listed previously can be the result of factors other than stress. Many physical conditions and disorders can also be the same as those seen under conditions of stress. If any of your symptoms persist, and/or are worrisome, be sure to speak with a medical professional. Your health-care provider is in the best position to tell you what your symptoms mean, and what you should do about them.

Knowing where your stress is coming from

This scale helps you assess not only the amount of stress you are experiencing now, but also helps you identify where that stress is coming from. Items in the scale includes major life-changes, important issues, and worries and concerns that you may be now be experiencing. Use this simple scale to help you:

- ✔ N = No stress
- ✔ S = Some stress
- ✔ M = Moderate stress
- ✔ G = Great stress

Conflicts or concerns about your marriage or relationship   _____

Concerns or worries about your children   _____

Concerns or worries about your parents   _____

Pressures from other family members/in-laws   _____

Death of a loved one   _____

(continued)

(continued)

Health problems or worries	_____
Financial worries	_____
Concerns related to work/career	_____
Long or difficult commute to work	_____
Change in where you are living or will live	_____
Concerns with current residence or neighborhood	_____
Household responsibilities	_____
Home improvements or repairs	_____
Balancing demands of work and family	_____
Relationships with friends	_____
Limited personal time	_____
Concerns with social life	_____
Concerns with your appearance	_____
Issues with your personal traits or habits	_____
Boredom	_____
Feelings of loneliness	_____
Feelings about growing old	_____

Note that this scale was not designed to provide you with a quantitative measure of your overall stress level. Rather, it is a tool than helps you pinpoint specific stresses in your life and assess the impact each might be having on your life at the present time. It is an index of what is "on your plate."

Gathering Your Basic Tools

This section provides you with some easy-to-use, stress-management tools that can help you maximize your stress-management efforts. Some of these aids are designed to help you monitor and quantify the ongoing stress in your life. Others help you identify and understand your stress. All of these tools make applying the stress-management approaches and techniques described in upcoming chapters easier for you to do. All of these tools are also relatively simple and painless, and they definitely won't add more stress to your already stressful life.

Keep a simple stress diary

One of the more useful items you can carry in your tool belt is a *stress diary*. To effectively manage your stress, you need to become aware of when you are feeling stressed and be able to identify the sources of that stress. A stress diary can help you do just that. Your diary shows you, very specifically, when you experienced stress and pinpoints the situations or circumstances that triggered those stresses. Your diary acts as a cue or prompt, reminding you that you should take some action and make use of one or more of the stress-management tools you have mastered. By keeping a longer-term record of your daily stress, you are in the best position to formulate a comprehensive program of stress management that can integrate the various stress-reducing strategies and tactics.

Maintaining a stress diary as you work your way through this book helps you focus your efforts and acts as a reminder that your stress needs tending to. Even after you complete your stress-management program, you should still monitor your stress on a less-frequent, yet ongoing basis.

Make your diary small enough and compact enough so that you can carry it with you. I find that using a small notebook works well, with each day on a separate page. If you are a high-tech kind of person, you can work your stress diary into your laptop or personal organizer. The form and format are less important than the fact that you use it on a regular basis.

Table 3-2 illustrates what a portion of a page in your stress diary may look like.

Table 3-2	Day: Wednesday, November 5, 1999	
Time	*My stress trigger (importance level)*	*My stress responses (stress level)*
7:45 a.m.	Couldn't find my keys (2)	Annoyed, upset (4)
9:30 a.m.	Subway stalled for 10 minutes (1)	Annoyed (3)
11:30 a.m.	Mail came; big credit card bill (4)	Upset, worried (6)
12:30 p.m.	Given a deadline for project (4)	Worried and anxious (8)

If you are uncertain as to what the terms *importance level* and *stress level* refer to, don't worry. That's next.

Find your stress balance

Determining your stress balance is one of the best ways of finding out whether you are overreacting to the stress in your life. Knowing your stress balance also helps you regain any lost perspective. This technique is invaluable, and you can use it anywhere, at anytime. It may quickly prove to be your favorite tool in helping to manage and reduce your stress. And it's simple to use. Just follow the steps in the next three sections.

Step 1: Rate your stress level

First rate the *amount of stress* you are feeling about a particular stressful episode using this 10-point scale:

10	
9	I was extremely distressed.
8	
7	
6	I was moderately distressed.
5	
4	
3	
2	I was only a little distressed.
1	
0	I wasn't distressed at all.

The term *distress* here refers to any one of the many forms of stress — frustration, aggravation, upset, annoyance, worry, anger, sadness, disappointment, and so on.

Step 2: Rate the relative importance of the stress

Whenever you experience some stress, attempt to identify what is the source of your stress and rate its *relative importance* on a similar 10-point scale.

10	
9	Major importance
8	

7	
6	Moderate importance
5	
4	
3	
2	Minor importance
1	
0	Not important at all

To help you get the feel of the scale, think of three *major* life stresses that could happen or have happened to you. These are your 9s and 10s, the major life-altering events that everyone fears, and some people dread.

If you are having trouble coming up with anything, you may consider these possibilities: the death of a loved one, a major financial loss, a life-threatening illness, the loss of your job, chronic pain, and so on. Again, these are given an importance rating of a 9 or 10.

Step 3: Evaluate your stress balance

Now simply ask yourself, "Does the stress I'm feeling match the importance of the situation?"

If it doesn't, you are off balance. Your stress level is out of line. I was off balance when I had a level-3 stress response when I had to wait for a while in a stalled subway car (a level 1 in importance). Similarly, my son's emotional outburst (a 7) when he when he was told that his favorite pair of pants was in the laundry (a 1 or 2), or my neighbor's great upset (from my house it looked like an 11) when he discovered that his newspaper was missing are examples of being off balance. In each case, the people were experiencing too much stress relative to the importance of the situations. These problems, situations, and circumstances do not deserve this kind of emotional investment. Knowing you are off-balance tells you that you are overreacting to a situation. Your stress button is bigger than it has to be, and you are causing yourself more stress than is necessary.

Test your balance

How would you rate the importance level and your estimated stress level if you were faced with the situations outlined in Table 3-3?

Table 3-3	Testing Your Balance	
Incident	*Importance Level*	*Stress Level*
Escalator broken; you have to take the stairs.	_____	_____
Salesperson serves someone else even though you were there first.	_____	_____
Someone cuts you off on the highway.	_____	_____
Your waiter is taking forever to serve you.	_____	_____
You just miss your train home, but another will be along very shortly.	_____	_____
You lose your house keys.	_____	_____

You get the idea. If you are off balance, you probably cause yourself more stress than is necessary. The upcoming chapters show you how to regain your balance and reduce your levels of stress.

Do a one-minute body scan

One of the best ways of learning how to recognize bodily tension is to create that tension on your own and see what it feels like. Try this simple one-minute scanning exercise.

With your eyes closed, scan your body for any muscle tension. Start with the top of your head, and work your way down to your toes. Ask yourself:

- Is my brow furrowed?
- Are my eyebrows knitted?
- Is my jaw clenched?
- Are my lips pursed?
- Are my shoulders hunched?
- Are my arms tense?
- Are my thigh and calf muscles tight?
- Are my toes curled?
- Do I notice any discomfort anywhere else in my body?

With a little practice, you'll be able to scan your body in less than a minute, finding your tension quickly. Try to do a body scan three or four times a day. This exercise is a great way of making you aware of your stress and then, of course, triggering you to do something about it.

Take the triple-A approach

To effectively manage your stress, you may need a systematic way of looking at your stress and then determining how to go about reducing it. I have found that a three-step approach, or what I call the *triple-A approach* to stress management, is a useful and easy way to help you plan a program of stress reduction. It tells you where to begin and what to do after you've started.

Here's what each of the three As refers to:

- ✔ **Awareness:** Know what your stress looks like and where it comes from. Your stress can be an unpleasant work environment, a major deadline, being caught in traffic, or any one of an endless number of other potential stresses.

- ✔ **Analysis:** The process of determining the best way or ways of managing this stress. Your options may include changing the situation or circumstances, changing yourself — the ways in which you react to a particular stress trigger — or possibly changing both.

- ✔ **Action:** What you do about your stress. Your action could be to do one of the many relaxation exercises, delegate more effectively, meditate, get some sleep — or use another of the methods and techniques described in this book.

In the pages that follow, you figure out how to do all of the preceding. The chapters in this book are designed to help you reduce and manage your stress at all three levels. You build a repertoire of skills, strategies, and tactics. The goal is to maximize your ability to manage and control the stress in your life.

Avoiding Roadblocks

If you recall your last attempt at losing a few pounds or getting rid of all the clutter in your house, you may recognize that good intentions do not always guarantee success. Almost always, you encounter one or two roadblocks. But being aware of potential obstacles in your path and figuring out ways of avoiding them makes reaching your goal more likely.

Here are some of the more commonly experienced roadblocks and some ways to help you avoid them.

✔ I don't have time.

✔ I'm too busy.

✔ I have too much stuff to learn.

✔ It's too much work.

✔ It's not my cup of tea.

✔ I tried it once and it didn't work.

Each of these excuses contains at least a grain of truth. But each of them can act as a roadblock, slowing or stopping you from getting the most out of your stress management efforts. In the following sections, I give you some ideas and suggestions to help you get around these potential obstacles.

Take it a step at a time

Learning any new skill takes time. The trick is not to tackle everything at once but instead spread your learning out over time. Start slowly. Don't overwhelm yourself. Set aside 15 or 20 minutes in your day and practice one of the methods and techniques described. It could be during a coffee break, your lunch hour, after work when you come home, or on your way to work in the morning.

Different strokes

No two people are exactly alike. One size rarely fits all. For one person, the picture of ideal relaxation may be lying on a beach in the Caribbean with a page-turner in one hand and a pina colada in the other. For someone else, this scenario may trigger some an eye-rolling "Do I have to?" His or her idea of a relaxing vacation may be visiting every museum that's open. Some people are hares and others are tortoises. What works for one, may not work for the other. The idea of meditating for 20 minutes may not fill you with anticipatory delight. Mental imagery may not be your cup of tea. Fine. The general rule is, if you aren't comfortable with a technique or strategy, you're less likely to use it and make it a part of your life. You need to put together a package of tools that reflects your personality and lifestyle.

Give it a try

A few of the approaches presented in this book may feel a tad foreign and not immediately comfortable. Yet, with a little getting used to, these techniques may be the very ones you routinely use later on. You may not think, for example, that the breathing exercises are "your thing." Yet, you may be pleasantly surprised to find them wonderfully calming and relaxing. Many years ago, when I first began exploring the various stress methods, I felt lukewarm about meditation as a relaxation tool. Now I swear by it. Hey, you never know. Keep an open mind. Give everything at least one good try.

Practice makes perfect

Most of the methods and techniques presented in these pages require some practice before you can master them. Even though they can be quickly understood at an intellectual level, to truly reap their benefits, you need to spend some time repeating a particular exercise or technique until it has the desired effect. Some of the techniques can be mastered fairly quickly. Others may take a little more time. Don't give up too easily. Learning to ride a bike, drive a car, and play tennis all take time. Why should learning how to manage the stress in your life be worth a lesser amount of time and effort?

Find a quiet place

You need a place to do all this practicing. Hopefully, you can find a place that's relatively quiet and relaxing, at least for a short period of time. Given the realities of your life, your quiet place may have to be a setting that is far from ideal. Your office — when the door is shut — may work for you. It could be your bedroom at home. Or your car, when you're stopped in traffic or commuting to work.

Work with a tape

Listening to a audio tape can be a marvelous way to learn and practice many of the relaxation and stress-reducing exercises presented in this book. The Appendix provides a script you can use to make a tape recording of the directions for many of the stress-management techniques. If you can, get someone else to be the voice on the recording. For most of us, listening to our own voices can be disconcerting.

Get a stress buddy

Doing something by yourself can be hard. Losing weight, going to the gym, stopping smoking are all easier when you do them with a friend. The same holds true for stress management. See if you can interest a friend in joining you. Your stress buddy can make your relaxation tape for you and gently prod you to practice and put your new skills into daily use.

Don't expect overnight results

Let's face it. It took you years to create your stress-producing styles and patterns. Fortunately, changing these patterns takes a lot less time, but it still takes some time. You need to change your behaviors and thinking, and modify your lifestyle and work style. You get there step by step. See yourself as being part of a program that looks at your daily encounters and experiences as opportunities for growth and change.

Part II
Mastering the Basics

The 5th Wave   By Rich Tennant

"No, Dave isn't big on exercise. About once every 3 years we take him to the doctors and have his pores surgically opened."

In this part . . .

1 present common-sense ways for you to deal with stress. I show you how to treat the physical symptoms of stress, quiet your mind, and deal with day-to-day issues that may be causing stress: Maybe you aren't as organized as you'd like to be, or maybe your career is taking time away from your family, or maybe you're not eating right. I can help.

Chapter 4

Letting Go of Tension

. . . .

In This Chapter

▶ Understanding the effects of tension

▶ Recognizing your tension

▶ Breathing properly

▶ Using suggestion to relax

▶ Stretching and massaging

. . . .

When you're under stress, your muscles contract and become tense. This muscle tension is nature's way of preparing you to cope with a potential threat — it's a part of the fight-or-flight response I describe in Chapter 1. Your body is now ready to fight that tiger. Unfortunately, this once adaptive response — and the accompanying muscle tension — can be triggered by less than life-threatening situations (like the disagreeable taxi driver who doesn't seem to have a clue where he's going but is breaking speed records to get there). Muscle tension can result in a wide variety of stress-related conditions and disorders. Fortunately, you can catch your tension before it does its worst. All you need are the right stress-busting tools in your toolbox.

This chapter describes those strategies and techniques that can help you let go of tension and relax your body. Chapter 5 shows you how to relax your mind. Together, these tools provide you with an important set of stress management skills.

Stress Can Be a Pain in the Neck (And That's Just for Starters)

The following is a short — and only partial — list of some of the effects tension has on your body. Unfortunately, many of these symptoms are all too familiar.

  ✔ Neck pain

  ✔ Headaches

  ✔ Stomach cramps

  ✔ Lower-back pain

  ✔ Clenched, painful jaw

  ✔ Sore shoulders

  ✔ Muscle spasms

  ✔ Tremors or twitches

And that's just on the outside. Inside your body other tension-related changes are happening. Here is a sampling of what else is quietly going on in your body when you feel tense:

  ✔ Your blood pressure goes up

  ✔ Your stomach secretes more acid

  ✔ Your cholesterol goes up

  ✔ Your blood clots faster

All in all, knowing how to prevent and eliminate bodily tension seems like a pretty healthy idea.

Funny, I don't feel tense

The fact is, you may not know when your body is tense. You get so used to being tense that you usually do not notice that you are feeling tense. Muscle tension creeps up on you. Slowly and often imperceptibly your muscles tighten and, voilà, the tension sets in. You don't feel the tension until you get a headache or feel the soreness in your neck and shoulders. The trick is to become aware of any bodily tension *before* it builds up and does its damage. Tuning in to your body takes a bit of practice. The next section gives you a simple awareness technique that helps you recognize your tension before it becomes a bigger problem.

Invasion of the body scan

One of the best ways to discover how to recognize bodily tension is to use this simple 1-minute scanning exercise:

Find a place where you can sit or lay down comfortably, and be undisturbed for a moment or two (see Figure 4-1). Scan your body for any muscle tension. Start with the top of your head, and work your way down to your toes. Ask yourself:

Figure 4-1:
A good position for body scanning.

✔ Am I furrowing my brow?

✔ Am I knitting my eyebrows?

✔ Am I clenching my jaw?

✔ Am I pursing my lips?

✔ Am I hunching my shoulders?

✔ Am I feeling tension in my arms?

✔ Am I feeling tightness in my thigh and calf muscles?

✔ Am I curling my toes?

✔ Do I notice any discomfort anywhere else in my body?

With a little practice, you can scan your body in less than a minute, finding your tension quickly. Try to do a body scan three or four times a day. It is a great way of becoming aware of your stress. When you find your stress, of course, you want to do something about it. The following sections give you some options.

Breathing Away Your Tension

Breathing properly is one of the simplest and best ways of draining your tension and relieving your stress. Simply by changing your breathing patterns, you can rapidly induce a state of greater relaxation. If you control the way you breathe, you have a powerful tool in reducing bodily tension. As important, you have a tool that helps prevent your body from becoming tense in the first place. This section shows you what you can do to incorporate a variety of stress-effective breathing techniques into your life.

Looking under the hood

Breathing provides your body with oxygen and removes waste products — primarily carbon dioxide — from your blood. Your lungs carry out this gas exchange. Lungs, however, do not have their own muscles for breathing. Your *diaphragm* is the major muscle necessary for proper breathing. The diaphragm is a dome-shaped muscle that separates your chest cavity from your abdominal cavity, and acts as a flexible floor for your lungs.

When you inhale, your diaphragm flattens downward, creating more space in the chest cavity, and permits the lungs to fill. When you exhale, your diaphragm returns to its dome shape. Diaphragmatic, or abdominal breathing provides the most efficient way of exchanging oxygen and carbon dioxide.

Your diaphragm works automatically, but you can override the process, especially when you are under stress. And that's where problems can arise. Too often you neglect to use your diaphragm when you breathe, and you interfere with the proper exchanges of gases in your system, which can result in greater tension, more fatigue, and more stress.

Your breath is fine. It's your breathing that's bad.

You probably take your breathing for granted. And why not? You've probably been breathing for years; you'd think by now you would have figured out how to do it right. No such luck. "Bad breathing" can take a number of forms. You may be a *chest and shoulder breather,* bringing air into your lungs by expanding your chest cavity and raising your shoulders. This description certainly fits if you have more than a touch of vanity and opt for never sticking out your tummy when you breathe. You also may be a *breath holder,* stopping your breathing entirely when you're distracted or lost in thought. Both are inefficient, stress-producing forms of breathing. And when you are under stress, your breathing patterns deteriorate even more. To make things worse, once your breathing goes awry, you feel even more stressed. Quite a nasty cycle.

Why change now? I've been breathing for years.

When you're feeling stressed, your breathing becomes faster and shallower. When you breathe this way, your body reacts:

- ✔ Less oxygen reaches your bloodstream
- ✔ Your blood vessels constrict
- ✔ Less oxygen reaches your brain
- ✔ Your heart rate and your blood pressure go up
- ✔ You feel light-headed, shaky, and more tense

Our primitive ancestors knew how to breathe. They didn't have to deal with the IRS, stacks of unpaid bills, or The Boss From Hell. These days only opera singers, stage actors, musicians who play wind instruments, and a couple of dozen moonlighting yoga instructors actually breathe effectively. The rest of us mess it up.

However, for a period of your life, you did get the whole breathing thing right. As a baby lying in your crib you breathed serenely. Your little belly rose and fell in the most relaxed way. But then you grew up and blew it. Thankfully all is not lost. You can re-teach yourself to breathe properly.

You probably think of breathing as a way of getting air into your lungs. However, in times past breathing was elevated to a more important status. Many religious groups and sects believed that a calming breath replenished the soul as well as soothed the body. In fact, the word *ruach* in Hebrew, and the word *pneuma* in Greek have double meanings, connoting both breath *and* spirit. If you remember your Bible, the book of Genesis says that when God created Adam, he "breathed into his nostrils the breath of life; and man became a living soul."

Evaluating your breathing

You may be one of the few people who actually breathe properly. But before you skip this section, read a little further. To find out whether the way you breathe is stress-reducing take this simple test.

1. **Lie on your back.**

2. **Put your right hand on your belly and your left hand on your chest, as shown in Figure 4-2.**

   Try to become aware of the way you breathe. Check to see whether your breathing is smooth, slow, and regular. If you're breathing properly, the hand on your belly rises and falls rhythmically as you inhale and exhale. The hand on your chest should move very little, and if that hand does rise, it should follow the rise in your belly.

Figure 4-2:
Evaluating
your
breathing.

Digesting and practicing new relaxation techniques is much easier when some-one reads them to you, rather than you trying to read them off the page — especially when the directions tell you to close your eyes. One idea is to go out a buy a blank cassette or two and tape the instructions. This way you can stick the cassette into your walkman and listen when you are on the train, on a plane, or at the office when your boss is away. Another idea is to find a friend with a soothing, mellifluous voice and have him or her be the reader. You do not want to listen to someone who sounds like Miss Jamison, my third grade teacher. A wonderful teacher, but oh that voice.

Cutting yourself some slack

I commonly find that people who want to adopt new patterns of breathing have a fervent desire to get it perfectly right. They frequently get so lost in body parts or lung mechanics that they wind up more stressed out than they were before they started. Don't let this happen to you. And remember that there is no one exactly *right* way to breathe all the time. Give yourself lots of room to experiment with your breathing. And don't overdo it. If you've been breathing inefficiently for all these years, changing gears may take some time. Above all, you are not taking a test. Do not grade yourself on how deep your can breathe or how flat you can make your diaphragm. Remember, the goal is to reduce your stress, not add to it.

Changing the way you breathe, changing the way you feel

Sometimes, all it takes to make you feel better is one, simple change. Changing the way you breathe can make all the difference in how you feel. The following exercises present various ways to alter your breathing. Try them, and discover whether all you need is one, simple change.

Breathing 101: Breathing for starters

Here is one of the best and simplest ways of introducing yourself to stress-effective breathing.

1. **Either lying or sitting comfortably, put one hand on your belly and your other hand on your chest.**

2. **Inhale through your nose making sure that the hand on your belly rises, and the hand on your chest moves hardly at all.**

3. **As you inhale slowly, count silently to yourself to 3.**

4. **As you exhale, slowly count to 4, feeling the hand on your belly falling gently.**

   Pause slightly before your next breath. Repeat for several minutes and whenever you get the chance.

Moving on to something more advanced: Taking a complete breath

Complete breaths (or *Zen breathing* as it is often called) helps you breathe more deeply, more efficiently, and maximize your lung capacity.

1. **Lie comfortably in bed, a reclining chair, or on a rug.**

   Keep your knees slightly apart and slightly bent. Close your eyes if you like.

2. **Put one hand on your abdomen near your belly-button, and the other hand on your chest so that you follow the motion of your breathing.**

   Try to relax. Let go of any tension you may feel in your body.

3. **Begin by slowly inhaling through your nose, first filling the lower part of your lungs, then the middle part of your chest, and then the upper part of your chest.**

   As you inhale, feel your diaphragm pushing down, gently extending your abdomen, making room for the newly inhaled air. Notice the hand on your abdomen rise slightly. The hand on your chest should move very little, and when it does, it should follow your abdomen. Do not use your shoulders to help you breathe.

4. **Exhale slowly through your parted lips, emptying your lungs from top to bottom.**

   Make a whooshing sound as the air passes through your lips, and notice the hand on your abdomen fall.

5. **Pause slightly, and take in another breath repeating this cycle.**

   Continue breathing this way for ten minutes or so — certainly until you feel more relaxed and peaceful. Practice this technique daily if you can. Try this exercise while sitting and then while standing.

With a little practice, this form of breathing comes more naturally, and automatically. Over some time and some practice, you may begin to breathe this way much more of the time. Stick with it.

Trying some "belly-button balloon" breathing

A simpler way of breathing more deeply and more evenly is to work with a visual image, in this case a balloon. Here's what you have to do:

1. **Imagine that a small balloon — about the size of a grapefruit — is replacing your stomach, just under your belly-button, as shown in Figure 4-3.**

2. **As you inhale through your nose, imagine that you are actually inhaling through your belly-button, inflating this once empty balloon.**

   This balloon is small, so don't overinflate it. As the balloon gets larger, notice how your belly rises.

3. **Exhale slowly through your nose, again imagining that the air is leaving through your belly-button.**

   Your balloon is now slowly and easily returning to its deflated state.

4. **Pause slightly before the next breath in, and then repeat, gently and smoothly inflating your balloon to a comfortable size.**

   Repeat this exercise, as often as you can, whenever you can.

Emergency breathing: How to breathe in the trenches

Breathing properly is no big deal when you're lying on your bed or vegging out in front of the TV. But what's your breathing like when you're caught in gridlock, when you're facing down a deadline, or when the stock market drops 20 percent? You are now in a crisis mode. You need another form of breathing. Here's what to do:

TIP

Standing up straight

Your mother was right! When you are under stress, you have a tendency to hunch over, making your posture lousy and your breathing impaired. You then breath less deeply, denying your system the proper supply of oxygen you need. As a result, your muscles get tense. When you stand or sit straight, you reverse this process. You needn't stand like a West Point cadet to correct bad posture. Overdoing it probably produces as much tension as you felt before. Just keep your shoulders from slouching forward. If you're unsure about what your posture looks like, ask your mother, or a good friend.

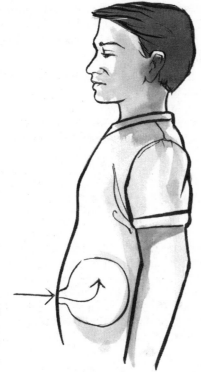

Figure 4-3:
Balloon
breathing.

1. **Inhale slowly through your nostrils, taking in a very deep diaphragmatic breath, filling your lungs and filling your cheeks.**

2. **Hold that breath for about six seconds.**

3. **Exhale *slowly* through your slightly parted lips, releasing *all* the air in your lungs.**

   Pause at the end of this exhalation. Now take a few "normal" breaths.

   Repeat Steps 1 through 3, two or three times and then return to what you were doing. This form of deep breathing should put you in a more relaxed state.

The yawn that refreshes

Yawning is usually associated with boredom. Business meetings you think will run well into the millennium, or painful telephone solicitors explaining (in detail) the virtues of *their* long-distance plan may trigger more than a few yawning gasps. However, your yawn may signal something more than boredom.

Yawning is another way Mother Nature tells you that your body is under stress. In fact, yawning helps relieve stress. When you yawn, more air — and therefore more oxygen — enters your lungs, revitalizing your blood stream. Releasing that plaintive sound that comes with yawning is also tension reducing. Unfortunately, people have become a little over-socialized, making for wimpy yawns. You need to recapture this lost art.

The next time you feel a yawn coming on, go with it. Open your mouth widely and inhale more fully than you normally might. Take that breath all the way down to your belly. Exhale fully through your mouth, completely emptying your lungs. What a feeling! Enjoy it. So what if your friends don't call you anymore?

Tensing Your Way to Relaxation

After you master the art of breathing (see the exercises in the preceding section), you're ready to discover another way of relaxing your body. One of the better relaxation techniques derives from a method called *progressive relaxation* or *deep muscle relaxation*. This method is based on the notion that you are not aware of what your muscles feel like when they are tensed. By purposely tensing your muscles, you are able to recognize what tension feels like and identify which muscles are creating that tension. This technique is highly effective and has been proven to be a valuable tool for quickly reducing muscle tension and promoting relaxation.

Exploring how progressive relaxation works

You begin progressive relaxation by tensing a specific muscle or group of muscles (your arms, legs, shoulders, and so on). You notice the way the tension feels. You hold that tension for about ten seconds, and then let it go, replacing that tension with something much more pleasant — relaxation. By the time you tense and relax most of your major muscle groups, you will feel relaxed, at peace, and much less stressed. The following general guidelines that set the stage for more specific muscle-group specific and relaxation instructions later in this chapter.

Appendix A gives you a complete set of progressive muscle relaxation instructions which you can tape, so that you don't have to remember all the various instructions and muscle groups.

1. **Lie down or sit, as comfortably as you can, and close your eyes.**

   Find a quiet, dimly lit place that gives you some privacy, at least for a while.

2. **Tense the muscles of a particular body part.**

   To practice, start by tensing your right hand and arm. Begin by simply making a fist. As you clench your fist, notice the tension and strain in your hand and forearm. Without releasing that tension, bend your right arm and flex your biceps, making a muscle the way you might to impress the kids in the school-yard.

   Do not strain yourself in any of these muscle tensing maneuvers; don't overdo it. When you tense a muscle group, don't tense as hard as you can. Tense about ¾ of what you can do. If you feel pain or soreness, ease up on the tension, and if you still hurt, defer your practice till another time.

3. **Hold the tension in the body part for about seven seconds.**

4. **Let go of the tension fairly quickly, letting the muscles go limp.**

   Notice the difference in the way your hand and arm feels. Notice the difference in feelings between the sensations of tension and those of relaxation. Let these feeling of relaxation deepen for about 30 seconds or so.

5. **Repeat Steps 1 through 4, using the same muscle group.**

6. **Move to another muscle group.**

   Simply repeat Steps 1 through 4, substituting a different muscle group each time. Continue with your left hand and arm and then work your way through the major muscle groups listed in the following section.

Relaxing your face and head

Wrinkle your forehead (creating all those lines that everybody hates)by raising your eyebrows as high as you can. Hold this tension for about 5 seconds, and then let go, releasing all of the tension in your forehead. Just let your forehead muscles become smooth. Notice the difference between the feelings of tension you felt and the more pleasant feelings of relaxation.

Now clench your jaw by biting down on your back teeth and at the same time force a smile. Hold this uncomfortable position for about 5 seconds or so, and then relax your jaw, letting your mouth fall slightly ajar.

Finally, purse your lips, pushing them together firmly. Hold that tension for a bit, and then relax, letting your lips open slightly. Now notice how relaxed your face and head feels. Enjoy this sensation and let this feeling deepen by letting go of any remaining sources of tension around your mouth and lips.

Relaxing your neck and shoulders

Bend your head forward as though you are going to touch your chest with your chin (you probably will). Feel the tension in the muscles of your neck. Hold that tension. Now tilt your head slightly, first to one side and then to another. Notice the tension at the side of your neck as you do so. Now relax, letting your head return to a more comfortable, natural position. Enjoy the relaxation for a moment or so.

Now scrunch up your shoulders as though you are trying to reach your ears. Hold it, feel the tension (again about 5 seconds), and let your shoulders fall to a comfortable, relaxed position. Notice the feelings of relaxation that are spreading through your shoulders and neck.

Relaxing your back

Arch your back, being careful not to overdo it. Hold that tension for several seconds, and then let your back and shoulders return to a more comfortable, relaxed position.

Relaxing your legs and feet

Either sitting or lying down, raise your right foot so that you feel some tension in your thigh and buttock. At the same time push your heel out and point your toes toward your head, as shown in Figure 4-4. Hold this tension, notice what it feels like and then let go, letting your leg fall to the bed or floor, releasing any remaining tension. Let that relaxation deepen for a while. Repeat this sequence with your other leg and foot.

Figure 4-4:
Relaxing
your feet
and legs.

Relaxing your stomach

Take in a deep breath and hold that breath, tensing the muscles in your stomach. Imagine that your are preparing yourself for a punch in the stomach. Hold that tension. And relax, letting go of the tension.

After you finish this sequence, let your body sink into an even deeper state of relaxation. Let go more and more. Mentally go over the sensations you are feeling in your arms face, neck, shoulders, back, stomach, and legs. Feel your body becoming looser and more relaxed. Savor the feeling.

Scrunching up like a pretzel

When pressed for time, you can use a quickie version of the progressive relaxation exercise that I talk about in the preceding section. Simply, this technique compresses all the muscle tensing and relaxing sequences into one. Think of it as one gigantic scrunch.

In order to do this, you have to master the gradual version first. The success of this rapid form of relaxation depends on your ability to create and release muscle tension quickly, skills you master by slowly working through all of the muscle groups individually. Here's what to do:

Sit or lie comfortably in a room that gives you some quiet and is relatively free of distractions. Now, tense all of the muscle-groups listed below, simultaneously:

- Clench both fists, bend both arms and tense your biceps. At the same time,
- Lift both legs until you notice a moderate degree of tension and discomfort, and
- Scrunch up your face, closing your eyes, furrowing your brow, clenching your jaws, and pursing your lips, and
- Bring your shoulders as close as you can to your ears, while you
- Tense your stomach muscles.

Hold this "total scrunch" for about 5 seconds and then release, letting go of any and all tension. Let your legs fall to the floor or bed, your arms to your sides, and let the rest of your body return to a relaxed position. Repeat this sequence at various points throughout your day.

Mind Over Body: Using the Power of Suggestion

Another important approach to bodily relaxation is called *Autogenic Training,* or *AT* for short. The word *autogenic* means self-generation or self-regulation. This method attempts to regulate your *autonomic nervous functions* (your heart rate, blood pressure, and breathing among others) rather than by relaxing your muscles. With Autogenic Training, you use your mind to regulate your body's internal stress levels.

AT relies on the power of suggestion to induce physiological changes within you. These *suggestions* are mental images that your subconscious picks up and transmits to your body. Just thinking about certain changes in your body produces those kinds of changes. As a result, you experience deep feelings of relaxation. AT may sound very mysterious, but it isn't. After you master this technique, AT is a highly effective way of putting yourself in a more relaxed state. The method I describe here is a more abbreviated form that the one originally devised. However it is better suited to a busy lifestyle. Here's what you do:

1. **Get comfy.**

   Find a suitably quiet, not-too-hot, and not-too-cold place. You can sit or lie down, but make sure that your body is well-supported and as comfortable as possible. Try to breathe slowly and smoothly.

Use your imagination? You're getting warmer!

With Autogenic Training, you may find that using the warm and heavy suggestions and images aren't effective for you. You may need a different image to release the tension in your body. Here are alternate suggestive images that I have found can induce feelings of warmth and heaviness.

✔ **Heat me up:** Imagine that the body part in question (arm, leg, and so on) is wrapped in a heating pad. Slowly but surely the heat permeates your body, relaxing your muscles more and more.

✔ **Get in hot water:** Imagine that you are immersing your arm or leg in very soothing warm water.

✔ **Sunny side up:** Mentally direct a sun lamp to a particular part of your anatomy.

✔ **Heavy metal:** Visualize weights attached to your arm, leg, and so on.

✔ **Get the lead in:** Imagine that your limb is filled with lead.

2. Concentrate *passively.*

For this approach to be effective, you need adopt a receptive, casual attitude of *passive concentration.* You want to be alert, not falling asleep, but you don't want your mind working too hard. You cannot force yourself to relax. Just let it happen. Be aware of your body and your mind but don't actively analyze everything or worry about how you are doing. Should a distracting thought come your way, notice it, and then let it go. If the relaxation doesn't come at first, don't worry. It comes with more practice.

3. Allow various body parts to begin feeling warm and heavy.

Although autogenic training utilizes many suggestions and images, the two most effective images are warmth and heaviness. Start by focusing on your right arm. Now *slowly* and *softly* say to yourself:

I am calm . . . I am at peace . . . My right arm is warm . . . and heavy . . . My right arm is warm . . . and heavy . . . My right arm is warm . . . and heavy . . . I can feel the warmth and heaviness flowing into my right arm . . . I can feel my right arm becoming warmer . . . and heavier . . . I can feel my right arm becoming warmer . . . and heavier . . . I can feel my right arm becoming warmer . . . and heavier . . . I am at peace . . . I am calm . . . I am at peace . . . I am calm.

Take the time to become aware of the feelings in your arm and hand. Notice that your arm *is* becoming warmer and heavier. Don't rush this process. Enjoy the changes your body is now begin to experience.

5. After you complete the phrases, remain silent and calm for about 30 seconds, letting the relaxation deepen; then focus on your *left arm.*

Repeat the same phrases again, this time substituting *left arm* for right arm. (Hopefully, by now you have memorized these phrases and can close your eyes and not worry about a script.)

6. Move to other parts of your body.

Focus on other areas, repeating the same phrases, but substituting other parts of your body. Here is the complete sequence: right arm, left arm, both arms, right leg, left leg, both legs, neck and shoulders, chest and abdomen, and finally your entire body.

Completing the entire sequence shouldn't take you more than a half hour or so. If you can fit in two or three autogenic sessions in a day, all the better. You may need some time to master this technique, but the results are well worth the effort.

"All this relaxing is making me tense!"

Believe it or not, you may find that practicing relaxation can be stressful, at least at first.

Changing your breathing patterns, tensing and relaxing muscles, and exploring autogenic exercises can result in some strange side effects. You may notice some tingling or a feeling of restlessness, and paradoxically, an *increase* in tension. This is not unusual, and although it is distracting, don't take this as a sign that you're doing something wrong. As you become more familiar with how your body feels when it is in a highly relaxed state, these sensations disappear.

Stretching Away Your Stress

Stretching is one of the ways that your body naturally discharges excess bodily tension. Waking up in the morning or just before retiring at night are the times you automatically feel the need for a stretch. But a good stretch can drain away much of your body's tension at other times, too. You may be desk-bound or sit for long periods of time during the day, causing your muscles to tense and tighten. Consider adopting one or more basic stretches and taking a "stretch-break" at various points throughout the day. Cats do, dogs do, why not you?

Following are two tension-relieving stretches that I find to be wonderful ways of draining off a lot of excess tension. They are simple and shouldn't evoke much comment or ridicule from friends or coworkers.

- ✔ **The Twist.** This stretch is great for your upper body. Sitting or standing, put both your hands behind the back of your head, locking your fingers together. Move your elbows towards each other until you feel some moderate tension. Now twist your body slightly, first to the right for a few seconds, and then slowly to the left. When you finish, let your arms fall to your side.

- ✔ **The Leg-lift.** This stretch is good for your lower body. Sitting in your chair, raise both your legs until you feel a comfortable level of tightness in them. Maintaining that tension, flex and point your toes toward your head. Hold that tension for about 10 seconds or so and then let your legs fall to the floor. If doing this with both legs together is a wee bit uncomfortable, try it one leg at a time.

Stretch slowly and don't overdo it. You're trying to relax your muscles, not punish them.

Massage? Ah, There's the Rub!

Massage, and other touch and pressure therapies are among the most popular ways of relieving muscle tension. These days you can get a massage almost as easily as you can get your hair cut. In the past, the idea of a massage usually conjured up an image of a liniment rubdown in a sweaty gym, or pampered caresses in a swanky health spa. No more. Massage and related treatment have come of age.

The range and the popularity of touch and pressure disciplines and therapies has grown enormously in recent years. A partial list of available methods and techniques include:

- Swedish massage
- Reflexology
- Shiatsu
- Chiropractic
- Acupressure

All of these methods have their origins in early medicine and healing. Many claim spiritual as well as physical changes. Rather than go into each of these disciplines separately, I am going to discuss several of the simpler stress-relieving exercises from the above list that I find to be particularly useful and easy to grasp.

You have several choices when it comes to massage. You can spend some bucks and get a professional to give you a massage. Or you can find someone who will give you a massage for free. Or you can give yourself a massage. I'm going to start with the last option, which is often the cheapest and doesn't require friends.

Massaging yourself

You can go two ways: High-tech or low-tech.

The high-tech route usually requires a wall-socket or lots of batteries. Many specialty stores stock loads of massage paraphernalia. My favorite is a mega-buck relaxation chair that transports you to relaxation heaven with the flick of a switch. On the less expensive side, a handheld vibrator massages those tight and tired muscles, leaving you much more relaxed. Alternately, you can forego the batteries and the cash by letting your fingers do the work. Fingers are cheaper, easy to control, and readily available. Following are three simple ways to rub out your stress.

For your hands

Hold your left palm in front of you, fingers together. The fleshy spot between your thumb and index finger is a key acupressure point that should spread a sensation of relaxation when massaged. Using your right thumb, massage this spot in a circular motion for a slow count of 15. Switch hands, and repeat.

For stress-related fatigue, pinch just below the first joint of your pinkie with the thumb and index finger of the opposite hand. (Pressure should be firm but not painful). Increase the pressure slightly. Make small circular movements in a counterclockwise direction while maintaining pressure. Continue for 20 seconds. Release. Wait for ten seconds and repeat up to 5 times.

For your feet

Try this sole-soothing exercise. Take off your socks and shoes and sit comfortably with one leg crossed over the other. (The sole of your foot should be almost facing you.) With both hands, grasp the arches of your foot and apply pressure, especially with your thumbs. Now kneading (like you would bread dough, using your thumbs and fingers) every part of your foot, work your way from your heel right up to your toes. Give each of your toes a squeeze. Now massage the other foot in a similar way.

If crossing your legs is more stressful than it used to be, go to the kitchen and get your rolling pin. Sit in a chair and position the rolling pin next to your foot. Gently roll your bare foot back and forth slowly for 2 minutes or so. Then try it with the other foot. Now wash the pin.

If you don't own a rolling pin, work with a tennis ball. Put it under the arch of your bare foot, put some pressure on that foot, and move the ball backward and forward.

Keep this rhythm going for about 2 minutes, and then switch to your other foot.

For your neck and shoulders

Stress most often finds its way to your neck and shoulders. To dissipate that tension, take your left hand and firmly massage your right shoulder and the right side of your neck. Start with some gentle circular motions, rubbing the muscle with your index and pointer fingers. Then finish with a firmer message, squeezing the shoulder and neck muscles between your thumb and other fingers. Now switch to the other side.

For your face

Start by placing both of your hands on your face with the tips of your fingers resting on your forehead and the heels of your palms resting just under your cheeks. Gently pull down the skin on your forehead with the tips of your fingers while pushing up the area under your palms. Rhythmically repeat this movement, contracting and releasing your fingers and palms.

You can also try pulling on your ears in different directions. My editor swears by it.

Becoming the massage-er or massage-ee

Having someone else give you a massage certainly has its advantages. When someone else does all the work, you can completely let go: Sit or lie back and totally relax. And another person can reach places on your body that you could never reach. You can, of course, visit a massage therapist; you can also ask a friend to give you a massage. Of course, you may have to reciprocate. But even giving someone else a massage can relieve some of your tension. Here are some general hints and guidelines to get you started:

- ✔ Use some massage oil or body lotion to add a relaxing aroma and smooth the massage process. (Warm the oil to room temperature so as not to shock you or your partner's system.)

- ✔ Lower the lights to provide a soothing, relaxing atmosphere. Calming music also adds a nice touch.

- ✔ Focus your massage on the lower back, neck, and shoulders — places stress tends to reside and cause the most discomfort.

- ✔ Start by applying pressure very lightly until the massage-ee is relaxed. Then increasing the pressure, using your palms to knead the muscles. Finish up with a lighter massage, and let your partner linger for a while after the massage to extend the sense of relaxation.

- ✔ Don't overdo it. A good massage shouldn't have the massage-ee writhing in pain. A bad massage can cause more stress than it attempts to relieve.

Taking a 3-Minute Energy Burst

Any concentrated expenditure of energy produces more stress by tensing your muscles, speeding your heart-rate, and quickening your breathing. However, after you stop expending energy, you find that your muscles, heart, and breathing slow down to a level that is lower than when you started. This energy boost can come from walking very briskly, a short run, jumping jacks, rope jumping, sit ups, push ups, running up steps — anything that gets your body going.

My own favorite way of relaxing my muscles

I am not a bath kind of guy. I am a shower guy. One of my more relaxing, soul-soothing experiences is luxuriating in a very hot shower with the faucets turned on full force and the spray massaging my body. My muscles go limp, my pulse slows, and I am transfixed. A key to all this physiological bliss is the right shower head. I have found that either the very old, large, flat shower heads with dozens of holes, or the newer models where you can manually dial the spray and pressure, and even pulse, work the best. I just stand there until I look like a prune.

✔ **Become a shaker.** Shaking off tension is fun. You can do this exercise either sitting or standing. Begin by holding your arms loosely in front of you and start shaking your hands at the wrist. Now let your arms and shoulders join in the fun. Continue for a short while, and taper off slowly, letting your arms fall comfortably to your sides. Now lift one leg and start shaking it. Then shift to the other leg. (If you are sitting, you can do both legs at the same time). When you finish, notice the tingling sensations in your body and more importantly, the feelings of relaxation. Admittedly, it looks a little strange, but it works.

✔ **Soak up your stress.** Think of your bathroom as a mini health spa and your bathtub as a pool of relaxation. Besides, not only do you emerge relaxed and de-stressed, but you're also clean. Here's the recipe for that relaxing soak:

- A spare half hour
- A tub of hot, soapy water
- Soothing scents
- Soft lighting
- Relaxing music
- A phone that is off the hook or fed into your answering machine

More Ways to Relax

A few relaxation techniques from off the beaten path:

✔ **Throw in the towel.** There was a time when barbers gave their customers shaves along with haircuts. In those days, your felt marvelous as your barber carefully placed moist, hot towels on your face. These days, stylists only cut hair. And other than flying first class to Europe or dining in an upscale Japanese restaurant, you are unlikely to experience the joys of a hot towel on your face — unless, of course, you put it there yourself. Simply take one or two washcloths and immerse them in hot water. Squeeze out the excess water, lie back, close your eyes, and put them on your face. Ah, nirvana.

And what if you don't have a towel or hot water? Use your hands. Rub them together till they feel warm. Place each hand on a side of your face. No, the feeling is not quite as good as a moist, hot towel, but it can still help you relax.

✔ **Go East young man.** Yoga is a wonderful way of relaxing your body and calming your thoughts. Through movement, breath, and body control, yoga exercises help you relax and release stress. Most people who have tried yoga swear by it. Find a good teacher and give it a try. (Ask friends about yoga classes in your community.) It's a commitment, but it's well worth the effort.

✔ **Relax in the bedroom.** Sex can be a marvelous way of unwinding and letting go of physical tension. Including some form of mutual massage into your love-making can increase the relaxation benefits.

Have a drink?

Dare I suggest that you use an alcoholic beverage as an agent of relaxation?

Yes and no.

Research literature, for some time now, has been supportive of the value of moderate drinking (that is, no more than one or two alcoholic drinks per day). At this level of intake, alcohol has been found to raise levels of HDL (the good cholesterol) and lessen the risk of heart disease.

However, the risks from excessive drinking far outweigh these benefits. For many, drinking can be a slippery slope, with the cure becoming the disease.

The bottom line: Don't put alcohol on the top of your stress-reduction list. If you have successfully integrated a drink or the occasional use of a pill into your life, fine. But always remember, you can reduce your stress in better ways.

Chapter 5

Quieting Your Mind

. . . .

In This Chapter

▶ Slowing down your mind

▶ Using imagery to relax

▶ Stopping unwanted thoughts

▶ Investigating meditation

▶ Hypnotizing yourself

. . . .

To be completely relaxed, you need to not only relax your body but also calm your mind. Chapter 4 shows you how to relax your body and how to let go of physical tension. This chapter details how to quiet your mind. For many people, and you may be one of them, stress takes the form of psychological distress, and you find that your mind is filled with distressing thoughts that prevent you from feeling relaxed and at ease. It may be that your mind is racing a mile a minute. You may be worrying about your job, your relationships, your finances, or simply how you are going to juggle the hundred and one things that are on your plate. Whatever the source of your worry, you clearly are not going to relax until you stop — or at least slow — this mental mayhem.

One of the best ways to relax your mind is to relax you body. When your body relaxes, your mind slows. (Check out Chapter 4 for some physical relaxation techniques.) But there are other ways of taming your unruly thoughts and calming your restless mind. This chapter shows you how.

Five signs that your mind is stressed

Below are some of the more common signs that indicate that your mind is working overtime. See how many of the following describe you.

1. Your mind seems to be racing.

2. You find controlling your thoughts difficult.

3. You are worried, irritable, or upset.

4. You are preoccupied more often and find concentrating more difficult.

5. You find it difficult to fall asleep or to fall back asleep once awake.

Distract Yourself

The simplest way to calm your mind is to distract yourself. This idea may sound obvious, but you'd be surprised how often people overlook this option. Psychologists know that concentrating on two things at the same time is very hard. Therefore, if your mind is flooded with distressing thoughts, change course. Find something else to think about. Here are some pleasant diversions you may want to consider:

- Watch some television
- Go to a movie
- Read a book, newspaper, or magazine
- Talk to a friend
- Work or play on your computer
- Play a sport
- Immerse yourself on some project or hobby
- Listen to some favorite music
- Think of something you are looking forward to

One of the best ways to distract yourself, calm your mind, and stop those unwanted, persistent worries is to use your imagination.

Imagine This

If you can replace that stress-producing thought or image with one that is relaxing, the chances are that you'll feel much better. Here's how:

1. **Find a place where you won't be disturbed for a few minutes and get comfortable, either sitting in a favorite chair or lying down.**

2. **Think of an image — a place, a scene, or a memory — that relaxes you.**

   Figure 5-1 shows an example.

   Use all your senses to bring that imagined scene to life. Ask yourself: What do I see? What can I hear? What can I smell? What can I feel?

3. **Let yourself become completely immersed in your image, allowing it to relax you completely.**

Figure 5-1:
Isn't this
relaxing?

"Sounds good," you say, "but what is my relaxing image?" Try taking one these mental vacations (airfare included):

- **The Caribbean package:** Imagine that you're on the beach of a Caribbean isle. The weather is perfect. Lying on the cool sand, you feel the warm breeze caress your body. You hear the lapping of the ocean waves on the shore and the tropical birds chirping in the palms. You are slowly sipping a piña colada. You can smell your coconut-scented suntan lotion. You feel wonderful. You are relaxed. Your mind is totally at peace.

- **The pool package:** You are lying in a large inflatable raft, floating blissfully in an incredibly beautiful swimming pool. The day is perfect. The sky is a deep blue, the sun is warming your relaxed body. You feel the gentle rocking of the raft in the water. You can hear the soothing voice of the waiter announcing a buffet lunch in a half an hour. You are very content. You could lie here forever.

- **The winter wonderland package:** Picture yourself in a small cabin in Vermont (if your tastes lean to the more extravagant, switch the scene to Aspen, or Gstadt — the cost is the same no matter where you go). You're snowed in, but that's fine because you don't have to be anywhere and no one needs to contact you. Also, you're not alone — a favorite person is with you and you're both lying in front of a crackling fire. Soft music is playing in the background. You're sipping hot toddies, mulled wine, or champagne.

- **A pleasing memory:** Try to picture a memory, possibly when you were growing up, or one from more recent times that you find particularly happy and satisfying. It could be a vacation long ago, a birthday party you loved, or frolicking with a childhood pet.

None of these examples do it for you? Then come up with your own personal relaxation image. You might try one of these:

- Soaking in a hot, soapy bath . . . soft music . . . candle light. . . .
- Walking in a quiet forest . . . birds chirping . . . leaves rustling. . . .
- Lying under a tree in the park . . . warm breezes . . . more chirping. . . .
- In your most comfortable chair . . . reading a great book . . . no chirping. . . .

What you see and hear usually dominates your imagination. But don't forget your senses of touch and smell. By adding these sensual dimensions you can enrich your images and make them more involving. Feel the sand between your toes; smell the freshly brewed coffee; taste the salt in the air.

Make Things Move

Your image need not be a static scene. It can change and move. You may, for example:

- Imagine a sports event that you enjoy. It could be a baseball game that you attended. Or make one up. Mentally follow the plays as you work your way through the innings. Not a baseball fan? Try imagining a tennis match.
- Try replaying favorite movies in your mind, visualizing different scenes and filling in bits of dialogue. Scenic movies work wonderfully.
- Remember the details of a trip you've taken in the past and retrace your journey from place to place.

This *Guided Imagery,* as it is called, can help keep you focused and interested in your image, and insure that unwanted, intrusive thoughts stay out of the picture.

Stop Your Thoughts

Sometimes distracting yourself isn't enough to quiet your mind. Sometimes you need stronger measures to eliminate, or at least slow, those unwanted and stress-producing worries and concerns. Perhaps you have an upsetting worry that continually intrudes into your thinking and keeps you from enjoying a pleasant evening with friends. Or maybe you're trying to fall asleep and the thoughts racing around in your head make sleeping impossible. You recognize that there is nothing you can do about your worry and that your worrying is only making things worse. You would be better off if you could somehow stop thinking about this. But how?

That's where a technique called *Thought Stopping* can be very useful. It is an effective way of not only keeping worries and upsets temporarily out of your mind, but it is also effective in weakening those thoughts, and making it less likely that they will return. Here are the steps you need to take to get this technique to work for you:

1. **Notice your thoughts.**

   When a worrisome thought runs through your mind, mentally step back and recognize that it is an unwanted thought. It may be a worry, a nagging concern, or a regret — anything that you feel is not worth the stress at this particular time.

2. **Find a stop-sign.**

   In your mind, picture a red and white hexagonal stop sign, you know, the kind you see on the street corner. Make your sign large and vivid.

3. **Yell, "Stop!"**

   In your head, silently shout the word STOP to yourself.

4. **Do it again.**

   Every time the worrisome or unwanted thought reappears, notice that thought, imagine your stop sign, and yell STOP to yourself.

5. **Find a replacement thought.**

   Find a thought or image that you can substitute for the distressing thought or image. It may be something taken from the list of relaxing images above, or any other thought that is not the one you are trying to weaken.

The image of the sign and the verbal "STOP" will disrupt your thought sequence and temporarily put the unwanted thought out of mind. Be warned, however: It probably will return, and you may have to repeat this sequence again. If your stress-producing thought or image is very strong, it may take many repetitions of this technique to weaken or eliminate it. Stick with it.

Snap out of it

One variation of the Thought Stopping that has proven useful for many people, is to use an elastic band to help interrupt the presence of a distressing thought. Simply take an ordinary elastic band and put it around your wrist. Now, whenever you notice an intrusive or unwanted thought crowding your thinking, pull the elastic and let it snap your wrist. This shouldn't be painful. Just a sharp reminder that you want this distressing thought to go. Use your mental stop sign and remember to replace your unwanted thought with something more pleasant.

What, Me Worry?

Worrying is one of the major ways your mind stays revved and keeps you stressed. You may find yourself worrying during your day or at three in the morning when you'd rather be sleeping. You may find yourself thinking about that brilliant comeback to that sarcastic coworker or that rude salesperson. Or maybe you're wondering how you're going to come up with the money to pay for all the things you charged this month. Whatever your worry, it may be keeping your mind running a mile a minute. Turning off these worries warrants a whole chapter by itself — Chapter 11. It provides you with a number of effective techniques and strategies that can help you reduce and control those distressing worries.

Strike up the band (or better yet, a string quartet)

As Congreve observed, music soothes the savage breast. He was right, though he may have added savage leg, arm, jaw, and others parts of our anatomy. Music therapists know that listening to music can result in significant physiological changes in your body: Your heart rate drops, your breathing slows, and your blood pressure lowers. But not all music does the trick. Some music can upset you, making you more stressed. (Think of that Metallica groupie living upstairs.) Other music may delight you, but still not having a calming effect.

Go for Baroque

Following is a short list of field-tested composers and compositions (Baroque and otherwise) that should slow your pulse.

- **Bach:** The slower second movements are particularly appropriate for relaxation. The Air for G-String is a real calmer.

- **Handel:** Water Music.

- **Chopin:** Nocturnes.

- **Shubert:** Symphony No. 8 in B Minor.

- **Pachelbel:** Canon in D.

- **Albinoni:** Adagio in G.

- **Mozart:** Piano Concerto #21.

- **Beethoven:** Pastoral.

- **Elgar:** Salut d'Amour.

Not a Fan of the Classics?

Of course, relaxing music need not be all classical. Bach and Mozart probably aren't as effective as Charlie Mingus if you're a jazz fan. Other forms of music can be incredibly soothing. Many of the "New Age" tapes and CDs work nicely.

No one piece of music works for everyone. Experiment. Find what relaxes you. Listen in your car while commuting, in bed before going to sleep, in your favorite chair in your favorite room. Headphones and a personal tape or CD allow you take your music — and a state of relaxation — wherever you go.

Visit the rain forest

Some years ago I was vacationing by the ocean, and as I was lolling by the water, I was transfixed by the soothing sounds of the waves rhythmically caressing the shore. Gee, I thought, wouldn't it be nice if I could have this sound lull me to sleep in my home in the city? Well, I can, and so can you.

These days, electronic sound machines can reproduce virtually any sound you can imagine. These machines cost dramatically less than they did just few years ago. So if — like me — you like the sounds of waves, no sweat. Or how about a tropical rain forest? Perhaps you like to be soothed by the sound of rain on a roof, the sound of a gurgling brook, or the sound of a beating heart. Your choice.

Use some common scents

Your ears are not the only road to mental relaxation. Your nose can work as well. People have been using scents to relieve stress and tension for centuries. An aroma can elicit feelings of calm and serenity. In fact, a school of therapy called *aromatherapy* is devoted to using your sense of smell as a vehicle for emotional change.

Studies carried out by Alan Hirsch, M.D., neurological director of the Smell and Taste Treatment and Research Foundation in Chicago, suggest that there is a connection between smell and mood: Your mood may have a biological basis.

Dr. Hirsch found that the part of the brain that registers smell may be biologically linked to the part of the brain that registers emotion. Certainly, the right scent can relax you and put you in a better mood. Here are some easy-to-find, soul-satisfying smells you may want to consider.

Eau de French-Fries?

You may think that sniffing food-related substances would send you immediately to your local fast food chain. It seems that the opposite is the case. Dr. Alan Hirsch in Chicago studied some 3,000 people, and found that smelling a banana, a green apple, or some peppermint whenever the person felt like eating, resulted in weight *loss*. Dr. Hirsch speculated that maybe it was the induced relaxation that led to less eating.

 ✔ A bowl of green apples on your table

 ✔ Suntan lotion

 ✔ Vanilla extract

 ✔ Freshly baked just-about-anything

 ✔ Soaps, hand creams, bath oils and perfumes, and aftershave

 ✔ Freshly brewed coffee

Light up

Candles can be a wonderful addition to your repertoire of stress-reducing devices. A burning candle connotes romance, warmth, peace, and a sense of tranquility. The flickering of the flame can be hypnotic. Burning scented candles only adds to the effect. Which scent to use depends upon what you find most pleasant and appealing. Vanilla and floral fragrances tend to be most relaxing. Often these aromas recall pleasant memories of childhood. And just think of the money you can save on your electric bill.

Mix your own aroma cocktail

If you have no time to bake bread or perk coffee, try concocting your own stress-reducing aroma by using commercially available oils. "Essential oils" and "natural oils" tend to produce better therapeutic benefits, but the synthetic oils are less costly. You can buy these pleasing fragrances from a number of shops or mail-order places. You can find essential oils in gourmet shops or at craft stores as a price far less than in a more upscale boutique or spa. If you are in a do-it-yourself mood, you can find books at your local library that show you how you can derive essential oils from flowers. Some of the more common oils used to induce a relaxed, calming state include lavender, rose, jasmine, chamomile, orange blossom, vanilla, bergamot, geranium, and sandalwood. Often, you can combine oils to produce a new, relaxing aroma.

The scent of a memory

A scent can trigger early memories. There appears to be some link in our brains between memory and smell. The trick, of course, is to find the smell that triggers a pleasant, relaxing memory. One of my very favorite smells is the one that comes from a dryer vent when clothes are drying, because I spent many happy hours in my aunt's laundry as a child. For most people, that smell just means work. Freshly mown grass tends to recall my days as a child playing in front of the house. Try to harness this phenomenon by discovering those scents that trigger happy memories for you.

Some oils can be inhaled directly, while others are better when added to your bath. Certain oils can be applied directly to your body, however, some oils act as irritants for some people. Certain oils should be avoided during pregnancy. It is best to get some knowledgeable advice before you begin experimenting. You can consult *Aromatherapy For Dummies* by Kathi Keville (IDG Books Worldwide, Inc.). In addition, The National Association for Holistic Aromatherapy in Boulder Colorado and the American Phyto Aromatherapy Association in Miami, Florida can help you with questions as to which oils to use and how to use them, and how to find a professional aromatherapist in your area.

Do Nothing: Meditation is Good for You

Of all of the ways available to help you relax, probably the one that evokes the most suspicion is meditation. When you think of meditation, chances are you conger up images of bearded gents in saffron robes sitting in the lotus position. You feel that this is hardly an activity that would go over well at the office. It is not surprising that you might be a wee bit leery about jumping in and joining the movement. Yet, it is likely that you have already meditated. You may not have been aware that you were doing so, but at those times when your mind becomes calm, uncluttered, and focused, and you're not processing your day, or thinking about a million things — you're doing something that closely resembles meditating.

The sections that follow present meditation as an important stress-reducing tool that fits nicely in your stress-toolbox.

East comes West

People in the East — especially those who subscribe to certain religious or philosophical beliefs — have been practicing meditation for literally thousands of years. These practitioners use meditation as a means to search for and find inner peace, enlightenment, and harmony with the universe.

Meditation has not received such ready acceptance in the western world, however. Westerners have tended to view meditation as foreign and remote, and sometimes as religious zealotry. In the '60s when the Maharishi — a then-popular guru — came along, westerners began to associate meditation with a somewhat wild fringe group of society.

But recently — in the last 10 years — researchers started taking notice of the positive effects of meditation. Herbert Benson, M.D., of the Mind/Body Medical Institute at Deaconess Hospital in Boston, was one of the first to adapt and introduce mediation to broader western audiences. Since then, the principles and practice of meditation have enjoyed widespread acceptance and enthusiasm in the west.

What can meditation do for me anyway?

The effects and benefits of meditation are wide and varied. Many of them you can notice immediately, while others are less obvious, affecting you in more subtle ways. Most importantly, meditation can help you relax your mind and body. It can help you turn off your inner thoughts. Meditating can help you feel less stressed; and your body will be less tense and your mind calmer. With some practice, after meditating you should feel rested, renewed and recharged. Meditation allows you to develop greater control over your thoughts, worries, and anxieties. It is a skill, that once mastered, can serve you well throughout your life.

But it's harder than it looks

Meditating for a very short period of time (like a minute) is pretty do-able. The challenge is being able to meditate for longer periods of time. Westerners in particular have some built-in resistances to meditating. You may share some of the following traits.

  ✔ **Westerners like to be busy:** You probably like to be active and do things, rather than be passive and let things happen to you. Lengthy periods of immobility tend to elicit feelings of boredom and restlessness.

✔ **Westerners need scorecards:** You may find yourself with a need to evaluate yourself on how well you're doing. If, after a very brief period of practice, you find that you're doing well, you may rate yourself — and your performance — accordingly. One of the keys to meditation is not rating yourself — good or bad.

None of this should discourage you or deter you from practicing your meditative skills. No, you won't become an accomplished meditator in 12 minutes. However, you may be surprised at how quickly you begin to see positive results. I repeat: Stick with it, the results are well worth it.

Preparing to meditate

Here is a step-by-step guide to preparing for meditation. Remember that there are a many ways of meditating. These suggestions help you prepare for different types of meditation, especially the exercises featured in this chapter.

1. **Find a quiet place where you won't be disturbed for a while.**

   No telephones, no beeper, no TV — nothing.

2. **Find a comfortable sitting position, like the one shown in Figure 5-2.**

   Contorting yourself in some yogi-like, snake-charmer squat (albeit impressive), may not be the best way to start meditating if you're a novice. Remember that you're going to remain in one position for 15 to 20 minutes.

Simply amazing

Some meditators make claims that are, well, a bit over the top. It is highly unlikely that you will levitate or that your I.Q. will improve dramatically through meditation.

However, those who study serious practitioners of meditation have noted rather remarkable results. A skilled meditator can attain a state of deep relaxation relatively quickly, and some can tolerate extreme levels of pain and stress. Through meditation, some people can slow their heart rate to surprisingly low levels — their breathing slows and their rate of oxygen consumption is greatly reduced. Practiced meditators are able to radically change their body temperatures. Brain-wave patterns associated with states of deep relaxation increase in intensity and frequency. Many claim the benefits of meditation go far beyond those of relaxation. They claim it helps you think more clearly, improves your relationships with others, improves self-esteem, and even offers enlightenment.

Enlightenment? Possibly. Levitation? I don't think so.

Figure 5-2:
Sitting in a
relaxed,
comfortable
position.

3. **Focus on a sound, a word, a sensation, an image, an object, or a thought.**

4. **Maintain your focus and adopt a passive, accepting attitude.**

   When you are focusing in meditation, intrusive thoughts or images may enter your mind and distract you. When those thoughts occur, notice them, accept the fact that they are there, and then let them go: No getting upset, no annoyance, no self-rebuke.

Try not to get hung up on the timing. Meditate for about 15 or 20 minutes. If you want to meditate longer, fine. If you find you're becoming uncomfortable, you can stop and try it again at another time. Remember, this is a non-pressured, non-ego-involved exercise.

After you have everything in place, you're ready to begin meditating. Although you have many forms of mediation to choose from, the most common ones are breath counting mediation and mediation with a mantra. The following sections deal with each type.

Meditative breathing

Breath-counting meditation builds on the controlled breathing techniques and exercises that I discuss in the previous chapter. (For more information on getting your lungs in shape for mediating, check out Chapter 4.) Breath-counting meditation is one of the basic and most commonly used forms of meditation. Here's what to do:

1. **Sit comfortably.**

   You can position yourself on the floor or in a chair. Keep your back straight and your head up. Dress comfortably as well — no tight shoes, tight belt, neckties, underpants, bra, or anything else that constricts you.

2. **Close your eyes and scan for tension.**

   Scan your body for any tension by using the one-minute body scan technique I describe in Chapter 4, and then let go of any tension that you find.

3. **Begin to breathe in a relaxed way.**

   Relax by taking some abdominal breaths (breathing using your diaphragm). Breathe slowly and deeply through your nose.

   To help you breathe in a relaxing manner, imagine a small balloon just under your belly button. As you inhale through your nostrils, imagine that balloon gently inflating and as you exhale through your nostrils, imagine the balloon slowly deflating.

4. **Focus on your breathing.**

   Your breathing now becomes the object of your focus. When you inhale, count this breath as "1."

   The next time you inhale is 2, and so forth until you reach 10. Then you start again at 1. Count silently to yourself, and if you lose count, simply start back at 1. If you lose count, don't worry — the number is merely something to focus on — there's no right or wrong number here.

5. **If you find a distracting thought or image intruding, let it go, and return to your count.**

   Continue this exercise for about 20 minutes, and — if you can — do this exercise twice a day.

Probably the most common complaint among beginning meditators is that their minds keep wandering off, especially at the beginning of a meditation. Even on those days when you face no major pressure or pending deadline, your mind can still come up with a million-and-one things to think about. That's normal. Expect it, and don't beat yourself up when it happens. Don't make this exercise into a test of your ability to concentrate. Getting good at focusing without undue distractions may take some time. Hang in there.

Meditating with a mantra

Probably the best known and most popular form of meditation is meditation using a mantra. A *mantra* is a sound or a word that you repeat; it can help you focus your mind and avoid distractions. After you select your mantra (see the sidebar, "Psst, looking for a mantra?"), you're ready to put it to use:

Psst, looking for a good mantra?

The word mantra comes from the Indian: "man" means "to think," and "tra" means "to free." Often mantras take the form of one or two syllables, such as *om* meaning "I am," or *so-ham,* "I am he." Many teachers of meditation believe that your mantra should have personal meaning.

In his book, *The Relaxation Response,* cardiologist and researcher Herbert Benson says that a personal mantra is not necessary for successful meditation. In his teaching of meditative relaxation, Dr. Benson suggests using the word "one" as a mantra. That word has very little meaning for most of us, and is therefore not terribly distracting. Your mantra can also be a soothing word such as "peace," "love," or "calm." Whatever you come up with, choose a word or sound that has a relaxing feel for you.

If you would like some additional information on mantras, and on meditation in general, take a look at *Meditation For Dummies* by Stephan Bodian (IDG Books Worldwide, Inc.).

1. **Sit quietly, either in a chair or on the floor as you did for the Breathing Meditation detailed in the preceding section.**

   Eliminate any distractions. Close your eyes and relax as much as you can.

2. **Start with some deep breathing and try to clear your mind of the day's hassle and worry.**

   Remember not to breathe with your chest alone. Breathe until you notice that you feel much more relaxed. (About a dozen breaths should do it.)

3. **Do a body scan to see where any residual tension may be hiding.**

4. **Focus on your breathing and begin to repeat your mantra to yourself, either silently or chanting it softly.**

   As you say your mantra, see the word in your head. Repeat your mantra over and over. Find a timing and rhythm that is comfortable for you. As before, if you find your concentration slipping, simply become aware of that fact and gently guide your mind back to your mantra.

   Do this exercise for about 20 minutes or so and try to squeeze in as many meditative sessions as you can in your week.

Find time for mini-meditations

Someone once asked a meditation teacher, "How long should I meditate?" "For about 20 minutes," the wise man answered, quickly adding, "But 5 minutes of meditation you do is better than the 20 minutes of meditation you plan on doing, but don't."

I recognize that you may not have 20 minutes twice a day to peacefully meditate in some quiet corner of your life. And even if you have the time, you may find that your boss — who is not nearly as enlightened as you are — frowns on your meditative sessions. Fortunately, you can practice "abbreviated" forms of meditation — they can be as long or as short as the time you have available. You can "mini-meditate" when you find a few extra minutes, for example, during the listed opportunities following. (I do advise not meditating in your car, unless you're the passenger.)

✔ Sitting in traffic (if you're the passenger)

✔ Waiting for your doctor or dentist to see you

✔ Standing (for what seems like forever) in line

✔ Sitting in a boring meeting (where you don't have to present anything, and won't be asked questions)

✔ Riding the bus, subway, or a taxicab

Hypnotize Yourself

When you think of hypnosis, two images probably come to mind. The first is from a B-grade movie where you see some Svengali-like doctor — usually deranged — dangling a pocket watch in the face of some innocent victim. The second is of some hypnotist on a stage with a dozen or so audience volunteers who are either dancing with brooms or are clucking like chickens. Fortunately, neither image is accurate.

Actually, hypnosis is less mysterious and far more mundane than you may think. Hypnosis is totally safe, but more importantly, it can be a very effective way of helping you relax and cope with stress.

No, you will not be turned into a clucking chicken

Probably no other psychological technique for stress reduction is as misunderstood as hypnosis. Some things you need to know:

✔ You are not asleep.

✔ You are not unconscious.

✔ You will not lose control or be under someone's spell.

✔ You won't do anything that you do not want to do.

Hypnosis is simply a deeply focused state that makes you more acutely aware of suggestions and allows you to be more receptive to those suggestions.

Some people are more susceptible to hypnotic suggestion. For hypnosis to be as effective for you as possible, try to adopt a receptive, non-critical attitude. Don't fight the process. Just go with it. If you remain totally skeptical and resistant, not much is going to happen. Have an open mind.

Surprise! You've already been hypnotized

You may not realize it, but chances are you've been in a *hypnotic trance* many times before. We slip in and out of hypnotic states all the time. Remember those times when you were driving on the highway and it scarily dawns on you that you haven't been paying attention to the road or your driving for the last five minutes? Or remember those times when you left the movie theater and realized that your attention was so glued to the screen that you had no idea who was sitting next to you or what was going on around you? Or when you were daydreaming, or just lost in thought. In each case, you were in a hypnotic trance.

The power of a trance

When you're in a trance, you're in a different mental state. You are still awake and in control, but your attention becomes narrow and incredibly focused. In this state, you're more receptive to any suggestions you may give yourself, or that a hynotherapist may offer. You basically give yourself a sort of shortcut to your subconscious. These suggestions can take many forms: cigarettes taste lousy, I'm growing taller day by day, I'm getting smarter, whatever. (Clearly some suggestions are more realistic than others.)

Some trances are deeper than others. In a light trance, you feel more relaxed and are able to respond to simple suggestions. In a heavier trance, you can learn how not to respond to pain and even to forget what occurred during hypnosis. In what follows, my aim is to induce a light trance, which is all you need to achieve a peaceful state of deep relaxation.

Inducing a light trance

You can induce a hypnotic trance in many ways (even the dangling watch can work). Here is one of the simpler induction techniques I have found to be useful in reducing tension and stress.

1. **Find a comfortable position in a quiet, dimly lit room where you won't be interrupted.**

Relax as much as possible. If you want, take off your shoes and loosen any tight clothing.

2. **Focus on an object across the room.**

The object can be anything — a smudge on the wall, the corner of a picture, it really doesn't matter. Just choose an object that is above your normal line of sight so that you have to strain your eyeballs a wee bit looking up to see your spot.

3. **As you look at your spot, silently say to yourself**

> *"My eyelids are becoming heavier and heavier."*

> *"My eyelids feel as if heavy weights are pulling them down."*

> *"Soon they will be so heavy they will close."*

Repeat these sentences to yourself about every 30 seconds.

4. **Focus on your eyelids.**

Soon you will notice that, indeed, your eyelids are beginning to feel heavier. Feel this heaviness deepen with time. Don't fight these sensations, just let them happen. Let your eyes close when you feel they want to close themselves.

5. **As your eyes begin to close, say to yourself: "Relax, and let go."**

6. **When your eyes close, take in a deep breath through your nostrils and hold that breath for about 10 seconds.**

7. **Slowly exhale through your slightly parted lips, making a "swooshing" sound.**

At the same time, let your jaw drop and feel a wave of warmth and heaviness spread from the top of your head, down your body, all the way to your toes. Continue to breathe slowly and smoothly. As you exhale, silently say the word "calm," or some other relaxing word, to yourself. As you breathe, let the feelings of relaxation deepen for another few moments.

Going a little deeper

After you induce a light trance, you're ready to move into a deeper state of hypnosis.

1. **Take a deep breath and hold it for about 10 seconds.**

Exhale slowly through your lips while saying the word "deeper" to yourself. Continue this process for several breaths more, saying the word "deeper" to yourself with every exhalation.

2. **Imagine that you're stepping onto a descending escalator, a long, slow escalator that will take you into a state of deeper relaxation.**

As you begin your descent, silently say to yourself,

"I am sinking slowly into a deeper state of relaxation."

3. **As you descend, count backwards on each exhalation, from 10 to 1.**

   When you reach the bottom of the escalator, imagine that you are stepping off this escalator and are stepping onto a second descending escalator. As you imagine your descent, deepen your trance with each breath, again counting backwards from 10 to 1.

4. **Continue to deepen your trance until you feel you have reached a comfortable level of relaxation.**

   You may need only one escalator ride, or you may need several. With practice, a deeper trance will come more easily and more quickly.

Get me out of this trance

Alright, you are now in a trance. You are feeling quite relaxed, and your mind is totally at peace. You can choose to remain in this relaxed state, and simply enjoy the benefits of relaxation and calm. You can also give yourself a suggestion that can extend this relaxation beyond the trance state. Here's what to do:

Simply count slowly backwards from five to one. Say to yourself beforehand,

"When I reach one, my eyes will open and I will feel totally awake and refreshed."

As you count, notice your eyes beginning to flutter and begin to partially open as you approach one.

Here are some suggestions that should help you overcome one or more of the possible roadblocks that may arise as you practice self-hypnosis:

- ✔ **Give yourself enough time to reach a trance state:** This process may take 15, 20, or even 25 minutes.

- ✔ **Don't ask yourself, "Am I hypnotized yet?":** This performance pressure only sets the process back. Don't force it or demand it; let it happen.

- ✔ **As you move into a trance, use the breathing and muscle relaxation skills that I discuss in Chapter 4.** These techniques speed the hypnosis process and help you attain a greater level of relaxation.

For more information, you can consult a certified hypnotherapist who can show you how to use self-hypnosis to achieve benefits other than relaxation. Hypnosis has been shown to be effective in helping individuals overcome insomnia, smoking, overeating, and a variety of other problems and disorders.

Want Some Feedback? Go the High-Tech Route

Biofeedback is a fancy term that means letting you know (the *feedback* part) what your body is up to (the *bio* part). Of course, biofeedback is nothing new. Getting the results of a blood test, having your blood pressure taken, or getting an EKG at your doctor's office are all examples of medical biofeedback. However, these days, the term biofeedback is usually used for the electronic devices that measure your stress level or more technically, your levels of *physiological arousal.*

Hard-wired to your own body

In the clinic or doctor's office, biofeedback is a wonderful tool that can tell you a lot about your stress and more importantly, help you learn ways of reducing that stress. Depending on the biofeedback device used, it may measure your heart rate, body temperature, your blood pressure, skin conductivity (sweating), levels of stomach acid, muscle tension, and even your brain activity (see Figure 5-3). Each of these can be controlled to some extent, and working with biofeedback can be useful in controlling each of these functions.

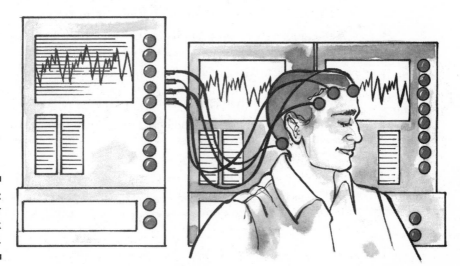

Figure 5-3:
Wired up for biofeedback readings.

Biofeedback is no substitute for learning the tools and techniques presented in these chapters. It can, however, help you use them more effectively. You may want to consult a certified biofeedback therapist who can work with you, showing you how biofeedback can help you learn to relax and reduce your levels of mental and physical stress.

Many companies now make inexpensive home biofeedback trainers that you can purchase and use by themselves or hooked up to your computer. Again, a certified biofeedback therapist can tell you whom to contact.

Biofeedback (without the wires)

But what if you can't afford the time or money to use biofeedback equipment? Not to worry. You can come up with your own biofeedback tools. For example:

- **A watch with a second hand.** By taking your own pulse (on your neck or even your index finger), you get a measure of your heart rate, which varies according to your level of relaxation.

  Also, by counting the number of breaths you make in a fixed period of time, you have a measure of your rate of respiration. This should decrease as you become more relaxed.

- **A thermometer.** Holding the bulb of a thermometer between your fingers can give you a measure of your skin temperature. Relaxing your body should raise your skin temperature.

- **A stethoscope.** By counting heart-beats, you have a measure of your stress level. Lowering your stress should result in a lowered heart rate.

- **A pressure cuff.** These days, a home blood pressure monitoring device is not all that expensive. Lowering your stress level and your levels of tension should result in lowered blood pressure readings.

- **A mirror.** The way you look can be a pretty good indicator of just how stressed you are. Furrowed brows, a clenched jaw, bags under your eyes — all can be signs of stress. Take a look!

Chapter 6

Stress-Reducing Organizational Skills

• •

• •

*I*f you've ever felt like screaming or maybe tearing out some hair when at the last minute you can't find your keys or the location of that very important appointment you wrote down on a paper napkin, you're probably sympathetic to the notion that disorganization can trigger a whole lot of stress.

Sure, a little bit of disorder doesn't rival developing a serious illness, getting fired, or having your house burn down. Yet being disorganized can fuel a long list of frustrations, delays, lost time, and missed opportunities — all accompanied by varying levels of anger and irritation.

Who needs it? Your stress level is already high enough. This chapter shows you how to get organized. It gives you the tools you need to overcome the disarray, chaos, and confusion in your life.

Just how disorganized are you?

Are you "organizationally challenged"? The first step in getting a handle on your disorganization problem is knowing just how bad your organizational skills really are. Read through the following statements and see how many you identify with.

✔ When people first visit my place, they always ask whether I've just moved in.

✔ I know that I have a pet, but it seems like months since I last saw it.

✔ I've bounced so many checks that the people at the bank have my number on their speed-dialer.

✔ When she quit, my cleaning lady's parting words were, "You couldn't pay me enough to stay."

✔ I think Quicken is the name of a fast-food chicken franchise.

If you find yourself identifying with any of the preceding statements, it's probably not a good sign. Not to worry. This chapter can help you get back on track.

Figuring Out Why Your Life Is So Disorganized

Okay, so your life is not a model of order and organization. Being disorganized is nothing to be ashamed of. In fact, it's totally understandable. Here are five major reasons why people get into this pickle. Yours should be among them.

✔ You don't have enough time.
✔ Your life is too complicated.
✔ You don't have enough space.
✔ You don't know what to do to become more organized.
✔ You know what to do to get organized, but you just don't want to do it.

Whatever the reason for your disorganization, you want to know what you can do about it. In the sections that follow you find the ideas and direction that can help you minimize your organizational roadblocks and get you started on the road to organizational bliss.

Clearing Away the Clutter

If you lived in a place with infinite space, had a live-in maid, and were independently wealthy, you may consider clutter a charming quirk, an amusing oversight. But I suspect that your clutter has become a pain and threatens to stress you out even more. De-cluttering can seem overwhelming. It's only a matter of time before you feel like you're lost in your clutter. You need help. You're ready to start. But where? The first step is finding enough motivation to start you off, and, more importantly, keep you going.

Get yourself motivated

Sometimes good intentions alone just don't cut it. You may find that you need a kick in the pants or some other form of external motivation to get you to clean up. Here are some field-tested ideas that can keep you on track:

- ✔ **Schedule it.** When you schedule things, you have a better chance of getting them done. People generally show up for dentist and doctor appointments, business meetings, and other engagements that they purposefully schedule. The same tactic can work when it comes to getting things done around the house. Commit to a definite time and write down the "appointment" in your calendar, daily planner, or whatever you use to keep track of your life.

- ✔ **Work with shame.** My wife and I discovered long ago that our home is at its organizational best about three minutes before a bunch of invited guests ring our doorbell. We're motivated and determined to make sure that others do not see how disorganized our place can be. You can do the same. Set a date and invite over some new friends whose approval you desperately need. It works like a charm for us.

- ✔ **Find your clutter threshold.** Frankly, I don't mind a little clutter in my life. For me, those minimalist, absolutely-nothing-out-of-place living spaces are scary. I require a touch of clutter to make me feel emotionally comfortable. Yet anything more than just a little bit of clutter begins to stress me out. Other folks are totally clutter-aversive. For them, any clutter is too much. You have to find your own clutter threshold, below which you get twitchy and above which you feel stressed. Then work hard to keep your clutter level at that line.

Draw yourself a clutter roadmap

Rather than seeing all the clutter in your life-space as one massive pile, see it as a succession of tasks that you can chip away step by step. One way to decide where to start, and where to go after you start is to create a *clutter roadmap*. Begin by choosing a number of areas of your life-space that desperately need organizing. These areas may be geographical (a specific room in your home, the yard, or the garage) or topical (your clothing, magazines, or toys). Then come up with a sequence of areas that you want to work on. After you deal with one bit of clutter on your list, move on to a second and then on to the next, so on. Think of your map as a kind of sequential 'to do' list. It takes you where you want to go.

A clutter roadmap gives you feeling that you know where you're going — and also a pretty good idea of how far you've moved toward your final goal. Be sure to make each piece on your map relatively small and doable. Also start by choosing areas of your life-space that will give you a great deal of personal satisfaction after they're organized.

Get your feet wet

One of my favorite bits of self-help advice is that Nike slogan, "Just do it!" However, my experience as a psychologist has taught me that "just doing it" for most people is probably not going to do it. My sweatshirt would read a bit more realistically, saying, "Just get started!" Deep down, you realize that you'll be better off if you get rid of much of that unneeded stuff. So jump in.

Have you ever noticed that once you start something, the momentum of doing keeps you going? This is especially true when you're de-cluttering. After you get yourself in de-cluttering mode, go with it. Don't stop just because you finish a small section. Keep going. Build on your success. You may be surprised at how much you can get down once you're into it.

Stop kidding yourself

It's easy to fool yourself. That's because some small part of you really does believe that you *will* clean out the basement, put those old clothes in boxes and give them to a thrift shop, and throw out those magazines that you've been hanging onto forever.

The reality is that unless you take your clutter seriously, it will continue to spread. If you're going to successfully de-clutter, you need to convince yourself that the quality of your life will improve measurably after you unload much, if not most, of those collected objects, and that it will be so nice when you find your last three TV remotes and all the mates to those single socks lying in your bedroom drawer.

Simplifying your life-space takes grit. Your attitude as you approach the task should be, "I'm sick and tired of this, and I'm not going to take it anymore!" You may find this approach a bit too merciless, but be clear; you're dealing with an evil force. Give no ground. Take no prisoners. Ask yourself the following questions to help increase your de-cluttering grit:

> ✔ Do I really want to spend the next 20 years living with this item?
>
> ✔ If my place were on fire and I could save only half of what I own, would I save this particular item?
>
> ✔ Would the quality of my life be seriously diminished if I didn't own this item?

In 90 percent of the cases, you may find that the answer to all three questions is no.

Avoid discouragement

A mistake that many people make when de-cluttering is thinking that they can finish their de-cluttering in one short Saturday afternoon. They get discouraged when they realize just how much stuff they have and how much de-cluttering they still have to do.

Face it: It took you years to amass all your wonderful possessions, so it's prudent to assume that reversing the process may take you some time. However, when you figure out how much time you can save by not having to look for misplaced items, you quickly realize that you'll be way ahead of the game after you finish. Accomplishing most anything in life that is worthwhile takes effort and persistence. Mastering golf or tennis, learning to ski, or figuring out how to get the most out of your computer didn't happen over night. Stick with it.

The top ten reasons for not throwing something out

At times, giving up your prized possessions is harder than pulling teeth. When pressed, you may vigorously defend your decision to hold onto some small thing in your life. Here are some of the most common reasons you may have used:

✔ Someday I'll need it.

✔ It was a present for my ninth birthday.

✔ Someone may want to buy this.

✔ I'm sure I'll find the matching one.

✔ It isn't broken.

✔ It can be fixed.

✔ If I just lose 20 pounds, I'll fit into this.

✔ It will be a collector's item one day.

✔ My kids will want to give it to their kids.

✔ I plan on reading this.

All these excuses contain at least a sliver of truth. And all guarantee that after your funeral, your relatives will hold the world's biggest garage sale.

Get down to the nitty-gritty

Okay, you've psyched yourself up for some serious de-cluttering. When you get into the trenches, try using the following clutter-busting techniques:

✔ **Pick any number from one to two.** When considering what to do with an item of clutter, remember that you have two basic options: Keep it or lose it. If you decide to keep it, you must figure out what to do with it. If you choose to lose it, you can chuck it or give it away. Clearly, the biggest obstacle to getting rid of anything is having to make this choice.

✔ **Take a second look.** It's never too late to get rid of some of the stuff that you decide to keep. Go back over your keeper pile and take a second look. Organizing even a small pile of things takes a lot of time. And although storage and filing plays an important role in managing all the possessions that clutter your life, simply getting rid of stuff often makes more sense.

✔ **Use the Triage Method of Clutter Control.** One approach I find useful in making difficult keep it/pitch it decisions is something I call the *Triage Method of Clutter Control.* First, I create three categories: Definitely Keep, Definitely Get Rid Of, and I'm Not Sure. Then I throw out or give away everything in the last two categories. The upside of unloading much more of your clutter far outweighs the downside of making a mistake. Don't look back.

✔ **Get a clutter buddy.** I've noticed that whenever I decide that it's time to de-clutter, I come up with marvelous ideas for organizing my wife's side of the room. I have even better ideas when it comes to our children's rooms. I've also noticed that my wife is equally creative in disposing of the stuff on *my* side of the room. You're probably less sentimental, less ambivalent, and more determined when dealing with other people's clutter than your own. Make this concept work for you. Ask your mate or a friend to help you de-clutter. Listen to that person, and do what he or she tells you.

✔ **Play the dating game.** Here's a variation of decluttering that Elaine St. James recommends in her delightful book *Simplify Your Life:* If you can't bring yourself to throw something out, put it in a box and put a date on the box that is exactly a year away. Don't list what's in the box — just the date. If you find that that future date has come and gone without your needing anything in the box, chuck it, without looking inside. Don't look back. And should you need and use some of the things from a box, find a good place to keep those items.

✔ **Find a clutter recipient.** Getting rid of stuff is much easier when you know that it won't end up in the trash, but in the hands of somebody who wants it and can use it. In fact, your rejects may be someone else's cup of tea. Clothing, sports equipment, books, and furniture are often welcomed by others. Give your relatives and friends first crack at your treasures. The Salvation Army, Goodwill Industries, thrift shops, and charity drives would all be delighted to take the stuff that your family and friends turn down. You can even get a tax deduction for donating to charitable organizations.

✔ **If it doesn't work, toss it.** Look around your home for a broken toaster, blender, vacuum cleaner, radio, or clock — any small appliance that hasn't worked for a long while. Once you find one, ask yourself whether you truly need it. If you decide to fix it, fix it. If not, replace or discard it. Sadly, these days you may find that replacing the item is cheaper than having it repaired. However, chances are good that if you haven't needed it in the last year, you probably don't need it at all.

Whatever you do, *do not* leave the broken item in your home. Throw it out or, better yet, give it to a charitable organization that will repair it and give it to someone who will use it. I often put a little note on the item explaining what's wrong with it and then leave it at the side of our building. When I come back to check in about an hour or so, the piece is usually gone.

✔ **Invest in doors and drawers.** If you absolutely must keep something, hide it. Unless the object in question is something you're very fond of or somehow adds to the visual aesthetic of your decor, keep it out of sight. Store things in cabinets and closets with drawers, in bureau drawers or file cabinets — anyplace that contributes to a sense of visual order. But remember that the space things occupy behind doors is still space that you could use for something else.

There are now shops and catalogues that are dedicated exclusively to storage furniture and containers. Catalogues are great fun to look through, but remember not to make them a new part of your clutter.

✔ **Take a sample.** I'm not sure at what point my wife and I realized that we couldn't keep absolutely *every* piece of artwork or craft project that our children came home with. I think it was when every major appliance in the kitchen was covered in crayon drawings. Then my wife came up with a brilliant idea: She brought home a large art folder and began taking *samples* of the masterpieces we were especially fond of. This folder is neatly stored in a back closet. When our children become famous artistes, we'll cash in. You can do the same.

✔ **Take a picture.** Often, items in your "I'm Not Sure" pile have sentimental value or are too big to keep around. You want the memories, but not necessarily the object. Take its picture. Pictures take up far less space and still can bring a warm smile to your face. I remember a rather large stuffed animal that our children had when they were smaller. There came a time when it had to go, but sentiment was holding us back. We decided to take its picture and give the teddy bear to a thrift shop. This compromise worked well. The photograph collects far less dust. You may also want to include someone in the picture. Looking at your daughter squeezing Cuddles is a lot more satisfying than just looking at Cuddles by herself.

Losing the Paper Trail

Those who have made the study of clutter their life's work say that *paper* is the real enemy. Your paper clutter can include everything from a toaster warranty to your last electric bill to the endless stream of circulars, catalogues, junk mail, and other unsolicited items that pass through your doorway every day. Take care of your paper clutter, and you're more than halfway home.

To merge or to purge? That is the question.

The two secrets to managing the paper in your life are fairly simple. In fact, they are amazingly similar to the two options you have when considering what to do with your non-paper clutter. You can either throw out the paper if you don't need it or find an effective way to organize it if you do need it.

This approach to paper sounds pretty easy, but the problem lies in actually *doing* the throwing out and organizing. Sorting through all that paper takes time and effort, and who knows — you might really need that coupon for a 10-gallon jar of spaghetti sauce or might actually read that article on skiing in the Himalayas. Yeah, right! You need help.

Cut 'em off at the pass

Much, if not most, of the paper in your life comes into your home via the mail. Your mailbox can be an insidious force, feeding you an unstoppable river of solicitations, announcements, catalogues, and bills. You can slowly drown in this incoming sea of paper. The trick is to catch it early, before it has a chance to collect.

- **Junk junk mail.** Keep a wastepaper basket near your front door. Throw out junk mail immediately. Do not open it. Do not be intrigued. Realize that no matter how much mail you receive telling you that you've probably won a million dollars, the chances of it actually happening are infinitesimal.

- **Please take me off your list.** I remember subscribing to something and when I received it, noticing that they had spelled my name wrong. Then I noticed that I was getting tons of other unwanted stuff in the mail with the same wrong name. Being on one list quickly put me on many others. Get yourself taken off mailing lists. Call the Better Business Bureau or look under "Direct Mail Associations" in the Yellow Pages. They'll tell you the number in your area to call to get yourself removed from many of the more annoying lists.

✔ **Need a catalogue to catalogue your catalogues?** Leafing through a catalogue and mentally shopping can be fun. Ordering items from catalogues is also useful because it cuts down on the legwork. The problem arises when your catalogues begin to collect and your life begins to look like a mail-order distribution center. If you must, keep one or two of your favorite catalogues. Peruse the rest and then chuck them. When a new catalogue comes, immediately throw out the old one.

Organize all the paper in your life

At this point in your life, I suspect that the notion of having a method of organizing the paper in your life does not come as an earth-shatteringly new idea. Yet I wager that you still don't have one, or if you do, you use it inefficiently.

Coming up with a system of organization takes thought and planning. And making use of it requires time and effort. In the short run, letting papers pile up is a lot easier. But in the long run, doing so can turn into a major headache. Taking the time and effort to develop a systematic way of organizing your papers can result in a lot less stress and hassle in your life. Try the following as you create your filing system:

Start simple

Come up with a filing system that's relatively easy to use. You don't want your filing system to be more stressful than the stress it's supposed to alleviate.

Be colorful

Files of different colors, or tabs and labels of different colors can not only turn your filing system into a work of art but also make it easier to find different subjects and interests. My travel files are red, my receipts are yellow, my restaurant files are blue, and so on.

Don't scrimp when you buy a filing cabinet

Invest in a cabinet of good quality. Poorly made filing cabinets tend to break down in the crunch. When your files get larger and heavier, their weight can strain a cheap filing cabinet and make it difficult for the drawers to open smoothly — or to open at all, for that matter. And try to find a cabinet that won't make your room look like an claim-adjusters office. Many of the traditional office cabinets are big and, frankly, pretty unattractive.

Keep important papers where you know they're safe

Keep your documents in a safe place, but make sure that you can easily get hold of them when you need them. Lest you forgot, here are some of the more important documents to keep track of:

Birth certificates	PIN numbers	Marriage certificate
Medical records	Wills	Loan agreements
Passports	Important receipts	Mortgage agreements
Tax returns (last 5 years)	Deeds	School transcripts
Insurance policies	Service contracts	Bank account numbers
Warranties	Credit card numbers	Instructions
Automobile information		

Some of the above categories will warrant their own separate file. Some, like your important numbers, can be combined. For the more important documents, you may want to keep the originals in a safe or in a safe-deposit box, and keep available copies in your files.

Avoid Lower Moravia

The most common error people make when creating a filing system is to come up with categories that are too specific. For example, a file titled "Travel articles about Lower Moravia" won't fit well in your system unless you're definitely planning on going there or you're writing your master's thesis on this topic. If you continue in this vein, you'll be overrun with file folders in no time, and you'll have a heck of a time ever finding anything — if you ever want to. Start with fewer, broader categories.

Never put all your papers in one basket

I like very much (and actually use) an approach described by organizational expert Stephanie Culp. She suggests that you have four baskets for your paper (in addition to the extremely important wastepaper basket):

✔ A "To Do" basket (The wire see-through kind works best.)

✔ A "To Pay" basket (Again, wire works best here.)

✔ A "To File" basket (Use a larger wicker basket.)

✔ A "To Read" basket (Try an even larger wicker basket with handles.)

Culp recommends that you stack your "To Do" basket on top of your "To Pay" basket on your desk. Keep the "To File" basket under your desk, out of the way of your more immediate paper needs. You can keep the "To Read" basket in a different part of your home — such as your bedroom or study — so that you can catch up on your reading whenever the opportunity arises.

Make filing a habit

Find a time during the week to empty your "To File" basket and file those needed papers away. This task really shouldn't take long — 15 or 20 minutes should do it.

Fine-tune later

At a later date, take a look at what's in your files. Usually, you find that a file is either underused or bulging. If you find that you have only one or two things in a file folder, find or create a file that's broader in scope. Alternatively, if you find that a folder is overflowing with contributions, create subcategories, either by topic or by dates.

Keeping Your Life Organized

Say you manage to reverse eons of disarray and disorganization and now, having applied much grit and determination, you have a clean slate. Rather than waiting for the disorganization to return, you can do a number of things to maintain the order and harmony that you've achieved.

Remember that an ounce of prevention goes a long way

Sometimes, the best way to fix something is to get to the source of the problem. If your roof is leaking, you can spend copious amounts of time figuring out where to put the buckets to catch the drips. But it's better to simply fix the leak. The same principle holds true for the disorganization in your life. Rather than coming up with more intricate strategies and systems to manage your overly complicated life, it may be better to catch the problem at the source. You can, for example . . .

- ✔ Put groceries and other purchases away as soon as you bring them home.

- ✔ Put photographs in an easy-to-load album as soon as you get them home from the photo shop and finish oohing and ahhing. Don't throw them in a shoebox and put off the task of sorting and marking them.

- ✔ Put it back as soon as you finish with it. No "Yes, but . . . ," no nothin'.

- ✔ Keep a container that can be recycled next to where you usually read the newspaper. After you finish reading the paper, put it immediately into the recycling container.

- ✔ Clean up as you go. Don't wait until the end, when you're looking at a big mess.

Buy less

One of the reasons your life becomes more stressful is that you probably have too many "things." Fewer possessions mean a less complicated life. You can really live very happily without many of the things you buy. So before you pull out your wallet at the cash register or pick up the phone or computer mouse to order something, ask yourself the following questions:

- Do I *really* need this item?
- Would the quality of my life be seriously compromised if I passed this up?
- How many of these do I already have?

If you're like most people, I suspect that your answers to these questions are No, No, and Enough.

Here are some other buying suggestions that you may want to consider:

- Don't buy stuff just because it's on sale.
- Don't buy in bulk unless you're sure that you have a place to put it all.
- Don't buy anything without considering where you're going to put it.

Shop but don't buy

I love to bake, but once the stuff comes out of the oven, I rarely eat much of it. I also love to shop, but I've gotten pretty good at not buying the items I see in shops or catalogues. I find that the vicarious satisfaction of shopping is usually enough, and actually buying and owning the item is not that critical. Indulge your desire to shop; curb your impulse to buy.

Chapter 7

Finding More Time

• •

• •

As a kid growing up, I was exposed to all those futuristic images of what life would be like when I was an adult. It was clear that I would be awash in time-saving devices that would leave me with very little to do but twiddle my thumbs. Or so I thought. Over the years, technology has, in fact, given us a long list of potentially time- and labor-saving devices that are now routine parts of our lives. We have computers, microwaves, the Internet, cell phones . . . the list goes on.

Yet we still don't seem to have all that free time we were assured of. If anything, our lives seems to have become more chaotic, demanding, and time-pressured. We have just too much to do and too little time to do it in. In any one day, a person might

✔ Sleep for 7 hours and 25 minutes. (You wish!)

✔ Work for 7 hours and 30 minutes. (Yeah, right!)

✔ Eat for 85 minutes.

✔ Groom for 49 minutes.

✔ Do chores for 66 minutes.

✔ Shop for 17 minutes.

✔ Prepare meals for 35 minutes.

✔ Commute for 51 minutes.

✔ Watch television or videos for 180 minutes or more. (Egad!)

Given that you have only 24 hours in each day — and realizing that this list leaves out the time it takes to take care of your children, your pets, your car, and so on — there appears to be little time for anything else. Time, or rather the *lack* of time, can stress you out.

Because it's highly unlikely that the days will get longer, you need better ways of using the time you *do* have. This chapter gives you the direction and strategies that can help you manage your time more efficiently and effectively, and reduce your time-related stress.

Manage Your Time, or Your Time Will Manage You

In life, you quickly learn that your days fill up incredibly quickly. You soon find yourself hurried, harried, and rushing to do all that you feel has to be done. Putting out fires, dealing with last-minute crises, and taking care of unending details leaves little spare time for anything else. Add to that a busy job, a family, and at least a few other obligations, and you notice that your stress level is escalating. You may also realize that something else is happening. You begin having little time to spend on those things that you really enjoy and bring you satisfaction. Fortunately, managing your time more effectively is something you can learn.

Ten signs that you're experiencing time-stress and that your management skills may need some help

Maybe you don't experience time-related stress. Let's find out. Take a look at the following list and check off those items that seem to describe you.

✔ I feel that I do not have enough time for myself, my family, or my friends.

✔ I feel that I waste too much time.

✔ I find myself constantly rushing.

✔ I find that I do not have enough time to do the things I really enjoy.

✔ I find that I frequently miss deadlines or am late for appointments.

✔ I spend almost no time planning my day.

✔ I almost never work with some kind of prioritized "To-Do" list.

✔ I have difficulty saying no to others when they make demands on my time.

✔ I rarely delegate tasks and responsibilities.

✔ I find that I procrastinate too often.

Checking off only one or two items on this list suggests that your time-management skills require only a tune-up. Checking off more than four of them suggests that your time-management skills may be in need of a major overhaul.

Knowing Where Your Time Goes

As the saying goes, "Time flies." Knowing *where* it flies puts you a step ahead of the game. Too often, you manage your time ineffectively and end up feeling that you've accomplished very little; and worse, you feel that you haven't devoted enough time to the things that really matter. Both result in a good deal of stress. An important step in changing the way you manage your time is becoming aware of how you use your time.

For a short period of time — a week or so — keep a time-log. A sheet of paper will do. A better tool, however, is an inexpensive "Daily Diary," which you can pick up at any stationery store. Find one that fits easily in your pocket or briefcase.

At convenient points during your day, enter what you did, or are doing, in the appropriate time slots. Don't become compulsive about this — you don't have to make it exact to the minute. Try to include anything over 20 minutes. A sampling of a week or two in your life should supply enough data to give you a good picture of the ways you use — or misuse — your time. Use the following headings to organize your time-log entry data:

✔ **Time Spent** refers to when the activity happened and how much time it took.

✔ **Activity** refers to how you spent that time.

✔ **Priority Rating** refers to the importance of the activity, (see the following section, "Rating Your Priorities").

✔ **Comments** includes any other description or explanation you might feel is relevant.

Rating Your Priorities

To help you rate the priority and importance of the things that you spend your time on, try using this simple rating system:

1 = High priority (Highly valued or important to me)

2 = Medium priority

3 = Low priority (Not especially important to me)

W = Waste of my time

There are activities that you *want* to do and activities that you *do not* want to do, but a third category also exists. This third category includes all those things that you had *better* do. Remember that necessity creates priority. Not all your Level 1 tasks are tasks that you *want* to spend time on. Clearly, there are times when certain self-maintenance activities, important details, and what you may consider the more ordinary aspects of your life become very important. Realizing that you're down to your last pair of clean underwear or your last clean plate, for example, can quickly elevate a less-desired activity such as laundry or doing dishes to Level 1 status.

A Sample Time-Log

Table 8-1 shows a sample of a possible time-log.

Table 8-1	Time-Log for Monday		
Time Spent	*Activity*	*Rating (1,2,3,W)*	*Comments*
7-7:20	Oversleeping	W	I didn't need it
7:20-7:45	Getting ready for work	1	
7:45-8:05	Ate breakfast	1	
8:10-8:45	Commuted to work	1	
9-9:20	Opened mail	2	10 minutes would do it
9:20-9:40	Returned phone calls	2,W	Could have been a lot shorter
10-10:45	Productive work	1	
10:45-11:00	Coffee break	2	
11-12	Sat through a meeting	3	Unnecessary meeting
12-12:30	Fiddled on Internet	W	Really doing nothing
12:45-2:00	Lunch with client	1, W	Too long
2:15-3:00	Productive work	1	
3-3:45	E-mailing	2	Could have done it another time
3:45-4:00	Solitaire on PC	W	

Time Spent	Activity	Rating (1,2,3,W)	Comments
4-4:30	Productive work.	2	
4:30-5	Paid bills	2	do at home?
5-5:30	Shot the breeze	2	
5:45-6:20	Commuted home	1	Listen to news and music
6:30-6:50	Talked with spouse	1	Don't do it enough!
6:50-7:15	Read newspaper	2	
7:15-8	Ate dinner	1	Over too quickly.
8-9	Watched TV	2	Love this program!
9-10	Watched TV	W	Not worth watching.
10-10:30	Watched news	2	
10:30	To bed		

Hopefully keeping a time-log gives you a better picture of where your time goes. You are now ready to take action and use this information to change the ways you spend your time.

Knowing What's Important

One of the secrets of effective time management is finding out what's important to you and figuring out ways to spend more of your time doing those things. Improving your time-management skills means more than finding ways to squeeze everything you might ever want to do into one day. Brushing your teeth and putting on your shoes at the same time may be admirable, and certainly efficient, yet it may not be the best way to manage your time. Being time-effective does not mean trying to do everything in the least amount of time. Doing it all is impossible, and trying to do it all is stressful.

Managing your time effectively means managing your priorities. Not all the things you have to do in life have the same importance or value. Your time-log may be loaded with W's and 3's. You may find yourself spending your time doing things that aren't really that worthwhile. Your next step is working to change that.

Figuring out what you want to spend more time doing

As an exercise, grab a sheet of paper and jot down activities that you would like to spend more time doing. This exercise helps you get in touch with those activities that you value and derive satisfaction from and those that you do not.

To help you identify those activities, the following is a sample of general items you may want to consider. (You can, of course, add others.)

- Spending time with your kids
- Spending time with your spouse
- Spending time with friends
- Spending time on you
- Spending time on your job or career
- Spending time on a hobby or interest
- Reading
- Exercising
- Nurturing your soul
- Spending time on community activities
- Traveling
- Sleeping

Knowing what you want to spend less time doing

Knowing what you want to spend more time doing is only half the battle. Knowing what you *do not* want to spend a lot of time doing is just as important. Here are some of my goals — make a list of your own:

- Spend fewer hours late at the office
- Spend fewer hours on office paperwork
- Spend fewer hours at events I don't enjoy
- Spend fewer hours cleaning the house

> ✔ Spend fewer hours doing laundry
> ✔ Spend fewer hours with people I don't enjoy
> ✔ Spend fewer hours watching television

Try to eliminate, or at least minimize, delegate, and generally avoid whenever possible those activities that you want to do less of. Encourage yourself to indulge in and savor those activities that you want to do more of.

Feeling a Wee Bit "List-less"?

You now have one list that tells you how you spent your yesterdays. You now need a second list to help you figure out how to spend your tomorrows. You need a master "To-Do" list. You can keep it on your desk, in your daily planner, in your purse or wallet, or in your electronic organizer — wherever is most convenient and accessible to you.

Review your list daily — either the last thing at night or the first thing in the morning — to plan for the day ahead and add any new to-do items that have come up in the meantime. During the day, review your list several times, putting a line through any item that you either have done or now deem unimportant.

As you use your To-Do list, keep the following points in mind:

Go the electronic route

If you're into technology and gadgets, chances are that you already have some kind of computerized time-management system. If you don't, consider using one. These days, the prices are very reasonable, and the things you can do with these small devices are truly amazing. Going electronic can add a little fun to the otherwise mundane business of scheduling your time. You might be surprised to learn that you already how the software needed hidden somewhere in you computer. Ask the office techie for some help, or consult *Microsoft Office 2000 For Dummies* by Wallace Wang and Roger C. Parker, or *Outlook 2000 For Dummies* by Bill Dyszel, both excellent references published by IDG Books Worldwide, Inc.

Set your priorities

After you enter an item, rate the item by using the 1-2-3-W scale.

Make time for your priorities

Keep your list of "Activities I Want to Spend More Time On" right next to your To-Do list. Refer to it every time you refer to your To-Do list. Your goal is to make time for and include as many of these activities as possible.

Use the 80/20 rule

Time-management guru Alan Lakein has long subscribed to and promoted the 80/20 rule, or Pareto Principle. Simply put, it states: Of the things you have to do, doing 20 percent of the most valued will provide you with 80 percent of the satisfaction you may have gotten by doing them all. In other words, by not doing many of your lower-priority items (your 3s), you don't really lose out on a whole lot in the long run. Don't get fixated on those less-valued, less-productive activities. Ask yourself, "Would it really be so awful if I didn't do this task?"

Unload the low-priority stuff

After you identify those activities and tasks that have a lower priority in your life, discover ways to reduce or even eliminate them. What follows is a number of useful strategies and tactics that show you how to do just that. For example, social engagements can easily eat up a good deal of your time. You probably attend many engagements out of a sense of obligation or habit. But you don't have to attend absolutely every party or dinner you're invited to. Nor do you have to attend every meeting posted by your church, temple, school, or any other organization you're affiliated with. Go to those events that you truly want to attend, but be selective and assertive. Give yourself permission to say no to many other invitations. You won't end up being hated by others or ostracized from the community.

Letting Go: Discovering the Joys of Delegating

Remember that old slogan, "If you want something done right, do it yourself"? Yes, it holds some truth. However, by doing it all yourself, you quickly discover that your stress level shoots skyward. Delegating tasks and responsibilities can save you time and spare you a great deal of stress.

You may have a problem delegating for several reasons. Here are some of the more common ones:

- ✔ You believe that no one else is competent enough to do the task.
- ✔ You believe that no one else no one really understands the problem the way you do.
- ✔ You believe that no one else is motivated quite the way you are.
- ✔ You don't trust anyone else to be able to manage the responsibilities.

All these reasons can hold some truth. But in many cases, these reasons aren't accurate at all. The reality is that other people can be taught. You may be pleasantly surprised by the level of work that others can bring to a task or responsibility.

Even if you're right, and others don't do the job as well as you do, you're probably still better off delegating than taking on everything yourself and feeling incredibly stressed.

The fine art of delegating

You may be from the "Do this, and have it on my desk by tomorrow morning!" school of delegating. Here are some tips to help you delegate more effectively:

- ✔ **Find the right person.** Make sure that your delegatees have the knowledge and skills to do the tasks asked of them. And if you can't find a person who has the knowledge and skills, consider investing the time in training someone. In the longer run, you'll be ahead of the game.
- ✔ **Package your request for help in positive terms.** Tell the person why you selected him or her. Offer a genuine compliment reflecting that you recognize some ability or competence that makes that person right for the job.
- ✔ **Be appreciative of their time.** Recognize that you're aware that the person has their own work to do, but that you would really be grateful if he or she could help you with this task.
- ✔ **Don't micromanage.** After you assign a task and carefully explain what needs to be done, let the person do it. Keep your hands off unless you clearly see that things are taking a wrong turn.
- ✔ **Reward the effort.** If the person did a good job, say so. And if he or she didn't do it quite the way you would have but put a lot of effort into the task, let him or her know that you appreciate the effort.

Delegating begins at home

You may associate the word *delegating* with working in an office and handing off a project to an associate or assistant. However, delegating tasks and duties at home is a major way to save a lot of time. Here are some suggestions:

- ✔ **Let one and all share in the fun.** Everyone in the family (assuming that he or she is old enough to walk and talk) can, and should, have a role in sharing household duties and responsibilities.

- ✔ **Start with a list.** Divvy up those less-desirable chores, such as washing dishes (or putting them in the dishwasher), doing laundry, cleaning up bedrooms, taking out the trash, and emptying the dishwasher.

- ✔ **Start small.** Don't overwhelm your family right off the bat. Give them one or two assignments and then add on as appropriate.

- ✔ **Don't feel guilty.** In the long run, your family will come to value the experience. (Recognize that it may be a very long run, however.)

Saving Time

You can save yourself a great deal of time by doing similar tasks all at the same time. Grouping tasks is much more efficient and much less stressful. You can, for example

- ✔ **Pay all your bills at the same time.** Designate a time when to go through the bills that you've put in your To Pay box, and write the checks, address the envelopes, and mail them.

- ✔ **Make phone calls in groups.** Rather than interrupting your schedule to make or return noncritical phone calls, wait until you have several calls to make and make them all at the same time.

- ✔ **Bundle your errands.** Rather than running to the store for every little item, group errands together. Keep a "Things We Need or Will Need Soon" list in a handy place and refer to your list before you dash out for that single needed item so that you can pick up other needed items as well.

An even simpler way to do this is to photocopy a master list with the common items you usually need to replace and stick it on the fridge. Check off a needed item when you notice that you're running low. When you've checked off a bunch of items on the list, head to the store.

- ✔ **Buy some things in bulk.** Many items around the house and office have to be replaced regularly. Buying office supplies, toilet paper, canned goods, paper towels, pet food, and so on in larger quantities can make sense, *if* you have enough room to store all your bulk purchases.

- ✔ **Cook ahead.** Preparing meals can be incredibly time-consuming. Whenever possible, prepare enough food so that you have several meals available. You can cook soups, stews, casseroles, and sauces in larger quantities so that you can freeze additional meals. A dismal day on the weekend is the perfect time to cook up a storm. Just make sure to clearly label those plastic containers.

Getting the most out of technology

You can also save yourself time by letting technology do some of the work for you. (After all, technology was supposed to make your life easier, remember?) Try the following techniques:

- ✔ **Shop by mail.** Shopping by mail can be great way to save time. Catalogues abound, and you can order just about anything over the phone, by fax, or by e-mail. If you order a dud, most companies let you ship the item back. And if you consolidate your orders or buy with a friend, you can save money on shipping costs. The downside? Finding things to buy that you really could live without is all too easy.

- ✔ **Work the Web.** The Internet can speed up your banking and make hotel, restaurant, plane, train, and just about any other kind of reservations a snap. You can also buy anything from books to automobiles and often save a lot of money, as well as time.

Enjoy technology, but curb your electronic dilly-dallying

I recognize that the Internet is here to stay and will probably add much satisfaction and joy to people's lives. However, at this point, it seems that you can easily lose the better part of a lifetime surfing through this stuff, not to mention just getting online. The Internet can easily become a black hole sucking in all your free time and energy with very little in the way of return. The same goes for computer games.

Limit your hours surfing the Internet by pre-scheduling when you will use it. Keep a simple log taped to the monitor, and check off when you use the Internet and for how long. Never sign in for more than a few hours in a week. Give some of your less-interesting computer games away and monitor the time you spend on the others.

Minimizing your TV time

As one of my children once commented, "Have you ever noticed how much longer the days are when you don't watch TV?" Although some television is terrific, a lot of it is not terrific. It's clear, at least to me, that people waste too much time watching television. I'm also convinced that the quality of our lives would be greatly enriched if we watched less television.

TV reduction tactics include the following:

- ✔ **Try to cut back drastically on the time you spend watching.** Never just randomly channel-surf, sticking with the least-objectionable program. Watch only those shows that you really want to watch. Try to keep your TV time down to less than two hours per night.

- ✔ **Try to make one evening a week a no-TV night.** Instead of watching television, do something else. Read a book. Go to the gym. Make soup. Make love. Go to bed earlier.

- ✔ **Use your VCR.** Try to not watch a television program when it's first broadcast. Tape the programs you like and watch them in a block, at a time *you* choose.

- ✔ **Avoid videotape pileup.** When you've collected more recorded tapes than you could possibly watch in one day of dedicated TV viewing, start winnowing. Begin recording over existing tapes rather than adding to your growing collection.

Minimize those pesky interruptions

It doesn't take long to realize that much of your time can be consumed by small interruptions that take you away from what you're doing and thereby lengthen the time that the task at hand should take. Some interruptions are triggered by others or by external events and situations. At other times, *you* may create the disruption.

If you're at home and you need to avoid interruptions, move to the room where you know you have the most privacy. If you're at work, close your office door, if you have one. Most important, curb those interruptions that you manufacture. (You do not need a break every two minutes.)

Although your telephone can be one of your best allies when it comes to saving time, it can also be a terrific nuisance. Have you ever noticed that your phone always rings exactly three minutes after you sit down for dinner, and the caller is someone who will gladly help you switch phone companies, review your financial situation, or want you to contribute to your alma mater?

Here are some useful ideas to help you free yourself from the time-stealing clutches of your telephone:

- ✔ **Screen your calls.** Monitor your calls via your telephone answering machine, and pick up those from people you want to talk with.

- ✔ **Use Caller ID.** With Caller ID, you can know who's calling immediately and can decide whether you want the machine to pick up or you really want to speak to that person at that moment.

- ✔ **Miss a few calls.** If you don't have Caller ID or an answering machine at home, try not answering the phone every time it rings. Missing a few calls (at home — not in the office!) will hardly handicap your chances of having a good life. If people really want to speak to you, they'll call back.

- ✔ **Deal with people over e-mail rather than on the phone.** Hand out your e-mail address to those people whom, for whatever reason, you really do not want to talk to on the telephone.

- ✔ **Leave a message.** If you just want to convey some information to someone but don't really want to speak with that person, call when you know that he or she won't be there.

- ✔ **Be specific.** If you're tired of playing phone tag and want to connect, give the person a specific time when you will pick up the phone, or ask the person to leave you a message telling you when he or she will be available to take your call.

- ✔ **Get off the lists.** Ask to be taken off those phone lists that are nuisances. If you ask the caller to take your name off the list, there's a better-than-average chance that he or she actually will — after all, it is the law. The same goes for unwanted faxes and e-mails.

- ✔ **Ask for the offer in writing.** If you're interested in what the person is selling, pleasantly ask him or her to put the offer in writing and mail it to you.

- ✔ **Get a cordless telephone.** A cordless phone enables you to walk around your house doing other things while you talk.

Getting up a wee bit earlier

Starting your day in a mad rush sets a harried tone that can stay with you all day. Why not get up a little bit earlier? This notion may seem radical, but having another half-hour before you leave the house gives you extra time to get ready, find the things that you need for your day, have a more leisurely breakfast, and otherwise get your day off to an unstressful beginning.

If half an hour is asking too much, try getting up 15 minutes earlier. If this approach isn't working, start going to bed earlier so that waking up becomes a little easier.

Buying Time

You may subscribe to the old work ethic, "Never pay anyone to do something that you can readily do yourself." This is a mistake. Hiring someone to help you can give you more time for the things you want to do and, in the process, make your life simpler and less stressful.

Am I being casual about your finances? I don't think so. I realize that you may not have a lot of extra money in your pocket. However, gone are the days when only the rich hired other people to help them out. Sometimes hiring someone else is clearly wise.

Here are some questions to help you decide whether hiring someone else or paying to provide a service makes sense:

- What chores do I absolutely *hate*?
- Which chores constantly provoke a battle between me and my spouse or me and my roommate?
- What chores do I merely dislike doing?
- What chores do I not do very well?
- What chores do I not mind doing, but really aren't worth my time and effort?

Tasks that you may want someone else to do for you, and in fact can do for you, include the following:

- Regularly clean your whole house or apartment (kitchen, bathrooms, dishes, and so on)
- Do your laundry
- Cook your meals
- Pick up your groceries
- Wash your windows and clean your rugs
- Repaint or refinish walls, furniture, or floors
- Water your plants while you're away
- Take care of your garden
- Take care of your pet
- Pick up your mail and newspaper while you're away

- ✔ Mow your lawn
- ✔ Shop for your clothing
- ✔ Purchase tickets
- ✔ Wait in line
- ✔ Wrap gifts
- ✔ Drive you places
- ✔ Cater a special event

Avoid paying top dollar

Getting someone else to do less-than-desirable chores need not cost you a bundle. You probably don't need an expensive professional. Lots of people who are "between opportunities" would be willing to do chores for you if you paid them. Look at supermarket billboards, neighborhood circulars, or your local newspaper for people looking for work. And check their references. Don't overlook high school and college students, especially during the summer. They can be cheaper, and surprisingly reliable.

Realistically assess your financial ability to hire someone to do a few or many of the items on your list. Remember, too, that the emotional relief and the extra time you gain is well worth the money in many cases. Spend the bucks.

Striving for deliverance

These days, many of the things you need can be delivered. If you live in a good-sized city, almost everything can be delivered. You can save time by dialing the right series of digits or clicking the right places on the Internet. In addition to take-out food, goods and services that you can have delivered to your door include the following:

- ✔ Groceries
- ✔ Laundry
- ✔ Videos
- ✔ Meats from the butcher
- ✔ Sweets from the bakery
- ✔ Liquor

Take-out or cook?

The take-out menu may not be the greatest invention of all time, but it's up there. Why not take advantage of the fact that more and more food can be delivered to your door or picked up on the way home? Yes, everyone knows about pizza and Chinese food. These days, though, the choice of take-out fare is far wider and more interesting than it was even a couple of years ago. Even supermarkets have gourmet-looking precooked items in their deli sections.

Will taking advantage of all this take-out food cost you an arm and a leg? Not really. Often, the cost of making dinner from scratch rivals the cost of bringing prepared food in. Sometimes, you may save by ordering take-out. Recently, I decided to make a curried shrimp dish at home. After I purchased all the ingredients, including the exotic spices that were needed, it was clear that I had spent much more than if I had ordered the dish from India Palace around the corner. Yes, I'm glad I made the dish. But I did not save money. And frankly, my rendition wasn't quite as tasty. And, oh, the time I saved!

Overcoming Procrastination

Procrastination may be one of the main time-robbers and ultimate stress-producers in your life. I have yet to see more than a handful of people who don't lose time by procrastinating. By avoiding the kinds of activities that are important and valued, you wind up spending a lot of time doing activities that are less valued and less satisfying. Procrastinating writing that letter to a loved one, or updating your resume, or making that phone call to a friend, almost always leads to regret.

You procrastinate for one of four major reasons:

✔ Doing the avoided task or activity involves effort and discomfort. Your low level of frustration tolerance slows you or completely stops you.

✔ You're afraid that you may not be able to do the avoided task as well as you'd like. Fear of failure and feeling bad about yourself make it less likely that you will do what you ought to be doing.

✔ You're afraid that somebody will be displeased with your performance. You over-value other people's opinions. You're fearful of rejection.

✔ You feel that you shouldn't have to do the task or activity, and you're angry at having to do it. You feel the world, or some of the people in it, are not treating you fairly.

All the preceding reasons can stop you in your tracks. The following suggestions can help you procrastinate less:

Pull a John Wayne: Bite the bullet

If you find that dislike and discomfort are steering you away from doing what you should be doing, see if you can challenge your assumptions. Ask yourself, "Why must I always do the things I like and want to do?" The answer, of course, is that you don't have to avoid difficulty and discomfort. Just do it! Then ask yourself a second question: "Wouldn't I be better off putting up with some discomfort and getting it out of the way?" The answer: Absolutely!

Motivate yourself

Sometimes your level of internal motivation doesn't get you where you need to go. You need external motivation. You can either reward yourself for doing something or penalize yourself for not doing it.

Try the reward approach first. Create your own motivational ladder by coming up with a list of rewards that can motivate you to get the job done and then rank them in order of their importance to you. For example:

- Treat yourself to a mini-vacation.
- Buy yourself something big that you've been dying to get but have been denying yourself.
- Treat yourself to a great meal or a dessert.
- Go to the movies, see a play, or do something fun.
- Buy yourself a small present.

However, being nice, even to yourself, doesn't always cut it. You may respond better to the threat of pain and suffering than to a positive reward. If pain is *your* thing, try creating a penalty for not completing a task:

- Give up a favorite pleasure for a day (TV, a movie, a dessert, going out, and so on).
- Give up a favorite pleasure for a week.
- Send a donation to a political candidate you dislike.
- Send cash anonymously to a person you know and dislike. (Make it one week's salary and I personally guarantee success.)

Use the smallest reward or penalty that gets the job done. If that doesn't work, more up to the next reward or penalty on your motivational ladder. Be creative.

To make sure that you do enforce a penalty, tell a friend about your plan and ask him or her to make sure that you follow through. I find that this approach improves your chances of successfully breaking through procrastination. If money is involved, put it in an envelope, address it, put a stamp on it, and give it to a friend, telling him or her to mail it if you don't come through on your end of the deal.

Go public

Make a public commitment. Tell a good friend about a task that you want to get done and tell him or her when you will complete it. Better yet, tell a bunch of people. Be sure to remind that friend or friends to ask follow-up and check to see what happened.

Using the "Will-Do" Approach

The *Will-Do approach* recognizes the reality that you're great planner, but your follow-through is usually weak. To use the Will-Do approach, follow these steps:

1. **Find a place to write things down.**

   A small notebook, a calendar, a set of index cards, or an electronic organizer can work well. Whatever you choose, make it something that you can easily carry with you.

2. **On the top of the left-hand page (or the back of a card) write the words** To Do. **On the right-hand page, draw three columns and title them** Will Do, When and Where?, **and** What Happened?

3. **Toward the end of your day, take ten minutes to think about the next day and update your planner. On your To-Do page or card, jot down** *all* **the things that you should or would like to do the next day.**

4. **Taking items from your longer To-Do list, write in the Will-Do column of your planner** *only* **those things that have high priority or importance in your life.**

   The list can be long or short. However, write only those items that you can truly commit to doing. Make a pact with yourself: "If I write something down, I will do it." This is not a "Things I would like to do" list, but a "Things I *will* do" list.

5. **Fill in the When and Where? column for each item on your Will-Do list.**

6. **As you go through the next day, fill in the What Happened? column for each item.**

   If, for some reason that's out of your control, you don't get something done and it's still important, put it back on the list. If you chronically leave tasks undone, shorten your list.

The following example shows a completed Will-Do list:

Will Do	When and Where?	What Happened?
Call for plane tickets	10:30, my office	Called. Got them.
Write report for Gerry	2:30, my office	Done.
E-mail to Beth	Evening, at home	Sent.
Call Donna	Morning, my office	Done

The secret of the Will-Do approach is that it minimizes procrastination and maximizes follow-through.

Avoiding the perils of perfectionism

The old adage "Anything worth doing is worth doing well" is misguided. There's nothing wrong with wanting to do something well, even very well. But when your standards are *too* high, and you aim for perfection, you will feel stress. Perfection is overrated. Being perfect for any longer than three minutes is very hard. Whenever you strive for perfection, you fall into one of two time-wasting and stress-producing traps:

✔ You spend more time on the task or activity than is warranted.

✔ You avoid doing the task altogether for fear that you won't do it well enough.

Strive for "pretty darn good" instead of "perfect." And, sometimes, let yourself strive for even "just okay."

Chapter 8

Eating, Exercising, and Getting Your Zzzs

In This Chapter

▶ Understanding how what you eat can affect your level of stress

▶ Exercising to reduce your stress

▶ Getting a good night's sleep

*R*emember when you were a very young child and you got cranky when you hadn't eaten or gotten enough sleep? Those were not your finest moments. Just ask your parents. Your ability to cope with frustration and disappointment were all but nonexistent.

Now that you've grown up, your stresses may be different, but your physical state still plays a major role in determining how stressed you become. What you eat, when you eat, your level of overall fitness, and the quality of your sleep all affect your ability to cope with stress:

✔ When your body is under stress because it is poorly nourished, insufficiently rested, or generally unfit; your body is more susceptible to a wide range of maladies and disorders, ranging from the common cold to something more dramatic.

✔ When you're stressed physically, you react to your world differently. You're less able to cope effectively with the many daily stresses that cross your path. In short, you become a lousy stress manager.

This chapter shows you how you can develop a more stress-effective lifestyle — through diet, exercise, and sleep — which can, in turn, strengthen your body's ability to cope with potential stress and help you resist its negative effects. Simply put: Your body is a temple. Treat it nicely.

Maybe I should just skip to the next chapter?

Who knows, you may be someone who eats right, sleeps tight, and has abs that would make even Arnold Schwarzeneggar feel insecure. Take this brief pop quiz to help you assess your health lifestyle.

For each of the five items below, circle the answer that best describes your current lifestyle:

1. For me, a *balanced meal* means:

a. Eating moderate amounts of red meat.

b. Eating more fruits, vegetables, and whole-grains.

c. Eating a taco and a soda while standing on a bus and not falling over.

2. For me, getting a *good night's sleep* means:

a. Eight or nine hours of sleep.

b. Six or seven hours of sleep.

c. Doing anything with my eyes closed for more than three hours.

3. For me, a *strenuous workout* means:

a. Lifting weights at my health club.

b. Running several miles a day.

c. Moving files from one part of my hard drive to another.

4. I find that the secret to effective meal planning is:

a. Cooking several meals at one time.

b. Using several good, low-fat, low-calorie cookbooks.

c. Having a wide selection of take-out menus next to my telephone.

5. The *best* way to lose weight is:

a. Cut your calories and get more exercise.

b. Become a member of a good weight-loss program.

c. Take up smoking and fill each day with as much stress as I possibly can.

Scoring:

Answering (c) for any question suggests that the rest of this chapter is required reading. The rest of you may find it useful as well.

Stress-Effective Eating

If you're like most people, I suspect that your dietary habits are less than perfect. Your eating is probably a hit-and-miss affair — inconsistent, rushed, and tailored to meet your busy schedule.

I know your life is already stressed enough without having to worry about what goes into your mouth. However, what you eat — and how you eat it — can contribute significantly to your ability to cope with stress in your life. Eating the wrong things, or eating at the wrong times can add to your stress level. Not to worry. Help is here.

Feeding your brain

In recent years, a lot of attention has been paid to the relationship between food and mood — what you eat and how you feel. Researchers now have a better idea of how different foods affect your psychological states and how food can increase or decrease the stress in your life.

One of the major biochemical elements involved in your stress experience is something called serotonin. *Serotonin* is a naturally occurring chemical neurotransmitter in your brain. Changing serotonin levels can dramatically change the way you feel. Antidepressant drugs like Prozac, Paxil, and Zoloft can alter the amount of serotonin in your brain, which can alter your mood and affect the ways in which you cope with a potential stress.

The foods you eat can also change the serotonin levels in your brain. Your diet is an important way of regulating your serotonin levels. Putting the right stuff on your plate means you have a better chance of giving your brain what it needs.

Choosing low-stress foods

The following are some specific food guidelines that can help you choose foods to lower your stress as well as help your body cope with all the stress in your life:

- ✔ **Include some complex carbohydrates in every meal.** *Complex carbohydrates,* such as pasta, cereals, potatoes, and brown rice, can enhance your performance when under stress. Foods rich in carbohydrates can increase the levels of serotonin in the brain, making you feel better. Too many complex carbohydrates, however, are not the best thing for you. Remember: Moderation.

- ✔ **Reduce your intake of simple carbohydrates.** Sweetened, sugary foods — simple carbohydrates — like soda and candy — can make you feel better in the short run, but feel worse in the long run.

- ✔ **Eat adequate amounts of protein.** This means eating more fish, chicken, and other lean meats. Foods high in protein enhance mental functioning and supply essential amino acids that can help repair damage to your body's cells.

- ✔ **Eat your vegetables.** Beans, peppers, carrots, squash, and dark-green leafy veggies, whether cooked or raw, provide your body with the vitamins and nutrients it needs to resist the negative effects of stress.

- ✔ **Get plenty of potassium.** Milk (especially the low-fat variety), whole grains, wheat germ, and nuts all can provide your body with potassium, a mineral that can help your muscles relax. Bananas, a personal favorite, are also a good source of potassium.

Stop feeding your stress

Are you an *emotional eater?* If so, you may eat whenever you are anxious, upset, nervous, or depressed. Although emotional eaters can still put it away when they're happy, delighted, non-anxious, and non-depressed (and yes, during those rare times when they're actually hungry), most emotional eaters eat when they feel they need to feed their stress.

When you feed your stress, a destructive cycle begins. You feel stressed, so your food choices are not always the best. For some reason of cruel fate, foods that tend to make you feel good are usually the foods that are not so good for your body. Chocolate, ice cream, pizza, cake, donuts, and cookies may make you feel terrific — but, unfortunately, only for about 17 seconds. Then, of course, your stress returns (plus a ton of guilt) and you feel the need for another bout of eating. The cycle then repeats itself.

The first step in breaking the cycle is becoming aware of exactly when you are distressed and identifying your feelings. When you feel the urge to open the refrigerator door, you need to realize that you are experiencing some form of discomfort. It could be hunger; but more likely, it is stress.

Before you put any food in your mouth, stop and take stock of your emotional state. Ask yourself, "Am I really hungry or am I feeling emotionally distressed?" If it is truly hunger, eat. Otherwise label your feelings (for example, "I'm upset," "I'm nervous," or "I'm a wreck!"). Simply breaking the stress-eating connection for even a moment can give you a different perspective and an increased level of motivation that can sustain you, until you find something a little more redeeming than filling your mouth.

The following are some other tips that you can use to improve your relationship with food when you're stressed:

Distract yourself

One of the better things you can do is involve yourself in some activity you enjoy that will take your mind off eating. Do something. Anything. Some eating substitutes that will keep you away from the kitchen include the following:

- ✔ Get out of the house. Often, simply changing your environment can rid you of the old eating cues. Go for a walk. Do an errand. Visit a friend.
- ✔ Get some exercise. Hit the stationary bike or treadmill, or simply do some floor exercises like sit-ups or even just stretching.
- ✔ Read a good book. Watch an interesting television program.

> ✔ Cook something. This may seem like asking for trouble, but often the process of cooking can serve as a substitute for your eating. A hint: Don't make cookies or cakes. Try something like a soup or a casserole, something that is filling, takes time to cook and prepare, and is not immediately ready to eat.

Substitute relaxation for food

Whenever you are about to open the refrigerator to calm your frayed nerves, consider substituting a relaxation break. Simple deep breathing, some rapid relaxation, some relaxation imagery, or any of the other marvelous techniques I describe in Chapters 4 and 5 can induce a feeling of emotional calm that can reduce your desire to eat. That's all you may need to ease you past a difficult moment.

Work with a stress-cue

Sometimes a little reminding goes a long way. Create a stress-eating reminder that you could put on your fridge or on the cabinet where you keep delicious snacks. One of my patients came up with what I thought was a beaut: She put a not terribly attractive picture of her in her heavier days in a small magnetic frame that she stuck on her refrigerator.

You may decide to be less brutal and opt for something more neutral. One friend has the question, "Are you really hungry?" taped to her kitchen door. Even more innocuous is a simple little colored circle of paper you can affix at strategic places in your kitchen. It reminds you that you shouldn't open the door unless you are hungry. Only you know what it represents and why it's there.

Eat your breakfast

Again, your mother was right! Research shows that eating a nutritious (low-fat, high-carbohydrate) breakfast makes you more alert, more focused, and in a much better mood than if you have a high-fat, high-carbohydrate breakfast; have a moderate-fat, moderate-carbohydrate breakfast; or have no breakfast at all.

Skipping breakfast can lower your body's ability to cope with the stress that lies in wait for your later in the day. Starting the day on the right nutritional foot is important. When you wake up in the morning, as many as 11 or 12 hours have passed since you last ate. You need to refuel.

And don't forget lunch

Lunchtime tends to be one of the busier times of your day. With a lot to do, eating lunch may be low on your list of priorities; but don't skip lunch. Your body functions best when it gets fed regularly. Missing lunch can leave you feeling tense and edgy.

TIP

The less-stress breakfast

What should you eat for breakfast? Avoid sugar and the usual high-fat villains — ham, bacon, and sausage. A cup of coffee or two won't hurt, but try not to go overboard with caffeine. Adding a low-fat, high-fiber, multi-grain cereal with some low-fat milk to your morning routine will get you off to a good start. I like to mix my cereals. Try combining a few Corn Flakes with some All Bran and some puffed wheat. What can I tell you. I'm a wild man!

I also like oatmeal. It's fast, too, especially if you use the instant kind, and it fills you up and keeps you full. Recent studies out of Pennsylvania State University have shown that oatmeal provides you with a sustained, long-lasting release of energy — longer, in fact, than any other kind of breakfast cereal.

When you do have lunch, don't overdo it. A big lunch can leave you lethargic and dreaming of a mid-afternoon siesta, a practice frowned upon by many businesses.

Eat like a cow

Eating a big meal can result in your feeling lethargic soon after eating. To digest that heavy meal, your body needs a greater supply of blood. This blood has to come from other places in your body like your brain, depriving it of some of the oxygen it needs to keep you alert. The solution? Graze like a cow.

Spread out your eating fairly evenly throughout the day. Avoid those huge meals that load you down with calories and leave you feeling ready for a nap. Instead consider smaller, lighter meals at your regular mealtime. Supplement them with healthy snacks. Have a mid-morning snack, and then a light lunch, another snack later in the afternoon (a piece of fruit is good), and a *moderate* dinner. A snack later in the evening (try some air-popped popcorn) should avert any hunger pangs. It seems to work for cows, doesn't it?

Drink like a camel

Most people do not get enough liquids into their bodies during the course of the day. The notion of drinking the recommended eight glasses of water, for most of us, is a joke. If you're like most people, you usually wait until you're thirsty before heading for the kitchen. Unfortunately, by then it's a little late. Your body needs the liquid *before* you feel that thirst. Coffee and tea can act as diuretics and therefore should not be considered as part of your "daily 8s."

Load up earlier in the day

For most people, the simplest way to lose weight is to eat more in the first half of the day than they do in the last half. Then they have time to burn off many of those earlier calories. Recall that old bit of nutritional wisdom, "Eat like a king in the morning, a prince at noon, and a pauper at night."

Simply supplement

If you think that you may not be getting enough of your needed vitamins and/or minerals, consider taking a daily multiple vitamin and mineral supplement. If your daily diet gives you all the nutritional good stuff you need, this may not be necessary. However, you may be one of the many whose diet is not nutritionally praiseworthy and could benefit from some supplemental help.

Mastering the art of anti-stress snacking

Feeling anxious, nervous, stressed out? Need a quick food-fix? Snacking, when done right, is an art. Anyone can down a candy bar or a bag of chips and a soda. The real skill is coming up with a snack that not only doesn't add to your stress level but helps you reduce the stress you already have. Here are some guidelines:

- ✔ **Avoid highly sugared treats.** They'll give you a boost in the short run but let you down in the long run. You'll crash.

- ✔ **Stick with snacks that have high-energy proteins and are high in complex carbohydrates.** They'll give you a longer-lasting sustained pick-me-up.

Here are some specific suggestions of quick bites and snacks that can boost your mood and help alleviate some of your stress:

- ✔ A piece of fruit — an orange, peach, apple, or banana — just about any fruit is fine.

- ✔ A handful of mixed nuts. (Until only recently, nuts were considered low on the health-food hierarchy. These days they're are on the okay list.)

- ✔ A bowl of whole-grain cereal with a sliced banana.

- ✔ A spinach salad.

- ✔ A bowl of fruit salad.

- ✔ A soft pretzel.

- ✔ Air-popped popcorn.

- ✔ An English muffin. (Go easy on the butter or margarine. A little jelly is fine.)

- ✔ A container of low-fat yogurt.

- ✔ A piece of chocolate (but just a piece!).

Don't fill your tank with the leaded stuff

Overdoing the caffeine is probably not a good idea if you'd like to lower your stress level. Although many people tend not to be sensitive to the effects of caffeine, many more are. Experiment and find out what your caffeine limits are. Biochemically, stressing your body only lowers your stress-threshold, and renders you more vulnerable to the demands and pressures around you. Limit yourself to what you know your body can handle without feeling edgy or nervous.

Noting that those tasty specialty drinks that your local coffee bar offers are often higher in caffeine is also important. That cup of mocha frappaccino you're sipping can have up to 250 mg of caffeine. That's about twice what you get from a regular cup o' joe. Opting for the larger "grande" size can also double the amount of caffeine in your system.

More jangled nerves are not what you need. The next time you ask for a skim, no-foam latte, trying hold the caffeine, too.

Eating out

These days it seems as though more of us are eating out or bringing in already-prepared foods. And to be fair, more fast-food places have modified their menus to include healthier fare. Still, temptations can run high, and the chances of you falling into some nutritional pothole is more than a little likely. Here are some fast-food guidelines:

- Go with turkey, chicken breast, or lean roast beef instead of salami, ham, and cheese.
- Avoid the chef's salad. It sounds terrifically healthy, but it isn't. The eggs, bacon, cheese, and dressing can turn it into a nutritionally bad idea.
- Tuna is great. But add a lot of mayo and it becomes a mistake.
- Have a hamburger instead of a cheeseburger.
- Never order a large-sized anything.
- Eat only half of your French fries or split a regular order of fries with someone.
- Have a slice of pizza without any meat toppings.
- Take the skin off your roasted chicken.

Curing "menu weakness"

Menu weakness is a condition that you may encounter when you sit down in a restaurant and the waitress hands you a menu. All you can see are the alluring descriptions of food possibilities. Any healthful habit or nutritional resolve vanishes. You wind up ordering things you later regret. Usually, the wonderfully tasty items such as the French fries, the cheeseburger, or that incredible dessert are the ones that get you.

To cure this affliction, you need a strategy. The best thing you can do is be prepared. Before you enter a restaurant, decide what you will order. By now, I suspect that you have a pretty good idea of what is on the menu. You don't need it to confuse and distract you. When the waitress comes, tell her what you want without benefit of the menu. Yes, in the short run it is less satisfying, but you will have fewer regrets later on.

Becoming salad bar savvy

I remember when salad bars first became popular. They really were "salad" bars. They contained mostly foods that were green in color, foods that are healthy and nutritious. That was the first week. Then the good-tasting stuff starting filling the trays, and there has been no going back. However, with some control over your tong-hand, you can again make the salad bar your body's friend.

Here is the secret to healthy salad bar visits: Never eat anything that is in a heated bin. The hot items are the most toxic. True, tuna salad loaded with mayo will not win any nutritional awards, but compared to the food farther down the line, it can be considered a health food. By steering clear of anything reheated, you can avoid such nutritional disasters as sweet-and-sour chicken, greasy lo-mein, ribs, fried rice, lasagna, and all the rest of the wonderfully tasting foods that beckon you from their aluminum trays.

Just don't go hog wild

At this point, you may feel that much of the joy and pleasure of eating has been taken from you. To some extent, yes. However my philosophy about food has always been "Everything in moderation" — including moderation. You really do not have to give up anything entirely. You can still have a steak, pizza, ice cream, or anything else that captures your fancy. Just eat less of it. *Bon appetit!*

Stress-Reducing Exercise and Activity

You already know how beneficial exercise can be as a way of keeping your weight down, your body buff, and your heart ticking well into the 21st century.

What you may not know is that exercise is one of the better ways of helping you cope with the stress in your life. Exercise and sustained activity — in whatever form — can decrease your blood pressure, lower your heart rate, and slow your breathing — all signs of reduced arousal and stress. Exercise is a natural and effective way of slowing and even reversing your body's fight-or-flight response. This section shows you how you can make exercise and activity your allies in winning the battle against stress.

Calming your brain naturally

When you exercise, you feel different; your mood changes for the better. This difference is not only a psychological response to the fact that you are doing something good for your body. It is physiological as well.

When you exercise, you produce *endorphins* (literally, natural morphine from within your body), which can produce feelings of well-being and calming relaxation. This positive feeling helps you cope more effectively with stress and its effects.

Think activity, rather than exercise

The word *exercise* has never been a favorite word for most people. It connotes too much work with too little fun, like taking out the garbage or making the bed. Exercise is something you endure and complete as quickly as possible. The word *exercise* is associated with sweating, stretching, straining, pulling, lifting, more sweating, and a long shower. At least the last part is fun.

You may think of exercise as something falling outside the range of your normal day-to-day activities. However, a better way of thinking about the goal of staying fit is to replace the word *exercise* with the term *activity*.

The word exchange is more than semantic. *Any* increase in your level of bodily activity — aerobically or non-aerobically — any muscle-toning or stretching contributes positively to your state of physical well-being. And whoever said activity has to be in a gym, on a court, or with a dumbbell? Many people mistakenly believe that to exercise you must engage in rigorous sports, go to a health club, or find some other specialized facility. Not so.

We all recognize that after a hard day of work, or taking care of the kids, the chances of your putting on a sweat suit and lifting weights or completing a 6K run are slim. The good news is, you don't have to. The trick is to find naturally existing outlets for activity that are readily available and easily integrated into your lifestyle and work style.

For example, I paid a health club big bucks to let me use a machine that simulates stair-climbing. I finished my encounter with the stairs feeling self-righteous and satisfied. Yet when I return home after my workout, I resented climbing the four flights to where we live. After several years it dawned on me that climbing my own stairs was not that different from climbing the Stairmaster stairs. "Wow," I realized, "A free health tool right in my own home!"

Exercise, cleverly camouflaged as daily physical activity, is all around you. The hard part is knowing it when you see it.

Never jump abruptly into a new program of physical exercise. Your head may be ready for the change, but your body may need more time to get used to the idea. This strategy becomes all the more important if you've led a rather sedentary life in the past. Check with your doctor first for an official okay, and then begin slowly, gradually adding more time and effort to your workout.

The following are some simple ways in which you can introduce small bits of activity into your day:

- ✔ **Park your car a little farther from your office and walk the rest of the way.**

- ✔ **Use your TV time effectively.** While you are watching TV, do some sit-ups, jumping jacks, push-ups, or stretches.

- ✔ **Walk away from your stress.** As an exercise, walking has always had wimp status. But if done consistently and for a sustained period of time, it can be a terrific way of staying in shape. The nice thing about walking is that it can be pleasantly camouflaged as strolling or sight-seeing — both painless activities. And if you crank up the pace and distance a bit, you have a wonderfully simple form of aerobic exercise that can enhance your feeling of well-being, mentally and physically. Walking is a great way to clear your head and calm your mind.

  And remember to take a mini walk or two during your day. Your walks can be as short as down the block to the corner store or a lap around your office or house.

- ✔ **Do something you like.** I was on the swim team in high school, but even though I was pretty good, I really disliked it. I dreaded the early-morning dips in that overly-chlorinated pool, and as soon as I could, I dropped out. The moral here is, if you don't like the exercise or activity you're doing, the chances of you sustaining it are small. Find something you really enjoy, like one of the following:

  - • **A favorite sport.** Golf, tennis, bowling, baseball, basketball, raquet-ball — whatever.

  - • **A favorite activity.** Horseback-riding, dancing, trampolining, swimming, ice-skating, or rope-jumping — or anything that gets your body moving.

  - • **Gardening.** Yes, if done for a sustained period, gardening can be considered a form of exercise.

  - • **Bicycling.** Find a place where you can bike safely and enjoyably. If you don't know where those places are, contact your local parks and recreation office. Or ask friends or people you see on bikes what they suggest.

  - • **In-line skating.** In-line skating is here to stay, because it's great exercise and one of the more painless ways of getting a physical workout. After you've figured out how to stop, no one will be able to hold you back. And be sure to wear the safety gear (a helmet, elbow pads, wrist pads, and knee pads). The stress of finding yourself in an ER should not be included in your already stressful day.

Be sure to wear a helmet and other protective gear when you're on your bike or on blades — even on short rides in your neighborhood. Accidents can happen anywhere.

✔ **Become a player.** One of the better ways of staying in shape is playing at something you like. Every big city has just about every conceivable kind of sports team; everything from Little League to pick-up games in the park on a Saturday or Sunday morning. You don't even have to be especially proficient at a sport to get on board. Check with your local YMCA or community center for teams forming, and ask at work if teams already exist.

✔ **Climb your way out of stress.** I have good news, and I have better news. The good news is, research done at Johns Hopkins University shows that, by climbing stairs for a mere six minutes a day, you can add up to two years to your life. The better news is, if you live in a big city, you encounter lots and lots of stairs every day. With land at a premium, most cities are designed with height, rather than width, in mind. Although some cities are more vertical than others, all have more than their share of opportunities to climb stairs.

And, if you don't live in a big city, you can find climbing opportunities in other places. Ask at your local high school to see whether you can climb the football stadium bleachers. Does your shopping mall have stairs? If so, become a mall walker! Opportunities for stair-climbing aren't limited to the big cities. Consider it a challenge to find stairs wherever you live.

Given a choice between a flight of stairs and an escalator or an elevator, you probably prefer the easier route. I'm not suggesting that you frenetically seek out exit doors to uncover hidden stairwells, but given a simple choice between stairs or no stairs, take the stairs.

Doing the gym thing

Maybe it's a case of misery loving company. Or maybe it's just more fun to do something with others around. Whatever the case, consider joining a gym or health club. After you enter the door of a gym, you rarely leave without some kind of workout.

The biggest obstacle to joining a gym is the cost. You'll find that, like the airlines, each gym charges a different price to do exactly the same thing. You have to shop around for the best deal. Generally, a YMCA or community center, though less trendy, offers better bargains. Also, if you can arrange your schedule so that you can go at off-peak times, many gyms will give you a cheaper rate. Almost all health clubs offer some corporate discount, especially if your corporation is in the neighborhood. Some companies even subsidize your membership.

Try out a club before you join. Ask for a guest pass or two. Many clubs offer short-term trial memberships that allow you to try them out first before signing on for a longer period of time.

Finding "hidden gyms"

These days more places are available to work out in than you may expect. More and more health clubs and gyms are scattered around in hotels, office buildings, and apartment buildings. No signs advertise their existence, but they are there. The equipment at a "hidden gym" may not be elaborate, but you probably don't need elaborate to get the job done.

To find these hidden treasures, you need to do a little detective work. Start with the newer apartment buildings and the bigger hotels in your area, and take a look. Some of these places offer memberships to non-building residents and guests at a reasonable cost. Ask at your place of employment if another company in the building where you work or in a neighboring building has any health facilities. You may be surprised by the number of companies that have installed workout equipment on their premises.

Sweating at home

Of course, you don't need to lay out money for a gym or health club if you purchase a piece or two of exercise equipment that you can use right in our own home. Alas, many pieces of home exercise equipment go badly underused. They become places to hang your clothes or serve as dust-collectors.

However, don't let this deter *you* from converting an extra bedroom or study into a home fitness center. To make sure that your killer ab machine doesn't just collect dust, schedule time with yourself when you commit to working out. And stick to it. Turn on the TV when you exercise to help ease any discomfort. I like to do the crossword puzzle and read the paper when I'm on my stationary bike.

And don't forget the many exercise videos and programs available. Daily new workouts ensure that you don't become bored. There are also tapes and programs on yoga, tae bo, dance-aerobics, and just about any other form of physical exercise.

Keeping yourself motivated

Often, remaining motivated is no small matter. You start with the best of intentions, but somehow run out of motivational steam fairly quickly. The following tips and suggestions should help you stay the course.

Get a workout buddy

A workout buddy or partner provides you with added incentive to make sure you get there. Working out can also be more fun if you go with someone whose company you enjoy. You find the time on the treadmill just whizzes by when you're lost in talk with the person next to you. As a bonus, many health clubs offer a membership discount if you bring in a friend.

Get your day off to an active start

Some exercise, especially aerobic exercise just after you get up in the morning, is a great way to get your juices going and get you prepared for any stress that may come your way later in the day. Aerobic activity introduces more oxygen into your body and makes you more alert and focused. If you make that activity a little more vigorous, your system will release those endorphins, which can produce a calming feeling of relaxation.

Remember that every little bit counts

You may have a mistaken idea that if you do something for only a small bit of time, it really is not worth much. The reality is, if you do it consistently, it adds up. For example, a recent research study found that if you walk briskly for only 10 minutes a day, 3 times a day, you get the same fitness and weight loss benefits as you would if you walked briskly for 30 minutes, once a day.

Do it; don't overdo it

Yes, you really *can* have too much of a good thing — even exercise. Anecdotal reports show that elite athletes complain of being more susceptible to colds and other maladies when they over-train, or merely train intensely. Recent studies further suggest that your immune system can be weakened with excessive, exhaustive exercise. So take a pass on that triathlon if you've never run more that 20 feet in the last 10 years.

Getting a Good Night's Sleep

The first thing you notice when you work with people under a lot of stress is how often they say, "I'm tired." For some, the stress of the day is what wears them out. But for most people, it is a matter of not getting enough sleep. And they are hardly alone.

The fact is, most people do not get enough quality sleep. Unfortunately, when you're tired, your emotional threshold is lowered. You are more vulnerable to all the other stresses around you. Stress breeds even more stress. Breaking the cycle and getting a good night's sleep becomes very important.

Just how much sleep should you get? Most Americans now get between 60 and 90 minutes less a night than they should for optimal health and performance. Though most people need about 7 or 8 hours of sleep a night, 20 percent of all Americans get less than 6 hours of sleep, and 50 percent get less than 8 hours.

Need more sleep?

Here are some of the more important signs and symptoms of someone who probably is not getting enough sleep at night. Answer true or false, depending on whether the following statements apply to you.

1. I notice a major dip in my energy level early in the afternoon.

2. I need an alarm clock to wake up in the morning.

3. On the weekends, when I don't have to get up, I end up sleeping much later.

4. I fall asleep very quickly at night (in about 5 minutes).

5. On most days, I feel tired and feel as though I could use a nap.

Answering "That's me" to any of the above suggests that you may want to re-evaluate how much sleep you're getting and how much sleep you truly need. Try experimenting by getting a bit more sleep at night and see if you notice any changes in your stress level.

No fixed rules will tell you how much sleep you need. So take the simple sleep quiz in the nearby sidebar to help see whether you're getting enough sleep at night.

To get the most benefit from your sleep, try the following:

✔ **Hit the sheets earlier.** I recognize that for many, getting to bed earlier is easy to suggest, but much harder to do. Face it, staying up at night is when you do the things you *need* to do (laundry, housecleaning, paying bills). Or, if you're lucky, late nights are when you do the things you *want* to do, whether that's vegging out in front of the TV or turning pages on the latest bestseller. You may try to burn the candle at both ends — stay up later and get up early. Often, this strategy just doesn't work, and you're tired the next day. An important element in helping you get the sleep you need is realizing that you have to get to bed earlier. It's as simple as that.

✔ **Try the 20-minute approach.** If you determine that you are, in fact, not getting enough sleep at night, try getting to bed 20 minutes earlier and see if the quality of your day is not improved.

To get to bed just a few minutes earlier, turn off the TV at a more reasonable hour. If you must watch that *Seinfeld* rerun or catch Leno's monologue, tape it and watch it earlier the next evening.

Getting quality sleep

Okay, you may get to bed earlier, but you either aren't falling asleep as you'd like or the quality of your sleep is somehow disturbed. Here are some suggestions and direction that can help you attain that night of restful bliss:

Develop a sleep routine

The best sleep comes from having a regular sleep pattern. Your body's internal clock becomes stabilized with routine. This means getting to bed at the same time and getting up at the same time.

Getting up at the same time may be controllable, but hitting the mattress at the same time every night is not that easy. I often get a second wind later at night and develop an unexplainable urge to work on some project that needs far more time than is reasonable. Burning the candle at both ends usually spells stress. Get to bed at about the same time each night. Save the parties for the weekend.

Bed = Sleep

Ideally, you want to establish a set of reminders and habits that promote an effective sleep routine. The relationship in your mind should be that lying down in bed means that you are going to sleep.

That's the ideal. However, if you live in a small house or apartment, you may not have the luxury of keeping a whole room dedicated to just one or two activities. You may be one of the many who uses the bedroom for just about everything. This is understandable, but unfortunately, it's less than ideal for purposes of optimizing your sleep patterns.

Create a sleep ritual

If you can't make your bedroom a room devoted only for sleeping, you may find that creating a bedtime ritual is more realistic. At a certain hour, make the bedroom a place where you wind down and relax. This means no upsetting discussions, no work from the office, no bill-paying, no arguments with the kids, no unpleasant phone calls, or anything else that may trigger worry, anxiety, or upset. You can read, watch some relaxing TV, or whatever else it is that calms your body and quiets your mind. I would advise against watching your local news. Hearing about today's robbery, fire, or general mayhem is not the last thing you want to hear before your head hits the pillow.

Don't exercise within three hours of your bedtime

Exercising is great, but doing it too close to your bedtime can rev you up and keep you awake.

Turn the noise down

You may have trouble sleeping soundly because of noise. This is especially the case if you live in a place where wailing car alarms or party-loving neighbors interrupt even the pleasantest of dreams. Worse yet, you may be a very light sleeper, and vulnerable to a host of far less dramatic noises. Here are some suggestions:

✔ **Sound-proof it.** Even with the windows shut, a lot of sound still comes through. Consider installing double-pane windows. Heavy drapes or shutters can add to the sound-proofing. Carpets, rugs, wall hangings, pictures, bookcases, and book shelves all help absorb excess noise.

✔ **Mask it.** The secret of masking is finding a more tolerable noise and making it the one you hear. Most of us first experience masking in the summers when the soothing hum of the air conditioner drowns out just about everything else. A *sound generator* can mask sound and calm you down. Inexpensive models, available at most discount and department stores, can reproduce a variety of soothing sounds: white noise, a waterfall, a rain forest, or the chirping of crickets in a meadow. A relaxing tape or CD can work just as well.

✔ **Block it.** That Metallica groupie upstairs or a deafening sanitation truck outside may call for stronger measures. These may be the times when earplugs are in order.

Watch the pills and the booze

The quality of your sleep is as important as the number of hours you sleep. A nightcap does little harm, but greater amounts of alcohol (even though they may help you fall asleep) can disturb the *quality* of your sleep and leave you waking up feeling tired. Sleeping pills have their place, and when used appropriately, they can be very useful. However, routine use of medication for sleeping can quickly become psychologically addictive and often impair sleep itself.

Look out for hidden stimulants

Besides that cup of coffee that will probably keep you up until the middle of next week, other less obvious sources of caffeine creep into your diet. Many teas and colas, and even some bottled waters have caffeine. Many people are unaware that some medications they are taking for a variety of medical conditions may have stimulating side effects. A large number of the drugs you buy over the counter also have sleep-disrupting properties. If you are taking any form of medication and are having trouble sleeping, speak with your doctor and/or pharmacist.

Nap carefully

As one who was never able to nap successfully, I always envied those who could drift off for a quick snooze and return to their world refreshed and ready to go. Naps can be a wonderful tool. However, if you are not sleeping well at night, you may seriously consider abandoning your daytime nap. Four out of five people with insomnia find that they do better during the night if they don't nap during the day.

Dealing with bedtime worries

Sometimes distractions are external — noise from the street outside or voices in another room of your house. Sometimes, the noises are internal — racing in your mind. You're worried, upset, angry, or otherwise distressed, and this keeps you revved and awake. You can try several techniques to help you stop this pattern of worry:

- ✔ **Jot it down.** Keep a small pad and pencil near your bed. Jot down the worrisome problem or thought on a piece of paper and decide to yourself that you will work on the problem the next day. This strategy will give you some closure and allow you to leave that little bit of business alone.

- ✔ **Just stop it!** Try something called the *Stop Technique*. I describe this in detail in Chapter 5, but it's worth summarizing here. Whenever you catch yourself obsessing or ruminatively worrying about something, visualize a large red and white hexagonal stop sign. At the same time as you're visualizing the stop sign, silently yell the word *stop* to yourself. What you'll find is that this temporarily interrupts your worrying. Then replace the worry with a welcome and pleasant thought or image. Keep repeating this process until you have sufficiently broken the worry cycle or have fallen asleep. This technique takes a bit of practice, but it really works.

Sleep tight!

Part III
The Fancy Stuff

The 5th Wave   By Rich Tennant

"I'm looking for someone who will love me for who I think I am."

In this part . . .

I cover more advanced techniques that you can use to decrease the amount of stress in your life. If you make minor changes in the way you think when you find yourself in potentially stressful situations, you can actually reduce and perhaps eliminate stress.

Chapter 9

The Secrets of Stress-Resistant Thinking

In This Chapter

▶ How you create much of your stress

▶ How to recognizing your stress-producing thinking

▶ How to change your thinking

▶ The importance of self-talk

*I*f someone cornered you at a cocktail party and asked you where most of your stress came from, chances are you'd tell them it was your job, or family pressures, or not having enough time or money. You probably wouldn't tell them that your thinking was creating much of your stress.

Yet, your thinking plays a larger role in producing your stress than you may imagine. Fortunately, learning how to change your thinking is not all that difficult. This chapter shows you how to spot those specific ways your thinking makes your life more stressful than it has to be. More importantly, it shows you, step by step, how you can turn that stress-producing thinking into stress-resistant thinking.

Believe It or Not, Most of Your Stress Is Self-Created

Feeling stressed is, and always has been, a two-part process. First you need something "out there" to trigger your stress, and then you need to perceive that trigger as stressful. Then you feel stressed. You empower these external events and situations by the ways in which you view them. Look at something one way and you feel major stress; look at it another way you feel less stress, maybe even no stress.

Your attitudes and beliefs about any potentially stressful situation or event determine how much stress you experience. By changing the way you look at a potentially stressful situation, you can change the way you emotionally react to that situation. This concept underlies a number of important approaches to psychotherapy and emotional change. The pioneering work of Drs. Albert Ellis and Aaron Beck are especially important. An important secret of stress management is knowing how you create your stress and knowing how to change that thinking.

In short, you can control the amount of stress you feel.

The notion that you play an active part in creating your own stress may not seem obvious. Consider, for example, some of these distressing scenarios:

- ✔ You feel stressed because you have to give a presentation at work tomorrow to win an important new client.

- ✔ You feel stressed at the supermarket because you got trapped in the slowest moving check-out line.

- ✔ You feel stressed because your picky Aunt Agnes is coming to stay with you for a whole week.

- ✔ You feel stressed because your neighbor is playing his music too loudly.

In each of these cases, the assumption is that the external situation or event produces the stress. That is, it is the presentation, the slow-moving line, the difficult relative, or the noisy neighbor causing you to feel stressed. And there is some truth in this. Let's face it, without those stress-triggers you wouldn't be feeling stress. However, the reality is, presentations, slow lines, difficult relatives, and loud music do not, in themselves, have the power to make you stressed. (Yes, I realize that I have never spent a week with your Aunt Agnes.) For a situation or circumstance to trigger stress, you have to see that situation as stressful.

Stress at 30,000 Feet: Flight and Fright

Consider this scenario: You're sitting in your plane seat, white-knuckled, downing your third Scotch. You're thinking:

> *Oh my gosh, I'm going to die! I know this plane is going down. We'll all be killed! That left engine sounds funny! This plane is in real trouble! Lord, just get me through this one and I promise. . .*

You're experiencing lots of stress. You notice your seat mate is smiling contentedly. She is experiencing absolutely no stress. She is thinking:

This is the best! I love flying. Nobody can reach me up here. I'll just relax with my Grisham novel and nurse this Scotch. Ah, here comes dinner. This feels so good! I'll think I'll have the fish.

If it were *only* the external situation that caused stress, then everyone would feel the same stress when placed in the same situation. Clearly, this is not the case. Whenever you take any group of people and expose all of them to the same stress or hassle, chances are you will get a range of reactions. What is stressful for somebody else may be less stressful for you, or maybe not stressful at all. Consider these slightly modified scenarios:

- ✔ A few days before your presentation, you learn that you have been offered a better job at another company. You are delighted. Do you feel less stress about the presentation? I think so.

- ✔ You're in the slow-moving supermarket line but pick up a magazine with a story that intrigues you. Now you're pleased that the line is moving so slowly because you want to finish the article.

- ✔ You are reliably informed that your Aunt Agnes has rewritten her will and made you the sole beneficiary to her rather large estate. You're staying only one week, Aunt Agnes?

- ✔ Noisy neighbor? Who cares? Just that morning, you signed the papers on a wonderful new place across town. Half the cost, twice the size. Knock yourself out, buddy!

Yes, I recognize that these scenarios are not likely, but they do make my point. It is not only the triggering event that causes the stress, but also your perceptions and expectations about that potentially stressful event that determine how stressed you feel.

Want to feel less stressed? Think straighter! Whenever you feel stressed, there's a very good chance that you're distorting or misrepresenting the event or situation triggering your stress. Your thinking is a wee bit crooked. You're making too many *Thinking Errors.* To remedy this, it is important to understand what your Thinking Errors are, and know how to correct them.

There are seven major Thinking Errors, and I cover them all in the following sections.

Stop "catastrophizing" and "awfulizing"

Having a low-stress day? Why not *catastrophize* or *awfulize*? These forms of distortion guarantee that your day has at least some stress. Put most simply, catastrophizing and awfulizing is making a molehill into a mountain. With very little effort, you can turn an everyday hassle into a major tragedy. Lest you are a novice in this area, here are some instructions as to how to become a better catastrophizer and awfulizer:

1. Find some commonly occurring situation or event in your life with the potential to stress you in some way. Using an example from the previous section, make it "waiting in a slow check-out line at the supermarket."

2. Now, exaggerate the importance and meaning of this situation. Say to yourself:

    Oh my gosh, this is the worst thing that could happen to me! I can't believe it! This is terrible! This is awful!

    It adds to the effect if you can summon up a pained look on your face as you say these things to yourself.

By escalating a hassle to a catastrophe, you also elevate your stress levels. The reality is, unless you are about to be married in 20 minutes, having to wait in a check-out line, being stuck in traffic, or not finding the remote for your TV is just a small hassle or inconvenience, and should be viewed as such. Even many of the bigger hassles — your 4s, 5s, and 6s (see Chapter 3 for tips on evaluating your stress) — can be emotionally exaggerated and blown out of proportion, creating more stress for yourself than is necessary.

Ask yourself these two questions to help reduce your catastrophizing or awfulizing:

- ✔ How important is this really? (Remember your 9s and 10s from your Stress-Balance Scale in Chapter 3.)
- ✔ Will I remember this event in 3 years, 3 months, 3 weeks, or 3 days (or even in 3 hours!)?

By challenging and disputing your exaggerated thinking, you begin to look at the situation differently. And as a consequence, you feel less stress.

Minimize your "can't-stand-it-itis"

Can't-stand-it-itis, which may sound like some rare neurological condition, is just another form of emotional distortion designed to increase your stress level. Here's how this little number works:

1. Find some hassle, situation, or circumstance that you do not like.

2. Then (and this is the important part) turn that "I don't like it" into an "I can't stand it!"

3. Now, utter with conviction:

    I can't stand it when I have to wait in long lines!

    I hate it when I'm caught in traffic!

When you say and believe that you can't stand, hate, despise, or loath something, your emotional temperature rises, and you become more upset — more stressed — than you would if you merely disliked that same something.

Even though you may not like the hassles and frustrations you're confronted with, you don't have to go ballistic and explode with inflated rage: "I just hate traffic (or crowds, lines, rude people, and so on)!" When you really believe you can't stand something, you produce a great deal of internal stress, far more than is warranted by the situation or circumstance. You make yourself very upset, angry, and distraught. When you recognize that some can't-stand-it-itis is contributing to your emotional stress, step back, and challenge and dispute your thinking. Ask yourself:

- Can I really not stand it, or do I really mean I do not like it?
- Is my over-reacting here helping me in any way? Or is it really making things worse?
- Couldn't I really stand it for quite a bit longer? And if someone were willing to fork over really big bucks, couldn't I stand this for even longer?

Cut out much of your "what-if-ing"

If you're having a slow day, here are some things you might consider stressing yourself out about:

- What if there's a transit strike!
- What if my company downsizes!
- What if my waiter has a transmittable disease!
- What if there are terrorists on my plane!
- What if I'm kidnapped!
- What if the stock market crashes!
- What if I get hit by a car!
- What if rock musicians move in next door!
- What if my mailman is a serial killer!

You may be a what-if-er. Whenever you what-if, you take a situation or event that *could* happen and make it into something that probably *will* happen. This way of thinking can and does add much unnecessary stress to your life.

In life, many unpleasant things can happen. Can they happen to you? Yes. Will they happen to you? Unfortunately, some will. However, many, if not most of the things you worry about never happen. But this doesn't stop you from worrying about the possibility of their happening. What-if, what-if, what-if. . . .

To cut out your what-if-ing, ask yourself these thought-straightening questions:

- ✔ Realistically, what are the chances of this feared event really happening?
- ✔ Am I over-worrying about this?
- ✔ When my life is nearing it's end, will *this* really be something I should have worried about?

Stop overgeneralizing

If you overgeneralize, you cause yourself to be more stressed than you have to be. Take a look at the following overgeneralizations and see whether you recognize yourself:

- ✔ "Nobody in this town knows how to drive!" (When someone cuts you off in traffic.)
- ✔ "I always have to do everything by myself!" (When your request for someone to take out the trash goes unanswered.)
- ✔ "The country is run by idiots!" (When you disagree with a political position.)
- ✔ "You never listen!" (When your spouse isn't listening.)

Though there may be some truth in these statements, they are all clearly overgeneralizations. When you overgeneralize, you create a distorted image of what is really happening, and create a reality that invites excessive and inappropriate anger and upset. By thinking in terms of all or nothing, good or bad, right or wrong, you make yourself more stressed than you have to be.

To help you curb any tendency to overgeneralize, here are some useful ideas:

- ✔ Ask yourself if you are seeing only one small part of a person's overall behavior and too quickly assuming that this sample truly characterizes that person as a whole.
- ✔ Try to think of individuals or situations that do *not* fit into your overgeneralization.
- ✔ Look out for language that reflects this all-or-nothing thinking — words like "always" and "never," as in "People are *never* friendly," or "People *always* take advantage of you when they have the chance."

The reality is, the world and the people in it rarely fall into discrete, easily identified categories. Try to find the gray areas and spare yourself a lot of stress.

Stop "mind reading" and "conclusion-jumping"

You *mind read* and *conclusion-jump* whenever you believe that you know something as true, when in fact, it may not be true at all. Some examples of mind reading and conclusion-jumping make this clear:

- ✔ You do not receive an invitation to a friend's party and conclude that she hates your guts.

- ✔ You see a brown spot on the back of your hand and conclude it's a terminal disease.

- ✔ You do a complete personality evaluation on someone you just met, based largely on what she was wearing.

There are times when you simply do not have enough information or data to come to a conclusion with any degree of certainty. But that may not stop you from trying. One method to determine whether you are mind reading or conclusion-jumping is to do a Perry Mason. Simply ask yourself, "Do I really have enough evidence to support my beliefs? Would a jury of my peers return a guilty verdict?" If the answer is no, reconsider your case, and hold off coming to any premature conclusions and reactions just yet. Who knows, you may be right. However, if you are like most people, you're also wrong much of the time. (By the way, if Perry Mason draws a blank, substitute Matlock.)

Curb your unrealistic expectations

Your expectations play an important role in determining just how stressed you feel in reacting to a potentially stressful situation. If your expectations are out of whack, there is a good chance you will overreact. The brief tongue-in-cheek Reality Test that follows should give you a better sense of what I mean.

The Reality Test

Take this short quiz to see just how realistic are your expectations are. Simply answer <u>T</u>rue or <u>F</u>alse to each of these items:

1. You've been searching for a parking place for the last 45 minutes when you finally see a spot opening up. The guy in the car ahead of you also sees the spot, and in fact, is closer to it than you are. You tell him how difficult it's been for you to find a parking place. You expect he will say: "Why don't you take this spot. I have lots of extra time today." <u>T</u> or <u>F</u>

2. You're waiting for the department store to deliver your new bed. They said that they would be there at 9 a.m. You expect that they'll be there by 9:15. <u>T</u> or <u>F</u>

3. You arrive at your doctor's office at ten minutes to 3, ready for your 3 o'clock appointment. You expect that promptly at three a nurse will emerge and say, "Follow me please, the doctor is ready to see you." T or F

4. You have an important report due early tomorrow morning. And, because you plan to write it at home tonight, it is essential that your computer and printer not give you any trouble. You expect that your computer and printer will not give you any trouble. T or F

5. Your two adolescent children have sworn that they will be totally responsible for taking care of a dog if you get them one. You expect that they, in fact, will honor their promise. T or F

If you answered True to any of these items, I wish you luck. Could any or all of the above expectations come about? Absolutely. However, the reality is, things often don't work out the way you'd like them to. Be realistic in what you expect.

Stop "musterbating"

Psychologist Albert Ellis has dubbed the use of unrealistic "shoulds" and "shouldn'ts" *musterbation* (with a 'u'!). You make this error whenever you hear yourself saying, in a rather rigid, angry way, things like:

> *People **shouldn't** be rude!*

> *People **shouldn't** cut you off in traffic!*

> *Life **should** be fair!*

What's that you say? There's nothing wrong with these statements? People *shouldn't* be rude, insensitive, and unfair? You're right. There would be nothing wrong with these statements if they were merely preferences, or a prescription for a better world. However, when these "shoulds" and "shouldn'ts" take the form of rigid demands and inflexible expectations, you are going to be mighty upset and angry when they do not materialize. When others (even you, for that matter) violate one of these unrealistic demands, you find yourself morally judging that person, and becoming indignant and angry. And there will be lots to get stressed about, because people often don't and won't follow your rules and guidelines for "correct living."

The antidote? Stop musterbating. Give up these rigid demands and replace them with healthier, more flexible, preferences. Try saying to yourself:

> *I would really **like** it if people were nicer.*

> *It certainly would be a better world if people were more considerate.*

Whenever you suspect you may be using an unrealistic "should" or "shouldn't," challenge this thinking, and ask yourself the following two questions:

✔ Is my *should* really a disguised *must* or a *have-to?* Am I really making a demand in disguise?

✔ Why *must* other people act the way I want them to? And then answer yourself by saying: "They don't, and often won't."

By changing your unrealistic demands to healthy preferences, you'll feel much better. And certainly less stressed.

Watch out for "exclamation mark" behavior

One way of finding out whether your expectation is realistic or unrealistic, is to look for *exclamation mark* behavior. Some examples of such behavior include saying any of the following to yourself when you're faced with a situation that angers or upsets you:

> *How can this be!*
>
> *I don't understand this!*
>
> *How could you do this!*
>
> *I don't believe this!*
>
> *Why would someone do this!*

What characterizes this behavior is the tone of surprise and disbelief in your reaction.

Accompanying such exclamations of disbelief are tell-tale "I just can't believe this!" gestures. Commonly seen examples include:

✔ Excessive eye-rolling and eyebrow-lifting

✔ Excessive and loud sighing

✔ Head nodding with accompanying "tsk-tsks"

✔ Hands thrown into the air indicating total frustration

The importance of this behavior is that it indicates the presence of unrealistic shoulds and musts. Implicit in your disbelief is the more magical demand: "Other people should and must be more like me. I wouldn't act like that; therefore, neither should they." But they do.

Stop "self-rating"

Whenever you equate your self-worth with your performance and/or the approval of others, you're *self-rating*. In either case, the end result is plenty of unnecessary stress.

The essence of this form of stress-producing thinking is that you believe you have worth, are a terrific person, and have a right to feel good about yourself because

✔ You have accomplished great things.

✔ You have marvelous traits (you're smart, good-looking, rich).

✔ Some important other person approves of you or what you have done.

Now I can hear you asking: "What's the matter with that? Don't we all want the approval of others, want to do well, and want to have terrific traits?" Yes, we do. The problem arises when you feel you *need* to do well or absolutely *must have* success or the approval of others. The reality is, there are many times in life when you will not do as well as you would like, when your performance will be less than stellar, and you will not get approval from others. By making your worth contingent on any or all of the above, you become vulnerable to unnecessary stress.

Frankly, giving up this self-rating tendency is not the easiest thing to do. It takes time and effort. To start, ask yourself the following questions:

✔ Do I really need to have others' approval to feel good about myself?

✔ Do I really have to be better than others to feel good about myself?

✔ I don't expect other people to be perfect, why should I expect it from myself?

✔ Can I rate my total worth as an individual on the basis of one or two traits or abilities?

The answer to each of the above is, of course, "No." None of the above is truly necessary for you to be happy in life — or feel good about yourself.

Putting It All Together: Systematic Stress Analysis

After you have a better understanding about the ways in which your thinking can produce your stress, you're in a good position to do something about your stress-producing thinking. *Systematic stress analysis* is a structured technique that shows you, step by step, how to take any stressful situation and determine exactly how much of a role your thinking is contributing to your stress level. More importantly, it shows you how you can correct your stress-producing thinking and replace it with stress-resistant thinking.

To start, make several copies of the Stress-Analysis Worksheet that appears at the end of this chapter. If you are somewhere where you are unable to make copies (the base camp on Kilimanjaro, for example), grab a sheet of paper and copy down the headings and format.

Write down what's stressing you

At the top of the page, where it says *My Stress Trigger,* write down what is triggering your stress. Be brief, such as the following description:

> *I was so upset when I got that flat tire on my way to the bowling alley. This was our big night. We were in contention. We could win the team title. That is, if Mable shows up. She's the real star.*

When shortened, becomes:

> *Flat tire on way to bowling.*

Write down your stress trigger.

Then, where it says *My Stress Response,* note your feelings — your reaction to that stress-trigger. It could be any one or more of the stress indicators: irritation, anger, upset, anxiety, worry, a headache, muscle tension, rapid breathing — or any of the many other stress-induced signs and symptoms.

Here, your stress-response may be:

> *Got upset and angry.*

Assess your stress balance

Lest you've forgotten how to do this (or skipped Chapter 3, where it is explained very nicely), first rate your **Level** of stress *about* that situation or event (on a 10-point scale, where 10 means major stress). Then, rate the **Importance** of the stressful situation on a 10-point scale (where 10 is a biggie). Enter your ratings in the appropriate places on the Worksheet.

Here's what your Worksheet looks like at this point:

My stress trigger (stress-producing event or circumstance):

Had a flat tire.

The importance of this stress trigger (0-10 scale): 2

My stress response (how I reacted to the stress trigger):

Got upset and angry.

My overall stress response level (0-10 scale): 5

Identify your stress-producing self-talk

Write down what you may be saying to yourself to create much of this stress. Remember that much of this self-talk is pretty automatic. You're probably not even aware of saying *anything* to yourself. But you are. To help you get in touch with this automatic self-talk, ask yourself:

What might I have been saying to myself about this stress-trigger?

In this situation, you may have said something like this:

Oh my gosh! This is awful! It couldn't have happened at a worst time. I coulda been a contender. Everything will be ruined! I just hate it when things like this happen! I'll never be happy again!

 Psychiatrist David Burns in his highly recommended book, *The Feeling Good Handbook* (Plume), suggests something called the *Vertical Arrow Technique* as a way of getting in touch with your less obvious, or hidden thinking. Here's how it works. Suppose your automatic thought in the example above was:

If I don't make it to the bowling alley on time, I'll miss the game.

Ask yourself

What would this mean?

Your response may be

That would be awful! I would be very upset.

The value of this technique is that it takes you to another level of your thinking, and uncovers the more irrational parts of your self-talk, which may be hidden by fairly sensible descriptive statements. You may have to do it two or three times to uncover all the hidden self-talk. Another example should make this clear.

My son wanted to play roller-hockey last week. He was very distressed because he couldn't. I asked him why he was upset, and he said, "It's raining out." Using the arrow technique, you can see how this statement could lead to more hidden thoughts, like:

It's raining out.

Ask yourself

What would this mean?

Which leads to

Therefore, I can't play hockey.

Ask yourself

What would this mean?

Which leads to

It's awful! My day is ruined!

You can use the vertical arrow technique to uncover layers of stress triggers, and then deal with them realistically.

Find your Thinking Errors

To recap, here are the seven major Thinking Errors, or ways your thinking creates excessive stress:

- ✔ Catastrophizing and awfulizing
- ✔ Can't-stand-it-itis
- ✔ What-if-ing
- ✔ Overgeneralizing
- ✔ Mind reading and conclusion-jumping
- ✔ Unrealistic expectations
- ✔ Self-rating

From your self-talk, try to identify the Thinking Errors that seem to be relevant. In the examples in the preceding section, you can see that there is more than a little *catastrophizing and awfulizing* going on, with a healthy dose of *can't-stand-it-itis* thrown in.

Use your coping self-talk

You are now ready to respond to your stress-producing self-talk, correct any Thinking Errors, and come up with a more stress-resistant way of looking at your stress-triggers. Finding yourself caught in horrific traffic jam — and becoming terribly stressed — you might say to yourself:

> *What a hassle. There's nothing I can do about it. If I'm late for the meeting the world won't end. Don't go ballistic here. Try some of that deep breathing you've been reading about . . . Hey, that feels pretty good. Put in that new CD and make the best of it. May this be my biggest problem all day!*

Or consider what my son's roller-hockey coping self-talk might sound like:

> *It's not the worst thing in the world. I can play tomorrow. Let me call Matt or Giddy and maybe we can go see a movie.*

Or consider your potential stress when you realize you've locked yourself out of the house (again!):

> *I'm an idiot! I've done it again. Calm down and try some Rapid Relaxation . . . and do it again. That feels better. Don't catastrophize or awfulize. Don't make this into a bigger deal than it is. On a scale of 1 to 10 this is still only a 2 or 3. Stay in balance. Just getting upset isn't going to help anything. Think. Who has another key? Nobody. Okay, Beth will be home in an hour. Go to the coffee shop, read the paper, and relax. I can handle this. I am handling this. Good for me. I may be a forgetful idiot, but at least I can cope with the consequences."*

Talk like an air-traffic controller

One way to help yourself use your coping self-talk is to think like an air-traffic controller. Consider this B-grade movie scenario:

> The weather at the airport is foggy. Very foggy. You are the air-traffic controller in charge. You learn that a novice pilot is having trouble landing and is panicking. He badly needs your help. You begin to talk him down. You say:
>
> *You're doing just fine, son. Hang in there . . . Take a deep, slow breath . . . Great!*
>
> *Now, remember what you learned in pilot school. Pull the throttle toward you. That's it. You can do this . . . Let her steady out. Begin your decent. Good. Take another deep breath. Don't panic. Hold her steady . . . you're almost down . . . You're doin' great . . . You're on the ground. You made it!*

You get the idea. Talk to yourself in a way that helps you cope better with the stressful or potentially stressful situation.

What to say to yourself

If you are at a loss for words, and can't seem to come up with what to say to yourself, use the following list as a reference. It includes most of the essential self-talk elements you need.

✔ Verbally correct your Thinking Errors by challenging and disputing their reasonableness. (Is this really so awful? Can I stand this for a little longer? Do I really need this person's approval? And so on.)

  If you're still a little shaky on how to do this, review the descriptions of the various Thinking Errors in the previous sections.

✔ Tell yourself to put the stress into perspective. Talk yourself into balance.

✔ Relax yourself. Include in your self-talk instructions to help you relax. Use the techniques and strategies described in Chapters 4 and 5.

✔ Problem solve. Give yourself some direction and instructions that help you cope with, and possibly remove, the source of your stress.

Here's what your coping self-talk might look (and sound) like in your Worksheet:

My coping self-talk:

> *This isn't really a major tragedy. Yes, I am disappointed, but I will live to bowl another day. It's not anything I can't deal with. Don't blow it up. Calm down and see what you can do to fix this situation. Start breathing . . . You're doing fine. What to do? Call the bowling alley and tell them what happened. Maybe they can send someone to get you. I hope Mable got there alright.*

You can use the same approach whenever you find yourself in a stressful situation. Yes, you *can* talk yourself out of being stressed.

Your Stress Analysis Worksheet

My stress trigger (stress-producing event or circumstance):

_____

_____

The importance of this stress trigger (0-10 scale): _____

My stress response (how I reacted to the stress trigger):

_____

_____

My overall stress response level (0-10 scale): _____

My Self-Talk:

_____

_____

_____

_____

_____

My Thinking Error:

_____

_____

My Coping Self-Talk: _____

_____

_____

_____

_____

Chapter 10

Overcoming Your Anger

• •

In This Chapter

▶ Understanding your anger

▶ Figuring out how anger affects your well-being

▶ Controlling your anger

• •

Are you angry because someone cut you off in traffic or kept you waiting for what seemed like an eternity? Are you angry because that clumsy guest spilled red wine on your sofa, or because your printer refuses to print? Everyone feels anger sometimes. Unfortunately, too many people — and you may be one of them — experience too much anger too much of the time. Anger is not only terribly stressful, it can be harmful to your physical well-being and destructive to your relationships with others. Fortunately, ways of reducing your levels of anger and limiting its consequences do exist. This chapter shows you how to control your anger — instead of letting your anger control you.

Figuring Out Just How Mad You Really Are

Does a big part of your stress come from your anger? Do you get just a little angry or does your anger get out of control? The first step in reducing your anger is knowing just how angry you are. In this section, I give you a simple, 12-item scale that helps you discover the role that anger plays in your life.

For the following 12 statements, indicate the extent to which each one describes you. Jot down one of the following responses for each statement: not at all like me, a little like me, or a lot like me.

1. My family and/or friends tell me I get angry too easily.

2. I feel my anger is excessive.

3. My anger has frequently gotten me into trouble in the past.

4. I get frustrated pretty easily.

5. I hold on to my anger longer than I should.

6. I hate waiting or being kept waiting.

7. Petty annoyances can make me fly off the handle.

8. I take criticism and disapproval badly.

9. Incompetence and stupidity in others makes me angry.

10. I get angry when traffic or lines don't move fast enough.

11. Being treated rudely or unfairly makes me very angry.

12. In arguments, I am usually the one who gets the most angry.

For each time you responded "a lot like me," give yourself 3 points. For each response of "a little like me," give yourself 2 points. And for each response of "not at all like me," give yourself a zero. If you have less than 18 points, anger is not a major part of your life. If you have between 19 and 30 points, anger is affecting your life moderately. And if you have 31 to 36 points, anger is a definite presence in your life.

The Pros and Cons of Anger

Anger, just like anything else, isn't all good or all bad: It has many pros and cons. The following sections explain those for you, so that you get a clear picture of anger and the effect it may have on your life.

Get a second opinion

I don't doubt that your answers to the anger quiz are frank and honest. *You,* however, may not be the best person to measure the length of your fuse. A more objective evaluation couldn't hurt. Why not have someone who knows you pretty well answer the quiz *for* you. You may not feel you have a problem with your anger, but the people who are closest to you may have a different opinion. Who knows? They may even see you as *less* angry than you see yourself. Compare your score with the score they give you, and see if they view you and your anger in the same way you do. Talk about any major discrepancies in scoring (but try not to get angry while you do so).

Looking at the positives of anger

Anger can be a highly distressing emotion that results in all kinds of negative consequences. Yet among the other possible stress emotions (upset, depression, grief, anxiety, and so on), anger remains the most popular and the most common. And not without reason. Anger has some appeal:

- **Anger is activating and mobilizing.** When you're angry, you feel as if you're doing something about what's triggering your stress. You feel there is a response you can make, a way of expending energy toward resolving the distressing situation. It can get you to take action and do something about the problem.

- **Anger makes you feel powerful.** Anger can make you feel like you're in charge, even when you aren't. When you tell someone off or give them a tongue-lashing, you feel stronger and in control. Anger allows you to express yourself in a forceful way.

- **Anger often gets results.** By becoming angry, as opposed to remaining calm and pleasant, you may get what you want. Many people are intimidated by anger and are more obliging when confronted with it than they normally would be.

- **Anger is often a respected response.** We often interpret anger as standing up for ourselves and not letting others take advantage of us. And other people may see it the same way. Our anger may be labeled as assertive, strong, and confident.

Anger has some advantages. But it also has some pretty strong disadvantages. Check out the following section for a list of them.

Examining the downside of anger

Although your anger does have its upside, the downside of anger far outweighs any positive benefits. Besides being emotionally distressing and making you a prime candidate for a black eye, your anger can give you other things to worry about.

Anger can make you sick

When you're angry, your body reacts much the same way it does when you are experiencing any other stress reaction. Your anger triggers your body to take a defensive stance, readying yourself for any danger that may come your way. (Check out Chapter 2 for more on this response, known as fight-or-flight.) When your anger is intense and frequent, the physiological effects can be harmful. Your health is at risk. And any or all of those nasty stress-related illnesses and disorders can become linked to excessive anger.

Anger can break your heart

Recent research now indicates that your heart (or more accurately, your cardiovascular system) is particularly vulnerable to your anger and its negative effects. In his book, *Anger Kills,* Duke University researcher Redford Williams describes a number of possible ways hostility can negatively affect your cardiovascular system. I highlight a few of the study findings here:

- ✔ **When potentially hostile individuals were angry, they had larger than normal increases in the flow of blood to their muscles (suggesting an exaggerated fight-or-flight response).** They also experienced an increase in their levels of important stress hormones, such as adrenaline and cortisol, which can have negative effects on the cardiovascular system as well.

- ✔ **Potentially hostile individuals with higher levels of blood cholesterol were found to secrete more adrenaline than those individuals with lower levels of cholesterol.** For these individuals, the linkage between higher adrenaline secretions and higher cholesterol levels means they have a greater likelihood of arteriosclerotic plaque buildup.

- ✔ **People who scored high on measures of hostility tend to have fewer friends.** This lack of strong friendships means a weakened social support system. Being able to talk to someone about what's stressing you can lower your blood pressure — and having no one to talk to certainly doesn't do anything to help you. Research has shown that socially isolated individuals excreted higher levels of stress hormones in their urine than those who had strong support systems.

- ✔ **Hostile individuals typically don't take good care of themselves.** They tend to engage in a number of destructive health behaviors, including smoking, drinking, and overeating. All of these behaviors can have negative effects on the cardiovascular system.

Anger can break other people's hearts

When you're angry, you're probably not a whole lot of fun to be with. Even worse, your hostility and aggression can be downright destructive. Your anger affects those around you — the people you live with, work with, and interact with. Anger can strain and damage your relationships with your children, friends, and coworkers. Together, anger and hostility can lead to conflict, mental and physical abuse, breakups, and divorce. Because of your anger, you may endanger your chances for career advancement or even lose your job. Anger tends to escalate as well. The other party involved often becomes angry, too, escalating and intensifying the levels of anger for everyone. When you're angry, you may do something or say something you regret later on, which can lead to other stress emotions, such as guilt, shame, upset, and depression.

Funny, you don't look like a Type-A

Remember all that hoopla about the Type-A Personality and how stress-producing it could be? The typical Type-A was the hurried workaholic, attempting to get more and more done in less and less time. The good news is that the most recent research has poked some holes in this picture and suggest that some of those old Type-A traits may not be as harmful as we once thought. What research does show, however, is that the most toxic traits in the Type-A pattern are hostility and anger. Working hard, by itself, probably won't give you that heart attack. But, if you're angry, mistrusting, and cynical; you may want to change your ways.

Anger can shorten your life

Research shows that your life can actually be shortened by anger. Psychologist John Barefoot measured the hostility levels of 118 law students. Then, he tracked these individuals for 25 years. The researchers found that nearly 20 percent of those who scored in the upper quarter of the hostility scale had died by the age of 50. This result was in comparison to a death rate by the age of 50 of only 5 percent for those who scored in the lowest quarter of the scale.

Understanding when and why anger is appropriate

Does this mean that *all* of your anger is inappropriate or destructive? No, not at all. In fact, in measured doses and expressed in the right way, anger can be appropriate and effective, helping you to take action, solve problems, or in some way better deal with the situation at hand. Anger clearly has a place in your emotional repertoire. But a big difference exists between feeling annoyed or somewhat angry for a brief period of time and having strong feelings of anger that simmer for hours. When it is intense and prolonged, anger can result in incredible amounts of stress and damage to your overall well-being. Understanding how you create your anger and knowing how to reduce that anger are the keys to anger control. The next section provides suggestions for doing exactly that.

Tempering Your Temper

Anger is not an automatic reaction beyond our control, even though it may feel like that at times. Instead, anger is a response that can be managed.

So, before your next outburst of rage and fury, take a look at some of these anger-reducing strategies and tactics. Who knows? They just may save you from a nasty argument, an upset stomach, costly litigation, or worse.

Keeping an anger log

The first step in managing (and ultimately eliminating) much of your stressful anger is knowing what it looks like and where it comes from. A simple anger diary, or anger log, can help you identify those times when you are angry and give you the information you need to begin feeling less angry.

Simply enter in your log (a small notebook, a piece of paper, a file on your laptop — whatever works for you) the times when you became angry and what triggered your anger. Also, rate the level of your anger using a simple 10-point scale, where a rating of 10 means "very, very angry," 5 means "moderately angry," and 0 means "not angry at all."

Take a look at the example in Table 12-1:

Table 12-1	Rating Your Anger	
What Happened?	*Importance*	*My Anger Level*
My child spilled juice on the couch.	3	6
I missed my train by 1 minute.	2	5
My boss blamed me for a mistake made by my coworker.	4	7
My computer crashed, and I lost the last hour's work.	3	8

Checking your stress balance

You can find out if your anger is excessive and inappropriate by checking your stress balance. Just compare the level of your anger with the importance of the anger-producing situation. Use a 10-point scale, where 10 means "incredibly important" and 0 means "not at all important." Insert that rating next to your description of the distressing situation as above. You are "in balance" when the two numbers match; you are overreacting if your anger level is higher than the importance of the situation.

If you are in stress balance, chances are your level of anger is appropriate and functional. If not, you are overreacting. If your level of anger is way up there (8s, 9s, or 10s), you may be experiencing rage and hostility and not just your typical garden-variety anger.

Using the examples in Table 12-1, the juice spilled on the couch is probably an importance level of 3; missing the train, a 2; being unfairly blamed, a 4, and the crashing of my computer, a 3. In each case, the person is overreacting and off-balance.

Modifying Your Mindset

Most often, your thinking and your perceptions of events are what make you angry.

Thoughts like, "I was angry because that idiot cut me off in traffic," or, "Missing my train made me angry," suggest that an outside event or circumstance is what caused you to feel anger. But the reality is that these situations and events are only *potential* triggers that can cause your perceptions and interpretations to create your anger. Like your other stress emotions (anxiety, upset, frustration, and so on), your anger is largely self-created. It is your *thinking* — your perceptions and interpretations — that play a very important role in creating (and ultimately reducing) your stress.

Thinking about your thinking

See if you can identify your anger-producing thoughts. Ask yourself, "What could I be saying to myself to make myself angry?" Take a look at Table 12-2, and try to complete it with your own experiences.

Table 12-2	Your Angry Thoughts and the Experiences That Triggered Them
Situation	*My Automatic Thoughts*
My son spilled juice on the couch	"The couch is ruined! He should have been more careful! How could he have been so careless? He knew he wasn't supposed to bring food into the living room!"
I missed my train by 1 minute.	"This is awful! This always happens! Now my whole day is ruined. I hate this!"

(continued)

Table 12-2 *(continued)*	
Situation	*My Automatic Thoughts*

Writing down these anger-producing thoughts helps you get a clearer picture of what you're saying to yourself to make yourself angry about a particular situation. By getting in touch with this thinking, you are now in a good position to begin changing that thinking, and thereby reducing the level of your anger.

Finding and fixing your Thinking Errors

Most likely, if your level of anger is excessive or prolonged, you're probably making at least one *Thinking Error.* Examine your automatic thoughts and see if there are any Thinking Errors to be found. Although just about any of the Thinking Errors can result in some form of anger, the two that most often trigger an anger response are unrealistic demands and can't-stand-it-itis. (If you're a wee bit rusty on what I mean by the term *Thinking Error,* take a quick look at Chapter 9.)

Expecting the expected

Your expectations play an important role in determining your level of anger. Having unrealistic expectations about your world and the way other people *should* think and act, as well as demanding that they be more like you, adds to your anger level. If you expect everyone else to be totally honest and completely fair, you'll probably wind up feeling more than a little angry most of the time, because your expectations won't always be met. Expectations are accompanied by shoulds and shouldn'ts; and when you create demands that are unrealistic, you end up judging the person who doesn't act in ways you think they should.

Am I suggesting that you become a complete cynic? Not at all. If anything, becoming more trusting is a better way of feeling less angry and less hostile. Becoming realistic in your expectations doesn't mean becoming cynical and untrusting. Not everyone out there is selfish, nasty, and only out for themselves. But other people *do* see things differently and *do* have priorities different than yours. At times, they will do things that you wouldn't do yourself. Expect the expected, and expect to see what probably will happen, given the world we live in. The following exercise helps you assess the extent to which your expectations are in line with reality.

Would you ever expect any of the following situations to happen? Answer yes or no.

At some point in the not-too-distant future,

- Someone will cut you off in traffic.

- Somebody you know and care about will disappoint you.

- You will just miss catching your bus or train.

- Your computer will crash at a critical time.

- Someone in front of you at the express checkout line will have more than the specified 10 items.

- Someone will play their music incredibly loud and disturb you.

- Someone will push their way onto your already crowded elevator, even though they know it's totally full.

- Someone you know will treat you unfairly.

Answering 'No' to more than one or two of the above may suggest that your expectations of the world (and the people who live there) are not totally realistic. You are probably in for some surprises — and some anger.

Lengthening your fuse

No one likes frustration. But, unfortunately, frustration is an integral part of our lives. When faced with a frustrating situation, you may find that you over-react too quickly, becoming too angry too fast. If so, your fuse is way too short. Here is one way of better tolerating frustration. This technique may sound a little far-fetched, but it really works: Do the opposite.

Sometimes, if you have the urge to respond in a certain way, you may find that doing exactly the opposite helps. For example, suppose you are having trouble falling asleep. By trying *not* to fall asleep you may be surprised to see that you *can* fall asleep. Therapists call this approach *paradoxical intention,* and it can help you overcome some of your excessive anger. Try some of the following suggestions:

- **Find a longer line.** If waiting in line triggers your anger, the next time you find yourself waiting in line, and you see an even longer line, move to that line.

- **Stay in a slower lane of traffic.** If you get angry when you're stuck in a stalled line of traffic, see if you can find a slow line the next time you're driving.

- **Pick the most inept sales clerk.** The next time you need some help to purchase something, see if you can spot the newest, most inexperienced, and most inept salesperson.

Now, when you are in these unusually difficult situations and you find your anger level rising with great speed, do the following:

1. **Practice some deep breathing to relax your body.**

2. **Repeat to yourself, "This is not the end of the world. I want to get a handle on my anger. This is only a hassle. I can cope with this."**

And indeed you can.

Using your coping self-talk

When confronted with a potentially anger-provoking situation, you can either say things to yourself that make you angry, or you can say things to yourself that reduce or even eliminate any anger that may have been triggered. By consciously and explicitly talking to yourself, you have a powerful tool that can help you regulate your anger.

Here are some useful examples of anger-reducing self-talk that can help you reduce your level of anger. Choose the ones that best fit your situation, and try coming up with some of your own.

- Is this really worth getting so angry about?
- My getting angry is not going to help anything.
- People can look at things differently than I do. They always have, and they always will.
- Don't take this personally.
- Let it go. It's not worth the emotional effort.
- I really do not have to feel angry about this if I choose not to.
- Relax. Take a deep breath. Hold it. And let it all out.
- Other people have different priorities.
- Just because someone says something, that doesn't make it true.
- How would Mr. or Ms. Mental Health handle this?
- Stay calm, stay cool.
- Don't go for the bait.
- People have the right to be wrong. And often they are.
- Don't judge the person. Judge the behavior.
- Is this really such a big deal?
- Will I remember this in three years? Three months? Three hours?

To vent or not to vent? That is the question.

Are you better off expressing your anger, or should you keep it in? Popular psychological wisdom would suggest that when you are feeling angry, you should get it all out, releasing any and all of that pent-up anger and hostility. Punch that pillow, wallop that punching-bag, smash some dishes. You'll feel better afterwards. Right?

Maybe not. As author Carol Tavris comments in her important book, *Anger: The Misunderstood Emotion,* "Expressing anger makes you angrier, solidifies an angry attitude, and establishes a hostile habit." Recent clinical studies have shown that *emotional catharsis* (the active expression of anger and hostility by physically releasing anger) can work against you. Researchers found that when people acted out their anger in this way (hitting or punching something), they felt *more* aggressive afterward, not *less* aggressive. Worse, by giving people permission not to control their feelings, the people experienced more episodes of aggressive behavior in general. Does this mean you shouldn't express your anger? No. It just means you may need to find better ways of doing it.

The following sections provide some answers to common questions about venting your anger. Take a look at the suggestions I offer here. They may help you get control of your own anger.

Can I at least yell?

Yelling doesn't appear to help reduce your anger. Screaming, "You're a stupid jerk and I hope you rot in hell!" to someone who has just done you wrong clearly has a lot of emotional appeal. And it may even feel pretty good in the short run. However, it may not be the best thing for your health and overall stress level. When you yell, your body becomes stressed. Your heart rate increases. We know that raising your voice, and certainly yelling can lead to an increase in your blood pressure as well. In some individuals — Type-A personality types, for example — the increase in blood-pressure levels may be even greater. But yelling can have psychological effects as well. In one study of 535 women, yelling, screaming, and lashing out resulted in greater feelings of low self-esteem. Because in most cases the yelling did little to resolve the problem, the women felt — and were seen — as being out of control rather than taking charge and acting competently. You can be sure that yelling — and feeling out of control or incompetent — doesn't elevate your sense of self-worth.

Should I suppress my anger?

Anger can be destructive when it steeps and simmers within you. Keeping your angry feelings inside of you, and keeping those feelings fresh by re-angering yourself over and over, is not the best choice. However, the long-standing belief that suppressed anger is the mother of just about every psychosomatic disease, from ulcers to constipation, may be ill-founded. A big difference exists between letting all of your angry feelings spew forth in an uncontrolled manner and packaging it so your message will express your feelings but not trigger World War III. And, of course, an even better option is to resolve the conflict or fix the situation that is triggering your anger, reduce your anger level, or both.

Rehearsing your anger

Often, you may become angry because you are caught off guard, and your gut reacts before your head has had a chance to evaluate the situation a little more sensibly. One effective strategy for combating this irrational response is to begin to anticipate which situations and circumstances may trigger some of your anger and plan ahead. Before the situation occurs, rehearse what you will say and how you want to feel. You can always identify upcoming situations in which you know that your chances of becoming angry are pretty high. These situations may be just before you're about to discuss some point of disagreement or contention with someone, and you know that the person will be less than receptive or downright opposed to what you have to say. You may be dealing with a client, a coworker, a relative, or the sales clerk at the local shopping mall.

When you can anticipate the situation, imagine it occurring, and then imagine what you will say and how you will act. Your goal, of course, is not to go ballistic or become excessively angry. Choose the words you think will work best. Also, imagine that the other person is getting angry and is close to getting you very angry in turn. Use your coping self-talk. Imagine telling yourself to calm down, to not go for the bait, and keep your anger level low. Rehearse this situation several times in your head. Chances are, when the situation does materialize, you will be much better prepared to handle it.

Doing an emotional replay

Okay, for whatever reason, you were unable to rehearse or get ready for that situation. You were caught off-guard and the situation resulted in an undesirable show of anger. All is still not lost. A useful technique in reducing future anger is something I call *emotional replay*. Here's how it works:

1. **At some point after you have had an experience or encounter where you have felt and maybe expressed what you now see as excessive anger (this could be an hour later, or maybe even days later), replay that situation in your mind.**

But this time, instead of seeing yourself becoming angry, imagine yourself responding in a calmer, more controlled manner. You're imagining the same situation, but your response is the one you want it to be.

2. **Try to get in touch with the kind of thinking and interpretation that may generate this less-angry state.**

   If you can, jot down some of these thoughts and beliefs and see if you can't begin to use them earlier in the anger sequence — like *before* you get angry.

Becoming an actor

Although your anger control may not be the world's best, you probably know one or two people whom you admire for their calmness and coolness under fire. The next time you are confronted with a potentially anger-provoking situation, try to see the situation through *their* eyes. Imagine how they would look at this. What would they say to themselves? How would they react?

By immersing yourself in their character, at least briefly, you can try to look at situations as they would. You role-play with a script, but instead of using your own, you choose the script of an anger role model, someone you feel has something to teach.

Being discrete and choosing your moment

Managing your anger does not mean letting it all out in some hostile manner, or keeping it in and letting it aggravate you. Being assertive and discrete means packaging and expressing your anger in a way that doesn't send your physiological system into orbit and doesn't result in you throttling someone — or finding yourself being throttled. The fact that you're angry doesn't mean you have to say your piece in that moment of emotional heat.

Most often, you're better off if you wait. Choose a time when your anger is reduced, and the other person is in a better mood.

Breathing your anger away

When you're angry, your body is probably running in high gear. Your heart rate and blood pressure are up, and just about all the other measures of physiological distress are elevated as well. You can speed up the process of dissipating your anger by adding some physical strategies to your psychological bag of tricks. Relaxing your body is a good place to start. And because you can *always* find time to breathe, a deep breathing exercise can be an effective way of lowering your body's level of physiological arousal and can make reducing your anger an easier job.

The next time you find yourself getting angry, follow these steps:

1. **Take a deep breath, inhaling through your nostrils.**

   Hold that breath for 3 or 4 seconds.

2. **Slowly exhale through your slightly parted lips.**

   Let a wave of relaxation spread from the top of your head, down your body, to your toes.

3. **Wait a little bit, and then take another deep breath.**

   Repeat the process.

You'll feel more physically relaxed and less angry in a very brief period of time.

Looking for the funny part

Humor can be an excellent tool to help you diffuse your anger. If you can find something about the anger-triggering situation to make you laugh or at least bring a smile to your face, you can be assured your anger will be lessened and possibly even eliminated. The following sections offer two ways of creating humor.

Blow things up

Exaggeration is a great way of diffusing a potentially stressful situation, robbing it of much of its impact. Try using the blow-up technique. Here's how it works: Suppose, for example, you find yourself standing in line at the Bureau of Motor Vehicles waiting to renew your license. The line is moving slowly. Very slowly. You can feel your stress level creeping higher. Now, introducing a touch of exaggeration, you imagine that it will take *forever* before you reach the front window. You picture your family coming to visit you on Sunday afternoons, bringing many of your favorite snacks. You strike up strong friendships with others in the line. There is talk of taking vacations together. You start planning your first five-year reunion. . . .

Try some therapeutic fantasy

A humorous fantasy can help you reduce and diffuse your anger. Here's what I mean. Imagine that you are a passenger in a taxicab and you notice that the cab driver is driving much too fast for your liking. You also notice that your anger level is creeping skyward. Before you yell at him, strike him, or blow some internal gasket, imagine this improbable scenario:

You tell him that he is driving too fast and he immediately slows down, and, with a sheepish look on his face, turns to you and says, "You're absolutely right! What could I have been thinking! I'll slow down immediately. In fact, I won't charge you for this ride, to make up for my unsafe and insensitive behavior. I'm sorry. This will never happen again."

By imagining this or another unlikely outcome, you can create a different mindset that is less angry and more accepting of the foibles and failings of others. Then, calmly tell him to slow down.

Revenge may be sweet, but forgiveness is probably less stressful

We've always given lip service to the value of forgiveness, but the reality has always been more lip than actual forgiveness. Psychologically, holding onto a grudge and our anger is always easier than forgiving the source of our anger for whatever he or she did. But the long-term effects aren't positive at all.

In a study conducted recently at Hope College, in Holland, Michigan, psychologists explored the effects of forgiveness on people's stress levels. They looked at their levels of stress when they were in a non-forgiving mode and compared those stress levels to when the same people were in a forgiving mode. The amount of stress was considerably greater when the subjects were entertaining revenge rather than forgiveness.

Forgiving for small indiscretions is usually no real problem. The major transgressions are the ones that are harder to swallow. You can reach a point of forgiveness by trying to understand where the other person is coming from, looking at their background, family history, and specific factors that may have played a role in determining their actions.

For some acts, forgiveness may be unrealistic. The best you can hope for in these situations is some form of acceptance. It's done. You can't change it. So try to move on. Maybe the best revenge truly is living well.

Chapter 11

Worrying Less

● ●

In This Chapter
▶ Understanding why you worry
▶ Controlling your worries

● ●

*E*verybody worries at some time or another. In fact, worrying can be a *good* thing. You *should* worry about some things in your life. Worrying is healthy and appropriate when it motivates you and leads you to attempt to resolve a problem in a productive, adaptive manner. Some people, however, worry far more than they have to, and they in turn do very little to effectively resolve their worries. For these people, much of their stress takes the form of excessive worry. This inordinate and often useless worrying can rob people of much of life's joy and can interfere with their day-to-day functioning. And if a person's worrying becomes chronic, it can result in a wide variety of stress-related conditions and disorders. Controlling and managing your own worries becomes an essential part of managing your stress.

Who, Me? Worry?

In this section, I provide you with a brief, 10-item self-assessment that helps you determine whether you are worrying too much. Simply indicate to what extent each of the statements below describes you ("not at all like me," "a little like me," or "a lot like me").

1. Worrying is a major source of stress in my life.

2. After I start worrying, I find it very difficult to stop.

3. People who know me well tell me that I worry too much.

4. I have trouble getting to sleep or falling back to sleep because of my worrying.

5. I often think of worst-case scenarios when I worry about a problem.

6. I frequently become anxious and worry about things that *could* happen but usually don't.

7. I have a great deal of difficulty coping with uncertainty.

8. I worry more than I should about small stuff.

9. When I worry, I usually just upset myself more, rather than try to resolve my worry.

10. Sometimes I literally worry myself to the point of sickness.

Answering more than one or two of these statements with "a lot like me" suggests that your worrying may be contributing greatly to your overall stress level. Don't skip to the next chapter just yet.

Don't Worry, Be Happy. Yeah, Right!

If you are a worrier, you know how difficult it is to stop worrying. Being told, "Don't worry so much!" or "Stop being such a worry wart," does little to curb the distressing and seemingly unending list of things you find to worry about. In fact, sometimes, actively trying *not* to worry about something actually causes you to worry *more*. Trying to stop your worrying is much like me asking you *not* to think of a pink elephant. Of course, the moment you read those words, you thought of a pink elephant.

We worry even when we are not aware we are worrying. We can worry in our sleep or at various levels of conscious awareness. Worrying can be an automatic response that can become persistent and seem out of control. Fortunately, a number of tools, strategies, and techniques really can help you worry less, and, when you should be worrying, they can help you worry more effectively.

"If I worry about something, that something won't happen."

Many worriers worry because of a misguided belief that the worrying actually will prevent the threatening or feared event or situation from happening. It's a little like "knocking on wood." For these people, worrying, paradoxically, brings some feeling of relief.

Will worrying keep that feared situation at bay or prevent it from happening? I'm afraid not. And worrying certainly won't prevent anything if you don't do something about that worry. This kind of thinking is magical or superstitious. The mistaken belief here is that worry will stave off disaster and prevent anything bad from occurring. Conversely, you may believe, "If I *don't* worry, then bad things *will* happen." Life doesn't work like that either. Thankfully, better ways of coping with worrisome situations do exist.

Get Off Your Worry-Cycle

Worrying is a process that starts when you perceive an event, situation, or circumstance as potentially dangerous or threatening. You think about that situation — at times unconsciously and automatically — and depending on what you say to yourself about that situation, you create varying degrees of emotional stress. If your self-talk is positive and sensible, your stress level will be lower. On the other hand, if your self-talk is negative and irrational, you will cause yourself to feel excessive worry. This worry not only manifests itself emotionally, but also physically, producing all of the symptoms that characterize the fight-or-flight response. And the fight-or-flight response can result in even more worry.

Situation/event⇨excessive worrying⇨physical/emotional stress⇨more worrying

Think straighter, worry less

If your worrying is excessive, chances are your self-talk and thinking are somewhat out of whack, which means that you're probably making one or more Thinking Errors. The following sections outline the major Thinking Errors that can result in excessive worrying and tell you how to avoid those errors yourself. Each of these Thinking Errors can add to your anxiety level, make you worry more than you should, and make your worrying more stress-producing rather than stress-reducing.

Minimizing the what-ifs

On the slowest day, some people can find a host of things to worry about. Chronic worriers can take just about any situation and find something to worry about. They dissect every potentially dangerous or threatening situation and ask themselves, "What if. . . ." Here are some examples of things chronic worriers worry about:

- ✔ What if that twinge in my shoulder means I'm having a heart attack?
- ✔ What if the plane crashes on my upcoming flight?
- ✔ What if my taxi driver is on drugs?
- ✔ What if this pimple turns out to be cancer?
- ✔ What if there's a snowstorm the day my daughter gets married?

You get the idea. One way of minimizing your "what-ifs" is knowing just how likely it is that your what-if will actually happen.

Knowing the odds

Just about every nasty, scary, threatening event you could imagine has *some* chance of happening. However, for many, if not most of these feared occurrences, the chances of them actually *happening* are really very slim. Most of us are not very good at estimating the odds that something will happen. Do you know the chances of your airplane crashing or being hijacked, or the odds that you're developing a brain tumor or contracting some strange disease? Probably not. Too often, we worry about the wrong things. We worry about getting rare or unlikely diseases or worry about dying in horrible ways. The irony is, we worry less about not putting on our seat belts, going to our doctor for a regular checkup, or having an accident in the kitchen, all of which have a greater chance of causing us grief than the things we do worry about.

Realizing that Murphy's Law is wrong

Remember Murphy's Law: "If anything can go wrong, it will." Well, even though this may seem like an accurate description of what happens in your life, it isn't. The reality is, most things that could go wrong in fact *don't* go wrong. We remember well the times when things go astray, but we tend to forget the times things go off without a hitch.

Cutting out your catastrophizing

Worriers are consummate *catastrophizers*. They are constantly vigilant, on the lookout for horrendous problems and imminent disasters. This vigilance in and of itself can be stressful, not to mention emotionally and physically draining.

And even if a feared event did happen, would it always result in catastrophic results like the following?

- ✓ If I lose my job, I'll wind up in a box on the street!
- ✓ If I fail the test, my life will be totally ruined!
- ✓ If I don't get into that college, my career is in the toilet!
- ✓ If I don't meet my deadline, they'll cancel the whole project!
- ✓ If I'm late, they'll never talk to me again!

Probably not. Whenever you emotionally exaggerate the importance of a situation (by saying, for example, "This is the worst thing that could ever happen!"), you can be sure that your stress level will rise accordingly. You can quickly turn something small that warrants some concern into a major catastrophe that elicits major stress.

Watching out for conclusion-jumping

We often come to a conclusion without having all (or at times *any*) of the evidence. Consider these worry-making interpretations:

- ✔ I'm going to be laid off because everyone seems to be avoiding me.
- ✔ She hasn't returned my call yet, so she must not like me.
- ✔ This headache means I have a brain tumor.

Could you be right? Yes. Are you? Probably not.

Getting more comfortable with not having control

A sense of not having control can easily trigger stress. We tend to feel uncertain when we feel out of control. In turn, feeling uncertain can create feelings of anxiety and upset. We would like to have control over the unpleasant and unsettling events in our lives, but frequently we can't. We cause ourselves to feel far more stressed than we have to. Becoming more comfortable with uncertainty and a lack of control is an essential part of your program of stress management. What should you do? What follows are some ideas.

Recognizing the limits of your control

A good deal of your stress comes from trying to control those events and circumstances that, in fact, you have little control over. The first step in becoming more comfortable with not having control is recognizing the *extent* of your control.

Take a moment to complete this little exercise. Use this simple point scale:

> 0 = No control
>
> 1 = A little control
>
> 2 = Lots of control

To what extent can you control the following events or circumstances?

Situation	My degree of control over this situation
Traffic	_____
Other people's personalities	_____
The weather	_____
The speed of elevators	_____
Crime	_____
Street noise	_____
Stopping people from acting like idiots	_____

You get the point. We can be incredibly limited when it comes to controlling our world and those who live in it. So, the next time you find yourself in a potentially stressful situation, ask yourself, "How much control do I really have in this situation?" And, if your answer is "not much," ask yourself a second question: "Then why am I making myself so stressed?" Sometimes, just acknowledging that you have no control can reduce your level of worry. Because you can't change it, maybe you can accept it. Worrying won't help.

Praying for serenity

You've most likely heard at one time or another what has become known as the Serenity Prayer. It still holds an important message — especially if you're a worrier:

> God, give us the grace to accept with serenity the things that cannot be changed, the courage to change the things which should be changed, and the wisdom to distinguish one from the other.
>
> —Reinhold Niebuhr

Coming up with a "worry ladder"

One way that you can cope with your worries is by listing them in order of the amount of stress they trigger.

1. Job security

2. Mother's health

3. Kids' safety in the city

4. Possible IRS audit

5. Condition of the car

6. Money for kids' college

7. Sticking door in bathroom

8. Losing hair

9. Repairing fence in yard

10. Upcoming meeting at work

11. Forgot the wife's birthday

12. Getting back to a friend about an invitation

Writing about your worries

You'd be surprised that by simply spending a few moments writing about your worries, you can weaken their power. Recent research findings reported in the *Journal of the American Medical Association* (4/13/99) have shown that writing about stressful and worrisome experiences can reduce stress-related symptoms. By writing down your worries, you begin to feel that you are more in control of them. Much of your worrying goes on in a somewhat vague, ill-defined manner. Sometimes even you aren't quite sure what you're worrying about. By committing your worries to paper, you are dealing with them in a more direct way. Instead of floating around out there somewhere, they are now in a concrete form, recorded forever. You don't have to write volumes. In the study cited in *JAMA,* patients wrote only 20 minutes a day over three consecutive days, and about half experienced positive effects that seemed to last for months.

Scheduling your worries

After you have a major worry, you quickly discover that the worry can be very forceful and insistent. One way of combating this is, oddly enough, to do your worrying at designated times. Build worrying into your day. Call this your worry time. Whenever you sense that your worries are creeping into your mind, remind yourself that it is not yet your worry time and that the worrying will have to wait. Jot down this worry in a *worry diary,* some notebook or day-planner that you use for other appointments. Assign a time for you to worry. Start with 20 minutes. It could be during a coffee break, or just after lunch, or on your trip home after work. If you find that 20 minutes is too much time, cut back by 5 minutes until you find your optimal worrying period.

The value of this approach is that it provides you with a sense of having addressed the worry. You will be able to worry about whatever is bothering you — but only at a specified time. This approach allows you to feel more comfortable *not* worrying (or at least worrying less) the rest of your day.

To practice this scheduled and concentrated form of worry control, start with a smaller worry and work up to your more distressing concerns. From your worry list, choose a worry that is manageable and not overwhelming. Then you can work your way up to your more formidable worries.

Having a place to worry

You now know when to worry, but do you have a place to do it? You may need a *worry corner* — a place where you go to worry and that you use *only* for worrying. This special places becomes associated with worrying in your mind. It shouldn't be your bed, because you don't want to associate sleep or sex with worrying. Try to make this place a tad uncomfortable, and not a place where you would like to spend a great deal of time. It could be in the bathroom at work or in a stairwell. It literally could be a corner. Find a corner in one of the rooms in your home that is infrequently used. Stick a stool there. Make that your place of worry. When you find yourself starting to worry in other places, gently remind yourself that this is neither the time nor the place to worry.

I have two places where I worry. The first is while I'm in the shower. While lathering up, I use that time and place to *productively* worry. When I turn off the faucets, I try to turn off the worries. The second place I worry is on my commute to work. With not much else to do, I find that I can usefully worry sitting on the subway or bus. By the time I get to my office, I often feel a sense of greater closure on a particular problem or problems. After the worrying turns nonproductive, I start to look for ways of turning off those concerns.

Asking yourself some good questions

People who worry too much tend to be somewhat limited in generating options, alternatives, and solutions to potentially stressful problems. This is mainly because their anxiety limits their ability to think outside the box and come up with more creative ideas. They continue to worry in nonproductive ways.

See if you can come up with some ideas and solutions that may resolve your worries or at least make your worries less troublesome. Some questions to ask yourself include the following:

- What am I afraid of?

- Is there another way, a more sensible way, of looking at this?

- Am I looking at worst-case scenarios?

- How likely is it that what I'm worrying about is really going to happen?

- How would someone else (a good friend or a role model, for example) look at this problem?

- How would someone who is more of an optimist look at this?

- What are some alternatives and solutions that I may have missed?

Using your coping self-talk

You probably have a pretty good idea of the importance I place on talking to yourself in a sensible, reasonable manner. This coping self-talk can help you change the way you feel. In short, it can help you reduce your stress. Using your coping self-talk to reduce (and at times eliminate) your feelings of anger is particularly useful. Here are some examples of coping self-statements that you can use whenever you find yourself over-worrying. See if you can come up with a few of your own.

- Don't assume the worst will happen.

- I can cope with this.

- Take a nice deep breath. Hold it. And let it all out slowly.

- Don't make this a bigger deal than it really is.

- I'm being a worrywart! Do I always want to be a worrywart?

- *Realistically,* what is the worst that can happen?

- Is this worrying helping me in any way?

- What can I do to distract myself from these worries?

- I will be able to figure out ways of coping with this.

- Stop what-if-ing.

- On my 0–10 scale of importance, how important is this really?

Going to yourself for advice

One of the quirks we have is that we seem to be terrible at dealing with our *own* problems, but we're usually pretty good at solving other people's. Why not use this bit of psychological irony as a tool to help you worry less?

Imagine that someone is sitting in a chair opposite you. He or she has come to you for advice. For whatever reason, this person values your opinion and guidance. Even more strangely, he or she has the *same* worry you have. Restrain yourself from your first impulse — throwing your hands up in frustration — and reach deeply into your storehouse of wisdom. You may find that you come up with some wonderful ideas. You are an incredible solution-finder. Now share these ideas with yourself.

Getting distracted

Worrying about something while you're doing something else at the same time is really difficult, especially if that other thing demands your attention. This means that if you are having trouble turning off a persistent and nagging worry, try to find some way to distract yourself. This strategy makes particular sense if, in fact, you can't do very much to fix or resolve the situation or circumstance you're worrying about. Your distraction could be watching TV, watching a funny or engrossing movie, reading a good book, cooking something you like, gardening, doing carpentry — any involvement that can hold your attention and take you away from your worry.

Sometimes the distractions can be even less obvious. You can distract yourself by window-shopping, people-watching, remembering the details of a favorite vacation, or simply getting into some kind of idle conversation with a neighbor, store clerk, or the person next to you in line. Anything that can take your mind off your worry will work.

Going for a walk

One of the frequently overlooked ways of coping with worry is to go for a walk. A brisk walk is even more effective. When you are walking, you are distracted, and you are releasing physical stress and tension — all terrific antidotes to stress.

Working up a sweat

Try worrying next time you are jogging, rowing, swimming, lifting, climbing, hitting a golf or tennis ball, or doing any other form of exercise or sport. It's not easy. After about ten minutes of working out on the stationary bicycle or on the treadmill at my gym, I find it very hard to concentrate on anything. Part of the positive effect comes from the physical relaxation that often follows physical exertion. With your body more relaxed, your mind slows. Also your body may be secreting *endorphins,* hormones that are known to have stress-reducing effects. The bonus: Not only can you control your unwanted worrying, you can stay in shape at the same time.

Talking about it

We feel better and worry less when we've had an opportunity to talk to someone about those things that are bothering us. When we can get our worries out on the table, it gives us some perspective, and with this perspective can come greater feelings of control and hope. You need, of course, someone to tell your worries to. This person could be a family member, a friend, or simply an understanding and sympathetic listener. Some of my best therapy sessions have resulted not from my brilliant insights, but from just letting my clients talk about their worries.

Humoring yourself

Humor is a marvelous antidote to worry. The problem is, when we are worrying, we are usually in no mood to joke. The following sections provide two of my favorite ways of using humor to diffuse a potential worry.

Exaggerate!

Exaggeration can be a useful tool in helping you reduce your worrying. Suppose, for example, that you are worrying about an upcoming presentation you have to make at work. Try imagining that, as you start your presentation, the audience begins to throw tomatoes and other assorted produce. A colleague comes to the front of the room and announces that this is the worst presentation he has ever heard in his professional life. The boos and foot-stamping are deafening.

Or how about this: You are worried that you may flunk your upcoming exam. Imagine that you not only flunk the exam, but your grade is so low it is entered into *The Guinness Book of World Records*. No college ever accepts you, and you live in a cardboard box on the street for the next 20 years. Mothers parade their children in front of your box warning, "See what happens when you don't study!" Hopefully a wee smile may help give you some perspective on your worry.

Play sitcom

Using this technique, you imagine that your worry is the theme for a favorite sitcom episode. It could be *Seinfeld, Frasier, Friends, The Simpsons*, or any show you enjoy. Imagine that one of the characters on the show is entrenched in your worry. But the other cast members manage to look at this worry in a less serious, more playful way. Looking at your worries through their eyes will, hopefully, dilute it and give you some emotional distance.

STRESS BUSTER

Worry harder!

One way of making your worry time and worry corner even more effective is to worry harder during those times. Research supports the notion that if you worry intensely for a brief period time (say, 15 or 20 minutes), you may actually reduce your need to worry at other times of the day — at least for that particular worry. This doesn't mean that you will never worry about that problem again. However, you will probably find that you worry about it less at other times.

The key word here is *intensely.* When you worry in your usual way, you worry inconsistently. You have worry lapses, you distract yourself, or you avoid thinking about certain negative scenarios. To get the therapeutic benefits of concentrated worrying, your worrying has to be constant and focused so that you become satiated with worry and get tired of worrying. In other words, you worry yourself out. By immersing yourself totally in a worry for a fixed period of time, you actually make it less likely that you will worry about that problem, at least for a while.

Relaxing your body and calming your mind

When you are relaxed, you'll probably find that worrying is much harder to do. When your body is relaxed, your mind slows down as well. Why not use this fact to help you control your worrying? The next time you notice that you are worrying, begin using one or more of the relaxation techniques described in Chapters 4 and 5. Try some deep breathing, progressive muscle relaxation, and various forms of meditation. The more relaxed you are, the less likely you are to worry.

Trying some positive imagery

Often, when we worry, we really don't allow ourselves to take the worry to a positive (and often more likely) conclusion. One method of helping you reduce your worry is to use something called *positive imagery.*

When you use positive imagery, you form a mental picture of that worry, including as much detail as you can — what you see, what you hear, and so on. Then imagine a positive resolution to your worry. All goes relatively well.

For example, if you have a presentation to give, imagine that as you approach the podium you are feeling calm. You feel remarkably at ease. You start a little nervously, but very soon you find your stride and the presentation is going swimmingly. You are even beginning to enjoy the process a little. You finish and hear appreciative applause. Several of your colleagues come up to you and tell you what a nice job you did. You feel great!

You don't have to go overboard with the positive nature of your imagery. Just make it more positive than your worries would suggest. Chances are, your revised image of what will happen may be a lot closer to what actually *will* happen. Trust me.

In a pinch, try this

This approach may sound a bit strange, but it can be highly effective in helping you turn off those unwanted and intrusive worries. It is a variation of the stop technique described earlier. Here's how it works:

1. **Whenever you sense that some recurring, unwanted, and distressing worry is ruminating in your thoughts, become conscious that you are fretting about that worry.**

2. **Pinch yourself on your wrist or some other part of your body. At the same time yell the word *stop* silently inside your head.**

3. **Replace that worrisome thought with a pleasant thought.**

   The pleasant thought could be a happy memory or a pleasant image. Hold that pleasant thought for about 20 or 30 seconds, then go about your usual business.

   Repeat this sequence if the distressing worry returns.

You may need some time before you weaken the troublesome worry. But stick with it!

Chapter 12

Reducing Interpersonal Stress

● ●

● ●

*Y*our relationships and interactions with others can be a major source of joy and satisfaction in your life. Unfortunately, your involvement with others can also be a major source of stress. Whenever you ask people where most of their stress comes from, they almost always answer "other people." The "others" may be family members, people at work, or just some incredibly rude so-and-so who is giving you a hard time, because he or she got up on the wrong side of the bed that morning. And unless you are hiding in a cabin in rural Montana, there is a better than average chance that you may run into someone very soon who will try to push your stress-button. Minimizing your levels of interpersonal stress means having the tools, strategies, and tactics that allow you to navigate the prickly world of other people. This chapter shows you how you can make your interactions and involvement with others far more satisfying and certainly far less stressful.

Developing Stress-Reducing Communication

Your ability to communicate affects your relationships with family, friends, co-workers, bosses, clients — everybody in fact. Ineffective communication can contribute to everything from an unhappy marriage to losing your job, from a so-so social life to a lousy sex life. And that usually means more stress in your life. Unfortunately, when you are feeling stressed, your ability to communicate deteriorates. So before you get to that point, following are some suggestions and strategies that can increase your communication smarts.

Start by listening

The fact is, poor listeners have more stress in their lives. If you are a poor listener, there is a better than average chance that your relationships are not as satisfying and effective as they could be. Good listeners have more friends, better marriages, function more effectively at work, and, as a result, usually have less hassle, friction, and conflict in their lives. Whether you are a terrible listener or a good listener, following are some ways that you can become a better listener.

Make a mental commitment

The next time you are in a situation where someone is talking and you feel it is important that you truly listen, make a mental commitment to do just that. Listen. Make it a priority. Put effort and energy into your listening. Don't be distracted. Don't look at your watch. Don't yawn. Don't look around. Don't daydream. If it's too noisy where you are, ask the speaker to join you in a quieter spot. Pretend that there will be a test on what the other person is saying and that your score will go on your permanent record.

Behave as though you are listening

A good listener does more than just stand there without saying anything. You should be an *active* listener. Acknowledge verbally and non-verbally that you are listening by responding with a nod, facial expressions, a raised eyebrow, an "oh really," an "I see," or anything that gives the speaker the idea that you are still conscious. If you are far away from the speaker, move closer. Lean slightly toward the person speaking. Look the other person in the eye. And uncrossing your arms and legs suggests a more open, verbally-receptive stance.

Give some feedback

One effective technique that helps to ensure that you are listening and that gives the speaker a real sense that you are actively following his every word is to reflect back or comment on bits of what you hear. For example:

> Speaker: "My job is getting worse. I'm there now till all hours. I'm beginning to hate it."
>
> You: "Yeah, it must be hard not having enough time for you and your family."

This response not only shows the other person that you are listening, but also that you are empathetic and can relate to what he or she is saying. Even if your feedback is off the mark, it allows the speaker to modify his or her remarks and clarify his thoughts and feelings, which is similar to what therapists may do in their sessions. The feedback may be as simple as paraphrasing the speaker's words in your own words. For example:

Speaker: "I'm at the office now from 8 to 8 at night! It seems like I'm there all the time!"

You: "8 to 8. That's a lot of hours to be at work."

This kind of active listening encourages the speaker to share more of his or her thoughts and feelings with you. It creates a feeling of connectedness.

Don't "one-up" the speaker

When someone else is talking, do not immediately begin formulating your own verbal comeback. Wait to start formulating your replies. Mentally rehearsing *your* wonderful story while the other person is telling his guarantees that you hear little of what the other person is saying. While most everything someone tells you can remind you of something that happened to you, resist, at least for that immediate moment, the urge to tell an even funnier joke or a better story. Withhold, for a while at least, that brilliant repartee. Do not interrupt. Don't put the other person down. Don't debate. Don't go for a win. In short, don't "one-up" the speaker.

Hold off on giving advice

Often, when others talk, they are talking about what is going on in their lives. They may be confiding in us and sharing some concern or problem. Upon hearing of a problem or predicament, our natural instinct is to give some advice. Men especially have difficulty *not* coming up with solutions and suggestions. However, while your ideas may be terrific and right on the mark, it may be that the speaker is not looking for your well-intended advice at this time and would really just like to express his feelings. You can always get back to the person later and ask him whether he'd like to talk some more and listen to some of your ideas.

Are *you* a good listener?

Most of us think that we are good listeners. Most of us also think that we have a great sense of humor, that we look terrific, and that we are wonderful drivers. Maybe yes, maybe no. The next time you are talking to someone, monitor yourself; notice whether you are truly listening and paying attention to what the other person is saying. Better yet, ask friends and family members if *they* think you are a good listener. You can also ask them about your driving, your looks, and your sense of humor.

Listening can be good for your health

Not only are you being polite when you listen, you may also live longer. In his book, *The Language of the Heart*, psychologist James Lynch found that the act of listening actually lowers your blood pressure. He looked at blood-pressure levels in hypertensive patients and found that there was a rather dramatic drop in blood pressure levels when patients were listening to someone else.

Practice listening

Think of a person in your life whom you care about and with whom you are not a great listener. Purposefully plan to listen carefully to that person every time you speak with her. Remember the guidelines that I describe in this section, and monitor yourself as to how you are doing. Practice listening with this person until you recognize your improvement. Then find another person to add to your list of people to listen to better, and so on.

Another way of honing your listening skills is to practice listening to something you find boring. Usually you do not have to wait long before such an opportunity presents itself. It could be a less than scintillating presentation at your next business meeting, or some fellow committee member going on and on about some trivial point. It may be some television program outlining economic growth in the newly-created province of Kalikistan. Force yourself to listen and pay attention to what is being said. You may find that you get much better at listening over time.

It's your turn to talk

Listening, of course, is only one part of the communication process. There are times when *you* have something to say. What you say, and how you say it, makes a big difference in terms of the amount of stress that you experience. Some communicational guidelines can help make what comes out of your mouth less stressful for you and for the people you care about.

Practice some damage control

What does come out of your mouth, and certainly the way it comes out, reflects how you are feeling at the time. If you have a particularly bad day at work, you may not come home feeling all warm and fuzzy. You may feel angry, or upset, or worse. And should you be greeted by any new demands or frustrations, your reactions may be less than delightful. You are in danger of feeling and spreading a good deal of stress. A little damage control is needed. Two suggestions:

✔ **Warn others.** As soon as you recognize that your mood has headed south and has real toxic potential, share that information with those around you. Let them know what you are feeling and warn them what to expect. Try the following:

"Hon, it's been a rotten day all round. I'm in a foul mood and not really fit for human company. I probably shouldn't be taken seriously for at least another hour. It's nothing you've done. Give me a little time and I should be my old wonderful self again."

The funny part is, once you have delivered this message, it is less likely that you will, in fact, interact negatively with those around you.

✔ **Make amends.** Should you screw up and manage to stress out everyone in sight, all is still not lost. As quickly as you can regain your emotional equilibrium, let the target of your negative fallout know that you are sorry, that it was not him or her that triggered your emotional over-reaction, and that you will work hard to make sure that it doesn't happen too often.

A little damage control up front can avoid a lot more stress down the road.

Use "I" statements

One sure way to escalate any interaction into a stressful confrontation is to start blaming or finding fault. For example, you find yourself becoming more than a little annoyed as you find yourself having to wait (yet another time) for a friend. Now, you could say:

"You are never on time! Can't you get your act together?!"

This approach can put the other person on the defensive. She may feel attacked and feel the need to protect herself. Rather than start with a blaming "you," start with an "I." Here's what I mean:

"I feel that when you come late, you don't care that much about me. I get annoyed and angry. I'd like it if you could try to be on time."

This approach allows you to express your feelings and tell the other person what you would like her to do differently, but in a non-attacking, non-hostile way. Following is a model, a template, to help you reframe your blaming.

Start with:

When you do . . . (describe the other person's behavior)

Then say:

I feel . . . (describe how this behavior effects you)

And finish with:

> *I'd prefer* . . . (describe what you would like to see happen)

Avoid kitchen-sinking

Kitchen-sinking describes what you do when you lump a bunch of grievances together and throw them all at once at the other person. For example, a parent may express his or her anger to his child in the following way:

> "You can't do anything right! You never take the garbage out, clean your room, get up on time, or finish your homework!"

This grievance may or may not be accurate, but expressing these complaints all at once usually ensures that the reaction is defensive and probably hostile.

If you have more than one beef, grievance, or issue, express them one at a time. And use the "I-statement" approach rather than blaming and putting the other person on the defensive.

Don't be a labeler

When we have a gripe about someone (even about ourselves), we tend to use simple, often one-word labels. We like labels. It simplifies things. Unfortunately, it *over*-simplifies things. People are not easily classified by a single descriptor. There are probably times when everyone does something that could be construed as lazy, selfish, mean, silly, and just about every other derogatory adjective you can come up with. The following illustrates how labels can be destructive, and how we take a single act or bit of behavior and turn it into a permanent character trait:

The Label	*The Behavior*
You're a slob	You didn't pick up after yourself
You're lazy	You didn't do your homework
You're stupid	You didn't know the answer to my question
You're inconsiderate	You didn't invite me to go shopping with you
You're selfish	You didn't ask me if I wanted some of your popcorn

A better way of avoiding this stress is to resist the label and go for the specific behavior. Instead of going for the global characterization, focus on the specific bit of the incident or situation that gets to you. It's simple. Instead of saying "You're lazy," just say, "You didn't do your homework." Instead of,

"You're inconsiderate," say, "You didn't invite me to go shopping with you." You'll find that the other person will be less defensive, and you stand a better chance of seeing some change or improvement in their behaviors.

Watch the "never" and "always" traps

"You never do anything right!"

"You always manage to hurt my feelings!"

"You never consider how someone else might feel!"

"Everything you do turns out badly!"

Statements with the words "always" and "never" usually are forms of exaggeration that distort what is happening and misrepresent the other person's behavior. They become traps that again put the other person on the defensive, and make it harder to resolve the potential conflict. Try to avoid these overly global characterizations. Whenever possible, catch yourself when you hear these words forming in your mind and replace them with less provocative descriptors. In their place, try substituting with the words or phrases "often," "too much of the time," "a lot," or "usually."

Time your response

If "location, location, location" is the formula for success in real estate; in stress-reducing communication, the formula might be "timing, timing, timing." *When* you say something is just as important as *how* you say it. For example, your child has come home far later than you would like. Your child knows this. You can have a heated discussion extremely late at night when both of you are emotionally ready for a fight, or you could leave it for the next day when you could more calmly (and effectively) present your dissatisfaction. Should you find yourself in an argument or heated disagreement, try to stop yourself and defer the interaction to another time when, hopefully, cooler heads will prevail. "Let's discuss this further tomorrow, Okay?"

Better timing usually means less stress.

Look for a pattern

Rather than complaining about every little bit of negative behavior, wait until you have collected a number of incidents of such behavior. And then complain. For example, suppose that you are upset because a friend appears not to be listening to you when you are talking, although you work very hard to listen when she talks. You could express your feelings to her the next time you find her not listening, or you could handle it a better way. After you have noticed that the behavior persists, bring it up at a time when you and she are not upset, angry, or defensive. Then raise it as a more general issue (using the I-statement). Should the pattern continue, express your feelings again — but at the right time, expressing even more strongly your displeasure at her behavior.

Discovering What It Means to Be Assertive

Are you assertive or non-assertive in your interactions with others? Becoming effectively assertive in your interpersonal relationships can result in much less emotional distress. Whenever you act non-assertively, you generally end up feeling more anxious and tense than you would like. There is also a good chance that you feel angry and resentful at not expressing your true feelings. You may feel frustrated at not getting what you feel you should have. You can feel victimized, pushed around, and taken advantage of. You feel less in control, and less hopeful that you are able to achieve what you would like to achieve. Your self-esteem is lowered. You feel less positive about yourself and about how others see you. And those times when you do act assertively, you may feel guilty or anxious, worrying about any repercussions of your behavior. Any or all of the above, of course, produces a good deal of stress. Fortunately, finding out how to become more comfortably assertive is something that can be mastered relatively painlessly. The first step is knowing just how assertive or unassertive you are.

How assertive are you?

In the following list, I outline several of the behaviors and traits of unassertive people. Read each statement and rate yourself on the extent to which that statement applies to you: not like me, a little like me, or a lot like me:

- ✔ I am very uncomfortable expressing my needs and wants.
- ✔ I hate confrontations and arguments.
- ✔ I have trouble asking for help or a favor from others.
- ✔ I find it hard to ask people to return things they have borrowed from me.
- ✔ When people ask a favor of me, I find it hard to say no.
- ✔ I am uncomfortable receiving compliments and praise.
- ✔ In social situations, I usually let others do the talking.
- ✔ Expressing feelings of caring and affection makes me uncomfortable.
- ✔ I find it hard to ask someone who is annoying me to stop.
- ✔ Maintaining eye contact when I am talking to others is difficult for me.
- ✔ Returning a purchase to a store makes me very uncomfortable.
- ✔ I have a lot of trouble speaking up in a group or in a meeting.

✔ I become anxious when I am in a conversation with people I do not know well.

✔ I feel that I am not assertive enough.

✔ Others who know me have said that I am not assertive enough.

Looking at your ratings, how many fall into the "a lot like me" category? If more than one or two do, it suggests that you may want to explore further the role that non-assertiveness plays in your daily dose of stress.

Following, I present four scenarios that can help you identify your interactive style. Take a pencil or pen and a piece of paper and circle the response that best reflects how you might react:

1. You have ordered dinner in a fairly nice restaurant — a big steak, in fact. You like your steak on the rare side and you told your waiter of your preference. The steak arrives far more well-done than you like. You would:

   a. Smile, say thank you, and finish as much of the steak as you could, unhappy with every bite.

   b. Tell the waiter that he is a complete idiot and that he needs a hearing aid, and yell this loudly enough so that everyone in the restaurant hears you and secretly wishes you dead.

   c. Politely explain that the steak is not the way you would like it, and ask him nicely for another.

   d. None of the above. I would _____.

2. You are in a taxi and the driver is driving far too fast for your comfort. You begin to feel nervous. You would:

   a. Grin and bear it, while mentally listing your heirs.

   b. Call the cab driver a reckless imbecile, while banging on the partition with your foot.

   c. Calmly ask the driver if he would please slow down.

   d. None of the above. I would _____.

3. You are in the middle of your dinner when the telephone rings. It is someone who would like to know if you would be interested in switching your telephone service. He drones on and on. You would:

   a. Listen for the entire 20 minute spiel and agree to sign on.

   b. Tell him you will be back in a second, and put the receiver in a sock-drawer while you return to finish your dinner.

   c. Interrupt the caller saying, politely, that you are not interested, and you hang up.

   d. None of the above. I would _____.

4. You are patiently waiting for a sales clerk to serve a customer next to you. Another customer shows up, and stands on the other side of the customer being served. Though you were there first, the newcomer seems oblivious of your presence. He quickly hands his purchase to the clerk before you have a chance to blink. You are not happy. You would:

   a. Say and do nothing.

   b. Grab the man by his lapel and throw him to the ground.

   c. Firmly, but politely, tell the sales clerk and the other customer that you were there before he was and that you would like to be served first.

   d. None of the above. I would _____.

In each of the above scenarios, you can respond in four very different ways:

✔ **You can respond *passively*** and keep your honest feelings and thoughts to yourself, or express them in a self-effacing, apologetic manner so that the other person doesn't take you seriously (the first of the answer choices). This response shows that you do not consider your own needs to be important and you feel that the needs of others always come first.

✔ **You can respond *aggressively*** by directly expressing your anger or expressing it in more subtle, passive-aggressive ways (as in my some- what exaggerated second choices). With this response, you disregard the other person's rights and feelings. You want to win, but at any cost.

✔ **You can respond *assertively*** with the third answer choices. You stand up for yourself, expressing the way you truly feel. You are considerate of other people's feelings. You do not attack or blame, nor do you become meek and withdraw.

✔ **You could respond with the fourth choice.** This form of response can be a combination of the first three. It can be part passive and part assertive, or some other mixture of interactive styles.

Not too hot, not too cold — just right

Acting assertively means knowing how to express your opinions, wants, and feelings in ways that do not compromise the rights of others or demean others. When you assert your own needs, you do not let others take advan- tage of you, nor do you feel guilty. Being assertive is more than returning a broken toaster or telling a waiter to take back your undercooked steak. Often, being more assertive means being able to express positive feelings to some- one, to express affection and caring. Being assertive also means being able to give and receive positives, be they compliments, thank-yous, or other expres- sions of praise and gratitude. You are not meek, you are not aggressive, and you do not blame and resent. You feel good about your actions. And you feel less stress.

Examples of assertive behavior

To help you get a better picture of what assertive behavior is, I list some assertive responses to common situations.

- ✔ **Refusing a request:**
  - I'm sorry, I cannot drop that package off for you.
  - That's not a good time for me.
  - I'm sorry, but I really do not want to do that.
- ✔ **Being given some unwanted advice:**
  - I really don't want your advice right now.
  - Thanks for your help, but I'll be fine.
- ✔ **Expressing disapproval:**
  - I don't like what you are doing.
  - I would like you to stop that.
- ✔ **Expressing a compliment:**
  - I think you are doing a terrific job.
  - I think you look terrific.
- ✔ **Receiving a compliment:**
  - It's nice of you to say that.
  - Thank you.

What assertive behavior is not

An old cartoon shows an office door with a sign on it reading, "Assertiveness class in session. Don't knock; just barge in." Back in the '70s there was great interest in the topic of assertiveness. A flood of books hit the shelves telling us that we could now say "No" with impunity, and to stand up, speak up, and to go get what we want. Assertiveness training courses flourished, and the streets were filled with course graduates all too eager to express their thoughts and feelings. While most people got the point of being more assertive, many others missed the point and interpreted being assertive as permission to express all their pent-up aggression and hostility.

Assertiveness is not:

- ✔ Simply getting what *you* want
- ✔ Disregarding the rights and feelings of others

✔ Acting belligerently or antagonistically

✔ Being aggressive or hostile

✔ Making fun of others

✔ Walking around with a chip on your shoulder

✔ Dominating, demeaning, or humiliating others

Becoming More Assertive

Looking around at those you know, you may be tempted to make a judgement on whether you are assertive or not, and you may think that you were born that way. Actually, there is some truth to this. We do come into this world with some hard wiring that predisposes us to be assertive or non-assertive. Then there are your parents, other people, and your life experiences, all of which contribute to the ways in which you interact with others. However, should you lack any or all of these influences, you can still become assertive. With a little time and some effort, you can readily see yourself becoming more assertive — and less stressed.

Observing assertive behavior

Following are some guidelines on how to become more assertive:

✔ **Watch others.** Notice how and when others act assertively. Pay special attention when you are with people you admire for their assertiveness skills.

✔ **Watch yourself.** Keep a brief record of when you do and do not act assertively. Nothing fancy — just make some notes to yourself.

✔ **Start small.** Start by working on situations where you feel only minimal or moderate amounts of anxiety. Work your way up to the harder stuff. Don't expect immediate changes. Becoming more assertive means changing years of behaving otherwise. Learning new ways of thinking and behaving takes a little time.

✔ **Cut yourself some slack.** Don't be too hard on yourself if you act non-assertively. Figure out what you did wrong and try not to let the same thing happen the next time.

Ten ways to stay permanently non-assertive

1. Never say no to anyone and avoid confrontations at all costs.

2. Always put the needs of others ahead of yours.

3. Feel guilty whenever you do something that *you* want to do.

4. Believe that your feelings do not matter; that only other people's feelings matter.

5. Believe that you are selfish if someone is unhappy with your decisions or actions.

6. Believe that being wrong or making a mistake is something to always be avoided.

7. Always do what people in authority tell you to.

8. Believe that you are not as smart or as competent as other people.

9. Believe that it is not polite to disagree or express a contrary opinion.

10. Never accept a compliment without putting yourself down in some way.

Watching how you say things

It's not just the words; it's also how you say them. While the words may be wonderfully assertive, the manner in which you deliver your message, and your body language that you use, may be saying something that is other than assertive. Ask yourself:

- ✔ Am I speaking in a loud, clear voice?
- ✔ Am I mumbling when I'm talking, or garbling my words?
- ✔ Am I looking at the person I am talking to?
- ✔ Am I fidgeting while I'm talking?
- ✔ Am I sitting or standing straight when I'm talking?
- ✔ Am I shouting or yelling?
- ✔ Is my tone sarcastic and demeaning?

The next time you get an opportunity to work on your assertiveness, pay attention to any or all of the above. When you're acting assertively, your non-verbal behavior is congruent with your message. All of you is saying the same thing.

Saying "No" (oh, so nicely)

Many times, a simple and direct "No" or other assertive response is totally appropriate and should be your option of choice. You need no further explanation or discussion. However, there are times when straight assertion is a little cold and may be taken as somewhat off-putting. Some tact and packaging may be required.

Here are some examples:

Situation: Friends sitting next to you in a theater are talking during the movie.

> Direct Assertion: "Would you please be quiet?"
>
> Packaged Assertion: "Guys, keep it down. I can't hear anything."

Situation: A co-worker asks you for help.

> Direct Assertion: "No, I can't do it."
>
> Packaged Assertion: "I'd like to help, but I really can't now."

Situation: You are interrupted while you're talking.

> Direct Assertion: "Don't interrupt me when I'm talking."
>
> Packaged Assertion: "Hang on. I'm not finished yet."

Situation: Being asked out for dinner by an acquaintance. (You don't want to go.)

> Direct Assertion: "No thank you."
>
> Packaged Assertion: "Thank you for the offer. But I really can't."

If you're caught off guard, and you find yourself tongue-tied, you can always defer your answer:

> "I'll have to look at my schedule. I'll get back to you."

It is also useful to have one or two wonderful excuses at your fingertips.

> "I really can't. My nephew is coming into town that weekend."
>
> "I'm sorry but we already have a dinner invitation for that night."

There are times when a convenient excuse or white lie works, and is the appropriate response. That may sound as though it's a violation of the principles of assertion, but there are times when the other person's feelings may be more important to you than to say, "No way. I just don't want to." Remember, discretion is often the better part of assertion.

The "good girl" syndrome

Women, in particular, face additional pressures to remain non-assertive. Culturally and historically, women have been taught to be "other-oriented." Women are taught that they should be passive, submissive, and compliant. They are told, "Be nice, and people will like you," "Never be the center of attention," "Don't look too smart." And while these messages are less strong these days, they still exist. Growing up with these early socialization messages lodged in women's psyche, life becomes even more complicated given the multiple roles that women now assume. More often than not it is the women who takes the lion's share of any child-raising responsibilities. Women are seen as the person primarily responsible for taking care of things at home, even if she works a staggering number of hours at an outside job. And should a parent get sick or require time and attention, you can guess who gives most of her time and attention. Couple this with a non-assertive headset, and the stress can become enormous.

Coping with Difficult People

You thought your Aunt Agnes was tough. Believe it or not, there are people out there who are even more difficult. They can be ill-mannered, grouchy, nasty, and appear to lack many basic interpersonal skills. They lose very little sleep over giving you a hard time. Sooner or later — and probably sooner — you will run into one of these types. You may have to bring out the bigger guns. More sophisticated strategies and tactics are required to spare you this unwanted and avoidable stress. The following sections outline what you need to do.

Staying calm

When you are seething and little puffs of smoke are coming out of your ears, the chances of effectively reacting to a difficult situation are not the best. Your first strategy should be to get yourself into a more composed, relaxed state. By relaxing your body at the first hint of conflict, you give yourself the best chance of responding well in a difficult situation. Some simple breathing exercises (see Chapter 4) should do the trick. I like using some Rapid Relaxation exercises in these situations. The following is what you can do to stay calm:

Inhale deeply through your nostrils, and at the same time press together your thumb and forefinger on one hand. Hold that breath for 4 or 5 seconds and then exhale fully through your slightly-parted lips. As you are exhaling, let go of the tension in your hand and let a wave of soothing relaxation spread from the top of your head to the tip of your toes. Repeat one or two more times until you can feel that your body is more relaxed.

Starting nice, and working your way up to nasty

I have always liked the strategy of *escalating assertion* when dealing with more difficult situations. Using this approach, you start as politely and as courteously as you can and then move up the assertion ladder, rung by rung. Should you find yourself nearing the end of that ladder with little hope of success, you may need to venture into the realm of more forceful behavior. Here's what I mean.

Suppose that you are enjoying a particularly good book. You become aware that your silence has now been disrupted. Your next door neighbor has turned up his television set to a highly disturbing level. It is loud. Very loud. You are very annoyed. You could let the incident go, but because this is not the first time this has happened, you decide that a little assertive behavior is required. You determine that escalating assertion is the way to go. Following, I give an illustration of how you might proceed:

Your Mood	*The Action You Take*
Mr. or Ms. Nice Guy	A polite note under his door.
I'm a little miffed	A courteous, but firm phone call
I'm pissed	A personal visit with strong eye-contact
No More Mr. or Ms. Nice Guy	Wall-banging; verbal threats
The Gloves are off!	The police; the super; lawyer's letter
Nuclear War	Lawsuit; You blast *your* TV
Defeat	Earplugs

Start modestly and hope that you can resolve your issue before you get to the end of your list. The key to escalating assertion is being in emotional control, which means working to not let your anger or upset overwhelm you and get you to do something you may regret later.

Talking like a broken record

Persistence pays at times. By repeating your request again and again, like a record with a scratch (remember LPs?), you often find that you get what you want. Consider this interchange. You purchase a lamp that works fine for the first day; but after that, you begin to hear some crackling in the socket that leaves you feeling a little leery of turning it on any more. You decide, rightfully, to take it back.

> You: "This lamp doesn't work properly. I think the wiring is defective. I'd like a refund."
>
> The Store Clerk: "Do you have a sales receipt?"
>
> You: "No. However you can see by the box that the item was purchased here."
>
> The Clerk: "We do not do refunds without receipts."
>
> You: "That may be, but I would like my money back."
>
> The Clerk: "I can't do that."
>
> You: "I would very much like my money back."
>
> The Clerk: " But we almost never give a refund without a receipt."
>
> You: "I really would like my money back."
>
> The Clerk: " Okay, but just this one time only."
>
> You: "Thank you."

As you can see, there is nothing brilliant going on here. Basically you wear down the other person. You are firm and repetitive. The tone of your voice doesn't vary. You stay on target. You are a Johnny (or Jeannie) one-note. This technique works best when you stick to a single sentence that you repeat again and again. Does this approach work every time? Nope. But by sticking to a consistent and unwavering demand, you find that in more instances than you may imagine, you get what you want.

Trying a little "fogging"

This technique is a nicer version of broken record, but includes some of the same ideas. Fogging recognizes that you may care about the other person's feelings or that the other person may have a valid point or be asking something reasonable of you, but that you would like to decline. The following example makes fogging clearer.

You are asked to donate money to a charity that you feel has merit, but you have decided that it is not one that you want to add to your give-to list. The fund-raiser is well-meaning, but persistent. Using the broken record approach seems a little harsh. You opt for fogging:

> The fund-raiser: "It's a great cause. It helps a lot of people."
>
> You: "I know it is a good cause. I don't want to donate to another charity at this time."
>
> Fund-Raiser: "You don't have to give a huge amount. Anything will do."
>
> You: "I realize that. But I'd rather not make a donation at this time."
>
> Fund-Raiser: "Why don't I put you down for $30. That's not an awful lot."
>
> You: "I know it isn't. I'd rather not make a donation."

Though it may sound much like the broken record strategy, it is a softer inter-action. You are actively listening to the other person, paraphrasing, or feeding back some of what he is saying. You appreciate his point of view, and you may in fact be quite sympathetic; but you still want to stick to your guns. It's the perfect technique when you are solicited for donations, membership on committees, volunteer positions, or asked for favors that are reasonable, but that you would like to decline.

Stop personalizing

A store clerk yells at you, your boss is in a foul mood, a friend is angry with you — any or all of these situations can trigger a good deal of stress. However, any stress that you may feel is greatly magnified when you believe you may be the reason for that other person's anger or upset. But you may not be. You may not have done or said anything that would merit the emo-tional outburst by the other person.

You *personalize* when you mistakenly assume that it is your personality or behavior that triggered negative reactions in others. If you've been around for any length of time, you quickly learn that everybody has an opinion, and usually a strong one, about everything. And, more often than not, they are negative opinions that these people will happily share with you. When you personalize, you fail to distinguish between opinion and fact. You assume that because people say something or voice a criticism, they are right. Sometimes they are right, but often they are not. Remember, other people may have problems. Many have disordered personalities and other forms of emotional dysfunction. Most are probably under too much stress, and cer-tainly all have priorities that are different from yours. So before you become too distressed, stop and ask yourself, "Am *I* really the one at fault here?"

Have a dress rehearsal

Interpersonal conflict and unnecessary stress most often results when we are caught off guard. Take some time to plan what you would like to say to the other person. Sometimes being caught unprepared is unavoidable. Many times, however, you can see it coming and have a chance to ready yourself for the interaction. Do some role-playing. Imagine what you might say and also imagine how the other person might react. Then imagine how you might respond. But go further than this. Also imagine that the other person becomes hostile and difficult. See yourself coping with this situation. Imagine yourself being calm, assertive, and in control. Play with different scenarios until you feel that you are ready for just about anything.

Following are some scenarios to mentally rehearse:

- You are quite unhappy about some things a coworker has been doing lately and you would like to make it clear that you would like it to stop.
- You know that a friend is going to ask you for a favor, one you definitely do not want to grant.
- You have to ask someone to do something that you know is going to make her angry.

Practice may or may not make perfect, but it certainly will reduce your stress.

Losing the battle, winning the war

Hardly a week (a day? an hour?) goes by without someone doing or saying something that has button-pushing potential. In everyone's life, there is no shortage of opportunities for conflict. You may be one of the many people who feel that they have to respond to every slight, insult, imposition, or provocation that comes their way, which can keep you very busy and highly stressed.

While this head on style should have a place in your repertoire of interpersonal skills, and there are times when direct confrontation may be the way to go, there are times when *avoiding conflict* may be the option of choice. Where is it written that you must respond to anything that comes your way? Sidestep, let it go, look the other way, keep your mouth shut. The trick is knowing when to act and when to retreat. It means not treating these encounters as though they are all of equal importance. It means choosing your battles wisely, and choosing to lose the less important battles so that you will be a winner in the longer run.

Using the "stoplight" technique

Using this technique, you put any conflict or disagreement into one of three groups: *green-light* interactions, *red-light* interactions, or *yellow-light* interactions.

You don't have to worry about the green-lighters. They are all the positive interactions you may have; you want as many of these as you can get. On the other hand, red-light interactions are encounters, issues, or situations where you feel something must be done. You must say or do something to deal with the situation.

Yellow-light issues are interactions that fall between the two. These are negative, but not so bad or distressing that they warrant red-light status. Yellow-light items can be let go, avoided, given the blind eye. Consider the following borderline situations:

Circumstance	*Red-light or Yellow-light? (R or Y?)*
Someone jostles you in a crowd	_____
You are interrupted when you are talking	_____
Someone cuts you off in traffic	_____
Your waiter is slow in serving you	_____
The person in front of you in line is taking a long time to pay for her purchase	_____
People are talking during a meeting	_____
Somebody says something stupid	_____
You are treated impolitely	_____

In each of these situations, you have the choice of responding to the situation or of ignoring it. There are times when you might consider one or more of these incidents and encounters as "Red-lighters." I'm suggesting, however, that you start to put more of these kinds of incidents and encounters into the "let it go," yellow-light category. Spare yourself the stress. Are you being unassertive? Not really. Save the emotional energy for the more important stuff.

Just because something goes into a yellow-light category now does not mean it can't later be given red-light status. When my son forgot to take out the garbage, I let it go. When it happened a second time, I didn't let it go. Similarly, when the painter didn't show up when he promised, I decided yellow-light. The second time he messed up, red-light.

Chapter 13

Stress-Resilient Values, Goals, and Attitudes

*B*y this point, you have mastered the skills of relaxation, your life is remarkably organized, you are eating like a nutritionist, and sleeping like a baby. But you're not finished yet. Just as your thinking plays an important role in creating (and relieving) your stress; your values, goals, and attitudes can increase or reduce the amount of stress in your life. This chapter helps you identify and clarify your personal values and goals and shows you how you can create more stress-resilient ways of looking at your world.

Recognizing the Value of Your Values

"What," you may ask, "have my values and attitudes got to do with the stress in my life?" The answer is, "Lots." Your personal values and your overall philosophy of life play a major role in determining your stress level. What you think is important and what you value act together in often subtle yet very important ways to either protect you from stress or make your life *more* stressful. Rarely a day goes by without some decision, some opinion, or some action being determined, or at least shaped, by your values and attitudes. Your values in large part determine your goals, your needs, and your wants. And when you do not reach these goals, or fulfill these needs and wants, you feel stressed.

You may not even be aware of holding such values and attitudes. Yet you do. And either consciously or subconsciously they guide many of your more important decisions — everything from what you eat to how you vote, from what work you do to how you spend your time and money. Clarifying your values and attitudes is an important first step in moving toward developing a stress-resilient philosophy of life. The greater the congruence between your values and your goals, and between your decisions and actions, the lower your stress level. Think of your values and attitudes as your roadmap in life. The better the map, the smaller the chance that you may make a wrong turn.

At various points in your life, you realize that some of your values and goals are not providing you with the kind of happiness and satisfaction you want. Many of your core values may not be the values you truly believe in. They may be the values you inherited from others, without much thought on your part. These values can come from your parents, your peers, your religion, your teachers, television and the movies, the corporation or organization you work for, or the community you live in. Such values can match your own values. However, in some cases, they may not reflect what is truly meaningful or important to you at this point in your life. Yes, you are climbing the ladder, but it may be the *wrong* ladder. What may have seemed worthwhile and important at one stage of your life, may not seem as important later on. Your values and goals change, and reevaluating and reconsidering your values from time to time is important.

Clarifying Your Values and Goals

In this section, I provide you with several exercises designed to help you discover and clarify what values and goals are important to you. These exercises aren't about passing or failing or being right or wrong, so just be honest. Does this mean some values are less stress-resilient than others? Absolutely. But you alone can determine which of your values and goals you should hold onto, and which of your values and goals you need to revamp or even throw out altogether.

The tombstone test

Contemplating your own demise may seem like an overly dramatic way of getting in touch with your core values and central goals, but it can be remarkably effective. The following exercise was designed to give you the ultimate perspective. Take a pen or a pencil, and a piece of paper (or your keyboard), and answer the following questions:

When I am gone, what would I like my tombstone to say about me? (Assume you have a very large tombstone).

Include in your tombstone description the answers to the following, more specific questions:

- How would I like people to remember me in life?
- What would I have liked to have accomplished in life?

This exercise should help you step back and look at the bigger picture. It forces you to consider what exactly you value as worthwhile and important. This approach worked for Ebenezer Scrooge. Give it a try.

Five-ish years to live

This section gives you another upbeat exercise. In this one, you aren't dead yet, but you will be shortly. You have been told that you have at least five years left, but not much more. You are reassured that you will experience no pain, and you can carry on a totally normal life until your death. This exercise differs from the "tombstone test" above, in that it looks less at the 'big' picture and asks that you re-consider and re-evaluate your present day-to-day involvements and concerns.

Ponder the following question:

If you had just five more years to live, would you spend the time you have left any differently than the way you are spending it now?

If yes, what would you do that is different? Would you stay at your job? Would you live where you are living? Would you finally call your mother? And so on. . . .

Play the rating game

One of the simplest ways of uncovering your values and goals is to rate a list of the most common ones. Use this simple 10-point rating system, where 10 means "Extremely important to me," and 0 means "Not at all important." You're not ranking the items in order of least to most important. You're just considering each item individually and rating it on a scale of 1 to 10. Take a stab at it:

____ Achieving financial success

____ Being seen as smart

____ Being powerful

____ Being a leader

____ Winning at most things

____ Helping others

____ Being seen as physically attractive

____ Being admired

____ Being seen as honest

____ Spending time with family

____ Spending time with friends

____ Achieving fame

____ Being respected

____ Being loved

____ Having a strong spiritual foundation

The purpose of this exercise is to get you to re-assess specific goals and involvements in terms of their value and importance for you. After you rate these values and goals, take a moment to consider which items you rated a 7 or greater. Elaborate on what that value or goal means to you. For example, does "financial success" mean having millions of dollars, or does it mean having enough money so that you don't have to worry about paying your bills? A sentence or two should do it. Hopefully, completing this exercise will help you discover something about what is important to you, and perhaps identify some aspects of your life that you may want to change.

Things I love to do

This exercise is a lot easier. Here I'd like you to simply list 15 things that you really enjoy doing. I'm not talking here about bettering the world, I'm talking about things you really like to do. It can be anything — traveling, playing a favorite sport, reading pot-boilers, learning, gardening, sleeping, watching TV, or whatever else you really like to spend your time on. Sometimes just putting these activities down on paper can trigger a realization that you're missing out. Then ask yourself:

"Why am I not doing more of these things?"

If you love playing golf or you'd like to spend more time traveling, ask yourself why you're not spending more time on these kinds of activities. Later sections in this chapter can help you figure out how to find the time to build in the activities you love into your busy life.

Some other intriguing questions to ponder

If your brain isn't completely drained by now, here are several questions that you can ask yourself to get to know your values and goals a little better. If you'd rather not ponder these questions now, jot down the questions and pull one out next time you find yourself waiting in a long line or sitting on a plane or train.

- ✔ If I could come back in another lifetime as someone else, who would it be? Why?
- ✔ If I had oodles of money, what would I do with it?
- ✔ If I could make only three phone calls before I had to leave this world, who would I call? What would I say?
- ✔ And the old job-interview favorite: Where do I want to be in one year? In five years?

Actualizing Your Values, Reaching Your Goals

Having identified some of your more important values, you may realize that there may be more lip service than follow-through. We have a tremendous ability to hold a set of values we feel are meaningful, yet in our day-to-day lives we can sometimes fail to recognize their importance. Thus, we may value highly the notion of spending time with our family, yet find ourselves, for whatever reason, actually spending very little time interacting with family members, even when we have the chance. The way to avoid this trap is to become more conscious of how exactly you do spend your time, money, and energy.

Staying on track

This exercise will help you organize much of the material culled from the preceding exercises and also permit you to assess the extent to which you are actualizing and achieving those goals and values you feel are highly important to you. The following sections take you through this process.

Step 1: Ranking your primary values and goals

From what you discovered about yourself by doing all the preceding exercises, come up with a ranked list of your top 10 values. These values can include more abstract ones (such as honesty and integrity), and more specific goals (spend more time with family, get more involved with community, and so on).

Step 2: Evaluating your progress

In a second column, rate the extent to which you feel you have achieved or actualized those values and goals listed in the first column. Again, use a simple 10-point scale, where 10 indicates "Completely," and 0 indicates "Not at all."

To help you think of specific goals and values, here are some categories to get you started: Job/Career, Family, Friends, Health, Money, Hobbies, Interests, Travel, and Spirituality.

My important values and goals

My success at actualizing these values or reaching these goals

_____   _____

_____   _____

_____   _____

_____   _____

_____   _____

_____   _____

_____   _____

_____   _____

_____   _____

_____   _____

Making the time

Actualizing your values and reaching your goals requires time. And because you are incredibly busy already, finding the time for the more important things in your life may take some planning. You need to schedule your priorities, rather than merely prioritizing your schedule. In other words, start out by determining which activities are more important in your life, and then make the time to do them.

To help you identify those activities, here is a starter list for you to begin with. For each of the items below, indicate the extent to which each is a priority and exactly how, when, and where you can find or create the time for that priority.

I would like to spend more time....	*How, when, and where can I do this?*
With my kids	_____
With my spouse	_____
With friends	_____
On my job or career	_____
On a hobby or interest	_____
Playing sports	_____
Reading	_____
Keeping in shape	_____
Nurturing my soul	_____
On community activities	_____
Traveling	_____
(Add any others you may have)	
_____	_____
_____	_____
_____	_____

No Joke: Humor Is Great Stress Medicine

If you take life too seriously, you can just about guarantee that your stress level will be higher than it has to be. Life is filled with hassle, inconvenience, and a myriad of other nuisances that can either drive you crazy or bring a smile to your face. And even the more serious problems that may come our way often contain a trace of humor. Humor gives you the ability to defuse much of the potential stress and pressure all around you. A sharp sense of the absurd combined with a dash of whimsy can make your life far less stressful.

He (or she) who laughs, lasts

Humor is a more serious stress-reducer than you may think. Here are some of the ways it can lower your stress level:

- **It relaxes your body.** We know that the physical act of laughing can result in an overall lowering of your physiological stress level. After rising briefly while you are laughing, your blood pressure drops and your heart rate slows. The brain may also release endorphins, which can induce a more calming physical state.

- **It can enhance your immunity.** Researchers are beginning to discover that humor may have even more important health-enhancing effects. Laughter reduces your body's production of stress hormones while increasing production of disease-resisting T-cells and the chemical interferon, all of which can result in a stronger immune system.

- **It gives you perspective.** Humor creates distance and objectivity. If you can find some way to see a potentially stressful situation in a humorous way, you reduce the stress potential of that experience.

- **It can get you to take *yourself* less seriously.** Much of your stress comes from giving too much importance to how you see yourself or how others see you. If you can learn how to laugh at yourself, you rob other people — and circumstances themselves — of their ability to trigger your stress.

Some humorous suggestions

Very few of us would admit to *not* having a good sense of humor. Yet too often, we lose the ability to laugh (or at least smile) at the nonsense and lunacy of life all around us. You don't have to be a standup comic or dazzle the group with side-splitting one-liners to make humor work for you. Here are some ways you can make humor one of your stress-reducing tools.

✔ **Reframe the situation.** Dr. Joel Goodman, director of the HUMOR Project in Saratoga Springs, New York, suggests that if you are having trouble finding humor in a potentially stressful situation, try to see that situation through someone else's eyes. Try to imagine how a friend with a particularly offbeat sense of humor may see it. Or ask yourself how not finding a parking spot or losing your wallet may have been handled on an episode of *Seinfeld*.

✔ **Be around others who make you laugh.** The humor of other people can be contagious. Not only can their laughter and humor lower your stress level, but you can begin to talk about your own stresses in more comical ways.

✔ **Tickle your fancy.** Try to find and collect bits of humor that you can use to induce a smile or a laugh. It could be that picture of you with that ridiculous look on your face. Stick it up on your bathroom mirror. Or it may be a humorous quip or cartoon that makes you chuckle. Put that on the fridge or stick it on your desk at work. Whenever I am stressed by the need to clean up the house, I recall that marvelous Joan Rivers quip: "I hate housework! You make the beds, you do the dishes — and six months later you have to start all over again."

Anything that can evoke a smile can change your mood for the better.

Blow things up

Exaggeration is a great way of diffusing a potentially stressful situation, robbing it of much of its impact. One form of exaggeration uses the *Blow-up Technique.* Here's how it works. Suppose you are angry because your neighbor has the TV sound turned up too loud. Let your imagination take it from there. Now imagine that he has turned it up full blast. Not only that but he has turned every radio he owns up to ear-splitting levels. You notice that you hear live music and realize that here is a high-school band practicing in his living-room. The walls are now shaking. You get a phone call from your cousin a half a mile away asking what's going on. The police and fire-department are arriving . . . and then you smile.

Or imagine this. Suppose you find yourself stressed in a crowded elevator. Now imagine that this already crowded elevator stops at the next floor and a dozen more people get on. Totally full, with no room for anyone else, imagine that the next stop has another dozen or so people all eager to join the group. And they do. People are standing and lying every which-way. You do not have enough room to move even a finger. There is talk of being listed in the Guiness Book of Records. Again you smile.

Exaggeration and distortion can help you put things into clearer perspective. Try it.

When funny is not so funny

Not all humor is that funny — or even stress reducing. Laughing at someone, or using sarcastic or hurtful humor is really a form of disguised aggression, and while it may lower your stress level for the moment, it can feed on itself and create a far more stressful result in the long run. If you are going to laugh at someone's foibles and failings, make that person you.

Do Something Good for Someone Else

Doing something for another person can act as a stress buffer, enhancing your stress resilience. Most often, you get as much if not more, than you give. And this can be achieved without drastic commitments on your part. You do not have to become a Mother Teresa, or have homeless families come and live with you. Small, simple acts of generosity and kindness can go a long way.

How helping helps

The rewards of helping others may not have to wait until the hereafter. Here are some ways in which doing some form of community service can be good for your stress level:

- ✔ **It gives you a sense of purpose.** For many of us, at least some of our stress comes from a feeling of uncertainty about the nature of our existence and a search for some meaning and purpose to our lives. Helping others can add to a sense of doing something worthwhile with our lives, and making a genuine contribution to others. We feel better when we help.

- ✔ **It connects you.** Almost all acts of community service (short of writing an anonymous check) bring you into contact with someone else. It could be the person or group you are helping, an agency or service, a board, a committee, or a fellow volunteer or care-giver. The act of helping adds to your social support system, and increases your sense of connectedness to the world around you.

- ✔ **It keeps you busy.** Helping others in your community, in whatever form, is an involvement that channels your time and energy. It can distract you from your cares and worries and focus your attention in a rewarding and certainly less-stressful direction.

✔ **It increases your sense of self-worth.** When we help others, we feel good about ourselves. Our self-esteem is enhanced; we feel valued. Because so much of our stress is related to a feeling of a lack of self-worth, doing for others becomes a truly valuable way of changing the way you see yourself.

Where do I start?

Often the biggest obstacle to volunteering is going to the trouble of figuring out what to do and where to go. Most communities have one or more umbrella organizations or volunteer clearinghouses that are aware of all the volunteering opportunities in your area. To find it, call up any major volunteer group. They will know where to send you.

Here are some ideas of ways to volunteer:

✔ Become a Big Brother or Big Sister.

✔ Volunteer to help out at a local homeless shelter.

✔ Help out at a library.

✔ Help at a local museum (serve as a tour guide or help with fundraising).

✔ Improve a neighborhood garden, park, or sidewalk.

✔ Coach kids in a team sport.

✔ Deliver food to the homebound or the elderly.

✔ Become a tutor in the public school system.

✔ Help administer a favorite charity.

✔ Help out at the ASPCA or Humane Society.

✔ Help organize a blood drive.

✔ Be part of a hotline.

✔ Teach literacy for adults.

✔ Become part of an ESL (English as a second language) program.

✔ Help with fundraising at a radio or television station.

✔ Work at a nursing home.

✔ Be a helper at a daycare center.

✔ Assist at a senior citizen center.

You'll live longer

Some research now suggests that the benefits of altruism may not be only psychological. In one study, researcher Allan Luks, executive director of Big Brothers/Big Sisters in New York City, found that volunteers who presented some of the more commonly reported stress symptoms — headache, arthritis pain, back pain — reported a reduction of these symptoms. The pain, it would seem, was masked by the positive involvement of the volunteers.

In a second study, Phyllis Moen, Ph.D., at Cornell University in Ithaca, New York, looked at the effects of volunteering on women's physical health and longevity. She found that those women who devoted time and effort to a volunteer organization lived longer than those who did not. They were less likely to be depressed, and felt more satisfaction with the quality of their lives. In a related study, conducted at the University of Michigan on men who volunteered their time and efforts at least once a week, the researchers found that the death rate for these individuals was about half that of those who did not volunteer. Maybe it really is better to give than to receive?

Random kindness works too

Remember, you can be altruistic in ways that don't involve a regular time commitment or membership in an organization. You can freelance. Dozens of opportunities exist for you to help someone or to do something positive for some other person. Random acts of kindness — a kind word, a small deed, a courtesy — all work to produce positive and satisfying feelings within you, and within the people you interact with.

Helping hints

In his book, *The Healing Power of Doing Good*, Allan Luks offers some guidelines as to what kinds of volunteering experiences are the most stress-effective. Here are some of his suggestions:

- **Find situations that bring you directly into contact with others who need the help.** Stuffing envelopes is okay, but you'll find greater satisfaction in a hands-on situation.

- **Find an area of helping where you feel empathy for those you are working with.**

- **Find an involvement that can utilize a skill or ability that you have.**

- **Don't overcommit yourself.** You're better off starting small and adding on.

- **Exert yourself to reach out.** Stretch yourself in some way.

Add a Spiritual Dimension

Having a belief in something greater than your immediate experience can be a powerful force in helping you create inner peace and cope with the stress in your life. We live in a universe that is both mystifying and, at times, overwhelming. We attempt to give meaning and purpose to our all-too-brief lives. Faith in something bigger, something cosmic can help us come to grips with the unknown and perhaps unknowable. No one right way exists for finding a sense of spiritual connectedness. For many, this belief may take the form of a belief in God and involvement in a traditional religious system of beliefs. However, your spirituality may take a different form. It may be a belief in a more global, more vaguely articulated higher power or higher purpose. Or it may take the form of a belief in such values as the human spirit, the human community, or nature.

How faith helps you cope with stress

Whatever the form your spiritual beliefs take, growing evidence shows that faith can be a powerful stress-buffer, enhancing your ability to cope with life's more serious stresses. Faith can help you cope with illness and it may even help you live longer. The reasons why faith helps are both direct and indirect:

- **Faith can provide meaning and purpose.** Having a deeply felt belief system can help us cope with many of the perplexing and distressing questions that surround the meaning of existence. Why are we here? What is the meaning and purpose of life? What happens when we die?

- **Faith can strengthen stress-effective values.** Virtually all religions promote values of love and kindness to others and condemn those stress-producing feelings and actions such as anger, hostility, and aggression.

- **Faith can provide hope and acceptance.** It encourages a sense of optimism and hopefulness that things will work out for the best. Faith also helps you accept what you know will not work out and what you cannot control.

- **Faith unites you with others.** It can create a sense of community that often brings people together in a mutually supportive way. Having others to be with and share with can lower your stress. Belonging to a religious organization can put you into contact with others in the wider community who are less fortunate in some way and allows you to play a helping role.

- **Faith can calm you.** It often involves prayer and contemplation, which, like meditation and other forms of bodily relaxation described earlier, can result in a range of physical changes that reduce stress.

The power of the Word

Dr. Herbert Benson, a pioneer in the field of faith, relaxation, and stress reduction, has studied the role of prayer and its effects on stress. Dr. Benson found that by having individuals include words or sentences with religious meaning in their program of meditative relaxation, the levels of relaxation they attained were significantly higher than in those who did not include religious content. The content could be as simple as a word or phrase taken from a traditional prayer (The Lord's Prayer, for example), or a word from the *Bible* (*shalom,* meaning "peace," or *echad,* meaning "one").

The power of belief

A number of studies now document the importance of faith in strengthening one's coping ability. Just take a look at these:

- A recent National Institute for Mental Health study, for example, found that for those for whom religious beliefs were a central element in their lives, the amount of depression experienced was lower than for a control group.

- In another study, researchers, in Evans County, Georgia, looked at the stress-reducing effects of regular churchgoers when compared with non-churchgoers. They found that blood pressure measurements were significantly lower for the committed churchgoers. In a different study, in Washington County, Maryland, researchers found that those who attended church on a routine basis were much less likely to die of heart attacks than were infrequent churchgoers. (They made sure the results had nothing to do with smoking, drinking, and other variables that may have clouded the results.)

- In a study conducted in Israel, researchers compared the health of groups of secular and orthodox Israelis, and found that the less religious or non-religious group had a four times greater risk of having a heart attack when compared with their religious counterparts. Also, the non-religious group was found to have higher levels of cholesterol than did the more religious group.

How to start

If you are a follower of a particular religious denomination and have been saying that you would like to spend more time attending services and getting more involved, now may be the time to do that. Again, spirituality doesn't need to involve worshipping in a traditional religious sense. It could be an ecumenical gathering or the Ethical Culture Society. Look around your neighborhood and see if you can find a group that reflects your beliefs and values. Try it out for a period of time and, if you feel good about the place, become a member. Join in on activities, both of a religious nature and a non-religious nature. Attend as regularly as you can. Volunteer for committees you may enjoy or derive satisfaction from. If you are already a member, but have let things slide, reconsider becoming more involved.

A Little Wisdom Never Hurts

A storehouse of collected wisdom can insulate you from many of life's stresses. If your collection is a little thin, you can begin collecting the wisdom of others. Kindergarten wisdom, chicken-soup stories, sayings, affirmations, insights, parables, and maxims can help you cope with a potentially stressful situation. Stick them on your refrigerator or bathroom mirror. Here are some of my favorites to start you off:

"When you get there, there isn't any there there." —Gertrude Stein

"If I had my life to live over, I'd try to make more mistakes next time. I would relax, I would limber up. I would be sillier than I have been this trip. I know of very few things I would take seriously. I would be less hygienic. I would take more chances. I would take more trips. I would climb more mountains, swim more rivers, and watch more sunsets. I would eat more ice cream. I would have more actual troubles and fewer imaginary ones." —John Killinger

"I am an old man and have known a great many troubles — but most of them never happened." —Mark Twain

"No one on their deathbed ever wished they had spent more time at the office."

"It's not the large things that send a man to the madhouse. Death he's ready for, or murder, incest, roguery, fire, flood . . . no, it's the continuing series of small tragedies that send a man to the madhouse . . . not the death of his love, but a shoelace that snaps with no time left. . . ."
—Charles Bukowski

"Live each day as if it was your last because someday you're going to be right." —Anonymous

"Life is what happens while you're busy making other plans."
—John Lennon

"Rule Number 1: Don't sweat the small stuff.

"Rule Number 2: It's all small stuff." —Robert S. Eliot, M.D.

"The true value of a person is to be measured by the objects he pursues."
—Anonymous

"If you never want to make a mistake, do nothing, say nothing, be nothing." —Anonymous

"Other people are not in this world to live up to your expectations." —Fritz Perls

"People are about as happy as they make up their minds to be." —Abraham Lincoln

"For every minute you are angry, you lose sixty seconds of happiness." —Ralph Waldo Emerson

Part IV

Managing Your Stress in Real Life

"I've tried Ayurveda, meditation, and aromatherapy, but nothing seems to work. I'm still feeling nauseous and disoriented all day."

In this part . . .

1 help you develop day-to-day habits for home and work that will ultimately help you live a less stressful life. For example, the simple act of taking a break and doing a few stretches can really reduce the effects of stress at work. And has it occured to you that if you do more fun things in life — hang out with friends or spend time on a hobby — you'll be better able to deal with stress.

Chapter 14

De-Stress at Work (And Still Keep Your Job)

In This Chapter

▶ Identifying your work stress

▶ Understanding why your workday really starts the night before

▶ Taking the stress out of commuting

▶ Building stress-management into your workday

▶ Creating a stress-resistant workspace

▶ Coming home more relaxed

*I*f you feel that your job is stressful, don't feel that you're alone. Ask a variety of people where most of their stress comes from; chances are that the answer will be "my job." The specific source of work stress can be impossible clients, a terrible boss, dreadful coworkers, ridiculous deadlines, nasty office gossip, or not having seen daylight or your first-born in the last two months. So before you're a candidate for a job-burnout seminar (and certainly before you do something you may regret later), read this chapter. You find out how to regroup, get a grip, and minimize your stress at work.

Ten Signs That Show You're Stressed at Work

Some people thrive on the adrenaline rush they get from diving into the "challenges" they face at work. But if you're not stimulated and feel that you're drowning instead, then work stress may be the problem.

See if you recognize the signs of work stress — check off the symptoms that describe you while you're at work:

_____ You're often irritable.

_____ You have trouble concentrating.

_____ You're tired.

_____ You've lost much of your sense of humor.

_____ You get into more arguments than you used to.

_____ You get less done.

_____ You get sick more often.

_____ You care less about your work.

_____ Getting out of bed on a workday morning is a major effort.

_____ You have less interest in your life outside of work.

A survey by Northwestern National Life Insurance Company found that twice as many workers today consider their jobs "highly stressful" compared with workers in 1985. The survey also found that about one third of respondents seriously consider leaving their jobs because they feel their jobs are too stressful. About one out of every seven workers will actually quit to escape the stress, according to the survey.

Know What's Triggering Your Work Stress

All right, so you're stressed at work. One of the key steps in managing your work stress is knowing where the stress comes from. Simply check off any of the items below that you feel are a major source of your stress:

_____ Work overload (too much to do)

_____ Work underload (too little to do)

_____ Too much responsibility

_____ Too little responsibility

_____ Dissatisfaction with current role or duties

_____ Poor work environment (noise, isolation, danger, and so on)

_____ Long hours

_____ Lack of positive feedback or recognition

_____ Job insecurity

_____ Lousy pay

_____ Excessive travel

_____ Limited chances for promotion

_____ Prejudice because of sex, race, or religion

_____ Problems with the boss or management

_____ Problems with clients

_____ Problems with coworkers, staff

_____ Office politics

_____ A grueling commute

You have others? Jot them down:

_____

_____

_____

Researcher Robert Karasek and his colleagues at the University of Southern California found that the two most stressful aspects of a job are:

1. **Lots of pressure to perform.** Tight deadlines, limited resources, productions quotas, severe consequences for failing to meet management's goals — any or all of these can result in a highly pressured work environment.

2. **A lack of control over the work process.** Stress often results when you have little or no input regarding how your job should be done.

What Can You Change?

Pinpoint your stress triggers at work and then ask yourself to what extent you can remove or at least reduce the impact of that stress. In some cases, you don't have the ability to eliminate some of the sources of stress at work: Getting the boss transferred may take some doing; and asking for a raise the day after the company announces downsizing plans may not be in your best interest. What you *can* change, however, is *you*. You can manage your stress and reduce its consequences by applying some of the ideas in this section.

Start your workday unstressed

Getting to your job in reasonable condition is half the battle. By the time you open your office door (if you have one), you don't want to feel as if you've already fought (and probably lost) several of life's minor skirmishes. Get a leg up on your work stress. Hit the ground running. Start your day the night before. Here's how:

- ✔ **Go to bed.** Not getting enough sleep the night before can be a real stress-producer. Your stress threshold is lowered. You find that you're more irritable and find it much harder to concentrate. People and situations that normally wouldn't get to you, now do. Arriving at work tired is a guarantee that this isn't going to be one of your better stress days. (If getting to sleep is a problem, take a look at "Getting a Good Night's Sleep" in Chapter 8.)

- ✔ **Get up a tad earlier.** Getting out of bed even a few minutes earlier in the morning can give you enough of a safety net so that you don't find yourself rushing, looking for something at the last minute, and racing out the door with a powdered donut in your hand.

- ✔ **Eat breakfast.** To manage your stress, getting off on the right nutritional foot is important. When you wake up in the morning, as many as 11 or 12 hours have passed since you last ate. Your body needs to refuel. You may feel fine skipping breakfast, but studies show that people who do not eat a reasonable breakfast more often report feelings of fatigue and more stress later in the day. (If you don't know what to eat for breakfast, check out Chapter 8.)

- ✔ **Work out before you shower.** If you can manage it, getting some physical exercise before your workday starts can put you ahead of the game. Hitting the stationary bike, working the stair climber, or even walking briskly around the block can throw you into gear and get you ready for your day. Studies show that even short periods of exercise can speed up your heart rate, increase the amount of oxygen to your brain, and release endorphins, which can exert a calming effect. You're ready for anything your job might throw at you.

Generally, most people feel that Monday is the most stressful day of the week. Studies show that you're more likely to have a stroke or a heart attack on Monday morning than at any other time during the week.

Overcome SNS (Sunday night stress)

As the weekend winds to an end, many of you may find yourselves dreading Monday morning. The real culprit is Sunday night. It is only after you get to the office and spent a couple of hours on the job when your stress level lowers. The trick is figuring out how to cope with the night before. Take in these tips:

- ✔ Get to bed even a little bit earlier Sunday night. (Many people find that their Sunday night sleep is their worst of the week.)

- ✔ Avoid eating that late-night heartburn special, which is guaranteed to keep you up 'til Wednesday.

- ✔ Plan something relaxing and enjoyable that you can look forward to on Sunday night — rent a movie, curl up with a good book, take a bubble bath.

- ✔ Try not to schedule something you dislike as the first thing to do on Monday.

- ✔ Plan something you can look forward to on Monday. (How about lunch with a friend?)

Calm your commute

I remember all those years I commuted to my teaching job about 40 minutes out of the city. I had a "reverse commute." I, along with a handful of domestic engineering consultants (some people may call them cleaning ladies), headed out of the city to the hinterlands, while most other people traveled toward the city. While on the train, I read my newspaper, drank my coffee, relaxed, and had a good old time. Most people have a very different experience. They either battle for a seat (if they're lucky) on a crowded train, or sit in stop-and-go traffic for what seems like an eternity. Far from fun, commuting can be a major stressor. Following are some tips to help you reduce the stress of coming from and going to work:

- ✔ **Practice some "auto" relaxation.** Try this simple technique while you are caught in traffic or even while stopped for a red light: Using both hands, squeeze the steering wheel with a medium-tight grip. At the same time, tense the muscles in your arms and shoulders, scrunching up your shoulders as if you were trying to have them touch your ears. Hold that tension for about 3 or 4 seconds. Release all tension, letting go of any muscle tightness anywhere in your body. Let this feeling of relaxation spread slowly throughout your entire body. Wait a few minutes and do it again.

✔ **Beat the crowd.** Often, leaving a little earlier or a little later can make a big difference in the quality of your commute. You may get a seat, you may find that the traffic is less congested, and you may find that what was horrific yesterday becomes a lot more endurable.

✔ **Amuse yourself.** Commuting can seem like a joyless endeavor. You can, however, make your time in your car (or on the subway, bus, or train) productive, entertaining, or at least pleasant.

Personally, my favorite pastime when I find myself stuck in traffic or sitting on the subway is daydreaming. I relish the opportunity to mentally veg and let my mind wander. Of course, I could also choose from other, more socially redeeming diversions. Have some interesting reading material in your pocket or purse whenever you go out. The reading material could be an amusing little paperback or an article you cut out of the paper last week but haven't found the time to read.

You can also turn to your radio, CD, or personal stereo for solace. A good selection of music can soothe your travel. These days, the selection of audio books is incredibly wide. You can pick and choose from a list that includes most popular novels, poetry, self-help tapes, or collections of short-stories. You can even learn another language should you be so inclined.

De-stress during your workday

One of the secrets of effective stress management at work is finding ways to incorporate a variety of stress-reduction techniques into your workday. By using these methods on a regular basis you can catch your stress early — before it has a chance to turn into something painful or worrisome.

Take a look at these surefire strategies to help you nip that stress in the bud:

Cut muscle tension off at the pass

A day at work is usually a day filled with problems, pressures, and demands, with little time to think about your newfound relaxation skills. Your stress builds, and much of that stress takes the form of tension in your muscles. Drain that tension before it becomes more of a problem using some of the techniques described in Chapters 4 and 5. This may include trying some relaxed breathing, rapid relaxation, differential relaxation, meditation, imagery, or one of the many other relaxation techniques presented in these chapters. Some potential relaxation opportunities include the following:

> ✔ Every time you hang up your telephone
>
> ✔ When someone leaves your office and closes the door
>
> ✔ Whenever you find yourself in a boring meeting

Collect some mileage points

Get up and walk away from your desk — get some coffee or water, make copies. Walk around a lot, and at lunch be sure to get out of the office and take a quick stroll.

Stand up when you're on the telephone — or, at least some of the time you're on the phone. And if you have a cordless model, walk around. This gives your body a chance to use different sets of muscles and interrupts any buildup of tension.

Stretch and reach for the sky

For many of you, your days are characterized by long periods of sitting at a desk or stuck in a cramped work area, punctuated only by trips to the coffee or copy machine. Other folks are on their feet all day. In either case, stretching is a great way of releasing any tension that has accumulated in your muscles. Here are some of my favorite ways of stretching:

The cherry-picker

This stretch works well for shoulders, arms, and your back. Sit in your chair, with feet flat on the floor, or stand in place. Raise both your arms over your head and point your fingers directly toward the ceiling. Now, pretend to reach and pick a cherry on a branch that's just a little higher than your right hand. Stretch that hand an inch or so, and then make a fist. Squeeze for two or three seconds. Relax your hand. Do the same with your left hand. If cherries aren't your thing, consider apples.

The pec stretch and squeeze

This move is good for relieving tightness in your pectoral and deltoid muscles and upper back. Sitting at your desk, or standing up straight, put both of your hands behind your head with your fingers interlaced. Bring your elbows back as far as you can. (See Figure 14-1.) Hold that tension for 5 to 10 seconds, release the tension, and then do it a second and third time. Find various times in your day when you can repeat this stretch.

Figure 14-1:
Unwind a bit
with the pec
stretch and
squeeze.

The leg lift

This stretch relieves tension in your quadriceps (in the thighs) and strengthens your abdominal muscles. Sitting in a chair, lift both of your legs straight in front of you. At the same time, curl your toes toward you. (See Figure 14-2.) Hold that tension for 5 to 10 seconds, and then let your feet fall to the floor. Repeat two or three times, and at other points in your day.

Figure 14-2:
The leg lift
works your
quadriceps
and abdomi-
nal muscles.

The upper-back stretch

This stretch is great for relieving any tension in your upper back. Put your fingertips on your shoulders, with elbows out to the side. Raise your elbows until they are in line with your shoulders. Now bring your elbows forward until they touch or almost touch each other. (See Figure 14-3.) Hold that position for 5 to 10 seconds, and then let your arms fall comfortably to your side. Repeat two or three times, and also at different times in your day.

Figure 14-3: Use some elbow grease to ease tension in your upper back.

If you'd like some more stretching ideas, take a look at *Workouts For Dummies,* by Tamilee Webb (IDG Books Worldwide, Inc.). It has dozens of great ways you can stretch and release muscle tension.

Create a stress-resistant workspace

You may not be able to control every single aspect of your job, but you do have the power to control your personal work area. Your workspace can (literally) give you a pain in the neck, straining your muscles and tiring your body. The culprit may be an awkwardly-placed computer monitor, uncomfortable seating, poor lighting, or simply a totally cluttered desk that's hiding that memo you remember writing and now urgently need. Your life is stressful enough as it is. You don't need your workspace adding to your daily dose of stress. This section shows you a few ways to make your workspace a lot more stress-resistant.

Lights! Sound! Action!

Here are a few ways to take some of the stress out of your workspace. I realize that your workplace may not be entirely supportive of all of your (or my) stress-reducing efforts. I also realize that if you share a tiny cubicle with three others, it may be hard for you to burn incense, move in a couch, or install a multi-speaker stereo system and personal video player. Nevertheless, see what you can do with some of the following ideas:

- ✔ **Soothe yourself with sound.** If you can orchestrate it, listening to calming music at your work site can unruffle your feathers. A radio, tape or CD player, and some appropriate music can be very relaxing. Classical music, especially Bach and Mozart, works nicely. If these composers are too highbrow, try one of the "lite" radio stations. Just keep the volume down, or use a headset.

  Recent studies at the University of California found that listening to Mozart, particularly the piano sonatas, can improve significantly a person's ability to reason abstractly. Not only do stress levels go down, but IQ goes up. On the other hand, listening to Philip Glass or Metallica didn't enhance anything.

- ✔ **Lighten up.** Although I'm sure that a naked, 300-watt bulb dangling from your office ceiling can provide you with more than enough light, I am also sure that by the end of the work week you'll be searching for a stool and a rope. The right lighting in your workspace can reduce eyestrain and make your environment a more pleasant place to work. Go for soft and indirect lighting. Just make sure you have enough light.

- ✔ **Create visual resting spots.** Give your eyes — and your mind — a break. At regular intervals, look away from your computer screen or paperwork and focus on a distant object to "stretch your eyes." You can also create visual relief to your office by adding a few interesting objects. For example:

  - Strategically place one or more photographs of those you care about to bring a warm glow to your heart. Better yet, have the picture include a scene — a vacation, a gathering — that reminds you of a happy experience.

  - Place a plant or flowers in your workspace to add an air of beauty and relaxation to your workday. Some plants (such as English ivy and spider plants) are even said to help clean the air of indoor pollutants — an added bonus! For more on the air-purifying benefits of plants, check out `hammock.ifas.ufl.edu/txt/fairs/30881`— the University of Florida's Cooperative Extension Service Web site.

  - Hang some artwork that you find calming and peaceful.

- ✔ **Be scent-sible.** Fill a bowl with green apples to add a relaxing scent to your office. From time to time I sprinkle a little aftershave on top of the papers in my waste bin. Hey, call me crazy.

- ✔ **Have more than one dumbbell in your office.** Keep a set of weights or mini barbells in your office. In a spare moment or two you can rip through a set of reps and feel a bit more relaxed. Alternately, keep an elastic stretcher in your desk that you can use for both your arms and your legs.

- ✔ **Keep a toy chest.** What's an office without a few toys? (Balls that knock into each other . . . a game on your computer . . . that peg-jumping triangle game. . . .)

- ✔ **Don't get tied down.** One of those headsets that attaches to your telephone can free up your hands to do other things, like look through your e-mail, lift those weights, or play that computer game. The better ones are cordless and let you move around your office so that you can file, play Nerf basketball, or rearrange your books in order of their color.

Does your desk look like a wreck?

Your desk can cause you stress. Yes, that polished piece of mahogany (laminated particleboard?) can be your enemy. Take this short true or false quiz to see if it's time to de-stress your desk.

1. When new company employees first see your desk, they ask if your office has been vandalized recently. True or False?

2. Your desk smells funny. You distinctly remember leaving half a tuna sandwich under some folders last month, but haven't seen it since. True or False?

3. If you had to find an important memo on your desk in the next hour, and let's say your job depended on it, you would be better off spending that time calling a headhunter. True or False?

Answering True to any of the above suggests that too much of your stress may be desk-induced.

How can a neater desk reduce stress? Well, because the source of many types of stress comes from a feeling of being out of control, of being overwhelmed. When your work area looks like a battlefield, you feel the tension growing. And when you can't find that report you need, your stress level soars even higher. By organizing your files and piles, you get a sense (perhaps mistakenly) that there is some order in all the chaos. So, at the end of your workday straighten things up. Doing so takes only a few minutes, but the rewards are large. Check out Chapter 6 for some ideas and direction that can help you to eliminate desk and office clutter, and give your filing and organizing systems a tune-up.

Become EC (ergonomically correct)

Your desk or workspace can cause stress for other reasons besides disorganization. The problem is, your body was not designed to sit and work in one place for long periods of time. When you sit in a stationary position for long periods of time, your muscle groups contract. The blood flow to these muscles may become reduced, resulting in oxygen-deprived muscles. This can lead to pain, strain, muscle aches, and fatigue.

Here are some suggestions that can help you avoid that ergonomic pain in the neck:

- If you spend long periods of time typing at your computer, where and how you sit becomes important. The height of your chair in relationship to your keyboard and monitor are important variables to consider in avoiding excessive muscle tension and fatigue in your shoulders, neck, and upper back. You do not want to be straining your neck while looking at your monitor. Adjustability is the key. If your chair or table is too high or too low, replace it. Better yet, find an adjustable chair and table. Seat heights should range from 15 to 22 inches, depending on what your dimensions look like.

- There should also be some padded support for your lumbar (lower back) region. The backrest should be full-length, extending some 18–20 inches higher than the seat of your chair. If your lower back is not supported sufficiently, consider a *lumbar roll* — a cylindrical pillow that fits nicely in the small of your back.

- Your keyboard should be approximately at elbow level when you are seated. When using your keyboard, make sure that you fingers are lower than your wrist. To avoid repetitive-stress injuries (such as carpal tunnel syndrome), you may want to consider an ergonomically designed keyboard that reduces the strain on your wrists. You should also consider a support for your wrist when you are using your mouse.

- Having a foot rest is a good way of taking some of the strain off your legs and back, especially if you're short.

  A study carried out by AT&T on their telephone operators found that switching to easily adjustable tables and chairs resulted in a significant reduction of the reported discomfort, particularly in the back, shoulders, and legs. Operators could adjust the height of the table that held their monitors, their keyboards, and their chairs.

- Not all writing instruments are ergonomically equal. Find a pen that is particularly comfortable to work with. The grip should not result in your fingers becoming easily fatigued.

- If you spend a lot of time on your feet, finding the correct footwear becomes a necessity. If you find you have to trade some style for greater comfort, go for the comfort.

Tennis (ball) anyone?

When you find that your bodily tension is over the top (better yet, try this *before* you get to that point), pick up a tennis ball or other soft ball, squeeze it for 8 to 10 seconds, and then slowly release all the tension in your fingers and hand. Let that feeling of relaxation spread out to the rest of your body. Repeat several times throughout the day.

Listen to your mother: Sit up straight!

Sometimes your stress comes from the most unlikely of places — your chair, for example. Sitting improperly for long periods of time can result in bodily fatigue, tension, and, ultimately, pain. Sitting actually puts more pressure on your spinal discs than does standing. When you slump or hunch forward, the pressure is even greater. Sit back in your chair with your spine straight. Your lungs now have room to expand, and you place less strain on your back. You may find that you have to invest in a more supportive chair. Spend the bucks — a good chair is well worth the money.

Delegate your stress away

And sometimes that approach is the way to go. When you have more than enough to do, however, doing it all yourself is a guaranteed recipe for stress. Most often, the greatest obstacle people face when deciding whether they should delegate or not is the fear that the job won't get done as well as it would if they did it themselves. In fact, it may be the case that having a coworker or assistant to do the job results in a less than perfect outcome in terms of performance quality and effectiveness. However, that may not be such a disaster — the outcome may be quite satisfactory without being quite perfect. Sometimes lowering your standards, and settling for a less than perfect job, can result in less stress.

If you can't find anyone who knows how to do what you need to be done, it may be worthwhile to make the investment in time and train someone. Yes, it will take longer in the short run, but you'll probably be way ahead in the long run.

Nourish your body (and spirit)

What goes into your mouth from 9 to 5 (or from 8 to 7) can make a big difference in your stress level. Eating the wrong foods, or even eating the right foods, but in the wrong amounts, and/or at the wrong times can make it harder for you to cope with the stress in your life. Also, when you eat poorly, your body doesn't work as efficiently as it should. This means that you're not in the best position to handle all the pressures and demands you must face at work. Here are some ideas and suggestions that can help make what you eat an ally in your battle against stress, and not the enemy.

Do lunch (with a difference)

Although the days of the three-martini lunch are gone, you can still find the harried worker overloading his or her plate with the kinds of food that ensure a high stress level for the rest of the day. Some suggestions for powering up your body (and not creating a meltdown) for the afternoon:

- Never skip lunch — no matter how busy your day gets.
- Eat less at your midday meal — no seconds.
- Eat stress-reducing foods. (Chapter 8 tells you what they are.)
- Don't drink any alcohol.
- Skip dessert.

Make your lunch break a stress break

Lunchtime isn't only about eating; it's a great time to work on lowering your stress. Try to get out of your work environment at lunch. Even if the outing is as simple as going for a walk around the block, go. Better yet, find a park, library, waterfront — anything relaxing — that can put you (however temporarily) into a different frame of mind. Find your lunch-time oasis.

Work it out

If you can swing it, one of the better things to do on your lunch break is to hit the gym or health club. Many clubs and gyms are conveniently located near work sites. A number of exercise facilities may even offer you a corporate discount for joining. Better yet, many companies and organizations have workout facilities right on their premises. Work up a sweat, take a shower, and then have a quick but nourishing bite to eat.

The coffee-free coffee break

The caffeine in two cups of coffee can increase your heart rate by as much as 15 beats per minute. It can also make you irritable and nervous. So forgo that third or fourth cup of coffee (and donut). Instead, eat something that adds to your body's ability to cope rather than weaken it, such as a:

- Cup of low-fat yogurt.
- Cup of fruit salad.
- Handful of mixed nuts.

✔ Piece of chocolate (one piece!).

✔ Piece of fruit.

✔ Cup of herbal tea.

✔ And, if you must have that nth cup of coffee, at least try going the unleaded (decaffeinated) route.

Avoid beans

Many people remember Ronald Reagan for his significant accomplishments, and rightfully so. What I remember, however, are those jars of jelly beans strategically positioned in his office. While admittedly colorful, having gobs of candy at hand at work may not help you with your stress. A sugar fix energizes you in the short run, but leaves you flagging later in the day. You're better off avoiding this and any other candy snack. If you need a pick-me-up, try to choose something from the list in the section "The coffee-free coffee break."

Coming Home More Relaxed (And Staying that Way)

You've had a long, long day. You're tired and dragging your tush. The last thing you want to do is take your work stress home with you. Consider these guidelines to make sure you arrive home in better shape than when you left work:

✔ **Create a to-do list for the next day.** Making lists is one of the simpler ways of getting control of your workday — and one of the easiest. All you have to do is make the list. You don't have to follow through, complete all the items on the list, or do any of them. Just having the list gives you a sense of personal control and provides you with a direction for your re-entry into work the next day.

✔ **After work, work out.** If early morning or lunch are impractical times to hit the gym or health club, consider exercising right after work. Take out your frustrations and worry on the stair climber or in a step class. Not only is this mode of venting healthier, you'll still have your job in the morning!

✔ **Leave your work at work.** One of the more common stress traps is to take your work-related stress and spread it around so that the other parts of your life now become stressful. I'm sure you have enough stress at home without importing more stress from your work. If you find that you absolutely have to take work home, be very specific about what you want to accomplish and how much time you want to spend doing it. Never take work home routinely. And try not to go to work on the weekends unless it is absolutely necessary.

Ah, home sweet home! But is it? Even if your ride home has been relatively non-stressful, opening your front door can lead to a whole new set of challenges. Walking straight into these stressors can catch you off guard and put you into a foul mood. When you get home, be sure to build in a short period of relative quiet — say 15 or 20 minutes — that can help you make the transition into your second world.

Following are some suggestions for low-stress segues:

- ✔ Take a relaxing bath or shower.
- ✔ Have a drink (one will do).
- ✔ Sit in your favorite chair and simply veg.
- ✔ Listen to some relaxing music.
- ✔ Read a chapter from a good book.
- ✔ Work out.
- ✔ Take a relaxing walk.

If, when you open your door, chaos descends, and it is clear that none of these activities are even remotely possible, you may want to consider implementing some of these relaxing segues *before* you reach home. I find that sipping a latte and doing the crossword puzzle at the local coffee shop near my home works for me. You can take that walk or spend a few minutes in a local park (with a good book?) before you open your door. You are now ready to cope with the chaos.

Chapter 15

Maintaining a Stress-Resilient Lifestyle

• •

• •

Managing your stress is a little like managing your weight. In the beginning, you're enthusiastic and, with much gusto and determination, you start dropping those pounds. Weeks (or maybe only days) later, your enthusiasm has begun to wane. You're even gaining back any weight that you may have lost. Your attempts at stress-reduction can easily fall victim to the same fate. Staying motivated and finding the time to practice your stress-management skills is not that easy.

You may also find that, even though you now have the right tools, you rarely use them. This common situation is much like belonging to a gym and never going. On most days, especially your busier ones, time flies by, and you don't even consider doing anything that even slightly resembles stress management.

This chapter shows you how to avoid many of the pitfalls that often derail your attempts to manage your stress over the long haul.

But there's more. Effective stress management means more than having the right stress-reducing tools and techniques. Stress management means knowing how to balance the pressures and demands in your life with positive satisfactions, personal pleasures, and a lifestyle that insulates you from the negative impact of stress. This chapter shows you how to create that balance and how to use these positives to enhance your overall stress-resilience.

Making It a Habit

One of the keys to successful stress management is turning your stress-reducing skills into habits. By integrating some bits of behavior into our daily life, we reduce our dependence on motivation and pure grit. Think of a habit like brushing your teeth. Rarely do you ask yourself, "Do I feel like brushing my teeth today?" No, you simply brush your teeth (or at least I hope you do). This behavior — brushing your teeth — has become a habit. You repeat this behavior day in and day out, with little effort or resistance on your part. This is what you need to do with your stress-management behaviors. The following sections provide some suggestions for making stress management a habit — and one of your better ones.

Making use of those found moments

Sometimes, the situation you are in makes you a prisoner of the moment. You cannot escape. You have to be where you are, and, to make things worse, you don't have much to do while you're there. You may be waiting in line at the grocery store or (gasp!) at the Bureau of Motor Vehicles. Why not capitalize on these situations and turn them into opportunities to bring some stress management into your life? Sneak in a little relaxed breathing, meditation, rapid relaxation, imagery, coping self-talk, or any of the many other stress-relievers you have mastered. Many of the stress-management methods in these chapters work quite well, even if you have only a minute or two.

And where exactly do I find these found moments?

When to use your stress-management skills isn't always obvious. Take a look at Table 15-1 for some potential times to use these skills, along with some suggestions of relaxation techniques you may want to use. If you want to find more detailed information on the relaxation techniques listed in the table, turn to Chapters 4 and 5.

Table 15-1 Places to Practice Your Stress Management Skills	
Place	*Relaxation Method to Try*
Sitting in a boring meeting	Diaphragmatic breathing
In transit — on a bus, train, or taxicab	Guided imagery
Flying in an airplane	Meditation
In an elevator or on an escalator	Rapid relaxation
Getting your hair cut	Autogenic suggestion

Place	Relaxation Method to Try
Sitting in the dentist's chair	Progressive muscle relaxation
A bathroom break	Deep breathing
Lying in bed, as you fall asleep	Personal imagery

While you're waiting, exhale

Having to wait for somebody or something is one of the better opportunities you have to build some stress relief into your day. Rarely a day goes by in which, at some point, you don't find yourself having to wait. Here is just a partial list of those all-too-common waiting opportunities. Try to take advantage of these opportunities in your own life.

- ✔ Waiting at a stoplight
- ✔ Waiting for an elevator
- ✔ Waiting in traffic
- ✔ Waiting for a train or bus
- ✔ Waiting for the microwave to cook your food
- ✔ Waiting on hold on the phone
- ✔ Waiting in your doctor's office
- ✔ Waiting for a TV commercial to be over
- ✔ Waiting for a file to download
- ✔ Waiting in line at the supermarket
- ✔ Waiting at the ATM machine
- ✔ Waiting in line anywhere

Relaxed breathing, deep breathing, imagery, meditation, and rapid relaxation, and other "Instant De-stressers" are some of the short, quick, and effective ways of taking the edge off your stress whenever you find yourself waiting.

Remembering Your Ps (Prompts) and Cues

In life, sometimes you need a little reminding. You need someone or something to nudge you to do things. In your younger days, your parents probably filled this role. (And what a fine job they did.) These days, however, you may

Using a "stress dot"

A *stress dot* is nothing more than a sticker to remind you to keep stress management an active part of your life. Stress dots can be very useful tools in triggering your memory. To create a stress dot, look at your local office-supply store for very small circles of brightly-colored sticky paper. (About ⅛-inch in diameter should do it.) Or you can make your own stress dots by cutting small circles out of anything with an adhesive back. Place this dot in a strategic spot, so that it becomes a cue or prompt and can signal you to do something stress-relieving.

Here are some places that may work for you:

- The face of your watch
- Your watchband
- Your steering wheel
- Your refrigerator door
- Your computer monitor
- Your keyboard
- Your pen
- Your coffee cup
- Your telephone
- Your television set
- A light switch

find that you have to do your own reminding. This section provides you with some ways you can remind yourself to use your new stress-management tools. All you have to do is use your stress prompts and your stress cues.

The idea here is to use naturally and frequently occurring behaviors — your prompts and cues — as reminders. The sight of my front door reminds me that I need to take out my keys. Getting into a car triggers me to fasten my seatbelt. These behaviors are automatic. I don't have to think about them much. The same principle can help you build in ways of managing your stress. Whenever you are presented with a prompt or cue, follow it up by doing an instant de-stresser exercise — deep breathe, meditate, use some imagery or rapid relaxation, and so on.

Here are some commonly found stress prompts and cues to get you started:

- Hanging up the phone
- Looking at your watch
- Shutting your office door
- Stopping at a stop sign

- ✔ Listening to your telephone messages
- ✔ Turning off your computer
- ✔ Turning off your TV
- ✔ Turning off a light

Make an appointment with yourself

When you schedule something, you're more likely to follow through with it. You almost always show up for appointments with your doctor, your dentist, your lawyer, your accountant, your dinner-date, and the person who cuts your hair. So why not use that same principle for other things in your life, like managing your stress? Try some of the following suggestions:

- ✔ **Schedule regular times during the week when you will do something to manage your stress.** Make Thursdays Lunch-with-a-Friend Day. Schedule Monday and Wednesday evenings as health club times.

- ✔ **Make your coffee break a stress break.** Set aside a few minutes mid-morning and mid-afternoon to drain some of that accumulating tension from your mind and body.

- ✔ **Commit part of each lunch hour to some stress-reducing activity.** Go to the gym or try meditating in a nearby park for 20 minutes.

- ✔ **Designate specific chunks of time during your week as times when you don't do the kinds of activities you normally wouldn't.** While these activities will be specific stress-management techniques, they can also be activities that are diverting and relaxing — listening to music, taking in a film, going for a swim, playing squash or tennis.

Log in once in a while

Try this suggestion for at least an entire day. On an index card, in your electronic organizer, or simply on a scrap piece of paper make a note of when you did something to reduce your stress. Be brief, making sure that your record-keeping doesn't add to your existing stress level. Here are some sample entries:

Time	Where	What I Did
9:30 a.m.	Bedroom	Meditated for 15 minutes
10:20 a.m.	Kitchen	Practiced deep breathing
Lunchtime	On the street	Did some stretching

(continued)

Time	Where	What I Did
3:30 p.m.	In the car stuck in traffic	Did some rapid relaxation
4:30 p.m.	Waiting for the elevator	Practiced relaxed breathing

You get the idea. You may find that by monitoring your stress-management attempts, you'll become more conscious of doing them and of doing them more often. Try it.

Become a freelance, unpaid, stress-management guru

The topic of stress frequently comes up in conversation, and if it doesn't, you can always bring it up yourself. When you do, you may find that most people have a great interest in your stress-management activities. People will ask you how you handle your stress. Tell them. In fact, show them. One of the best ways of mastering something is by teaching it to others. Teach a friend or interested listener one or more of your favorite stress-management techniques. You'll begin to feel somewhat proprietary about these tools and, as a result, feel more motivated to use them yourself.

Finding Your Oasis (Sand Optional)

To effectively manage your stress, you need a place where you can escape the pressures and demands of everything going on around you. In fact, you need *several* such places. Ideally, these should be places that are quiet, peaceful, and relaxing. These places become your oasis — your places of refuge in a stress-filled world. Places like this usually aren't that easy to come by. A wood-paneled study or a Zen garden may only be wishful figments of your imagination. The reality is, the place you use as an oasis may be your bathroom or your bedroom. But these can just as easily serve as places you retreat to when your soul needs a little peace and tranquility. Continue to add to your list of peaceful places. Your oases don't need to be magnificent. All you need is a place where, for at least a small part of the day, you won't be disturbed. In the following sections, I start you off with some suggestions.

Create an inner sanctum

Try to create a space within your home that you really like to spend time in. Have at least one feel-good room or an area that is emotionally welcoming. Your private corner can be anyplace — maybe a window seat, a warm kitchen, an inviting bedroom, or a cozy study — where you can close a door and feel hidden away from it all, where you feel unhurried and unhassled. This place is your inner sanctum, a space within a space to which you can retreat when the world outside feels less than hospitable, a place where you can sit, read, write, think, meditate, or just daydream. Designate this space as somewhere that you don't worry, pay bills, answer the phone, or do anything else that could even remotely increase your level of stress. The rewards of having a quiet retreat are immense.

Note, by the way, that these places are not the same places you designated as "worrying places" in Chapter 11. These are your "worry-free" places.

Take a bath

The bathroom may be the only room in your house where you feel like you can lock the door and be alone. One of the many things you can do in a bathroom is take a bath. A hot bath is a wonderful place to relax and totally let go. Stretched out and surrounded by warmth, in a bath you can give yourself permission to relax. Adding some soft lighting, gentle music, and a soothing drink, can make this place feel like heaven.

Park a while

Most towns and cities have wonderful parks where you can stroll aimlessly, taking in the activity around you, or becoming lost in your own thoughts and images. In the larger parks, you can often find yourself quite alone, one of the few places were there is no one else around. But the park doesn't have to be large. Some are no more than a small patch of grass, a few trees, and a bench or two. When I can, I find that walking through the park on my way to my office or coming home after work is a wonderful way of mellowing out and disassociating from my busy day.

Jogging, bicycling, or inline skating in the park are great ways of combining exercise with a sense of solitude. You can bring headphones or, better yet, simply enjoy being alone with your thoughts.

Seek sanctuary

We tend to think of houses of worship as religious sanctuaries, places for prayer. And, of course, they are. But churches and temples can also be visited for non-religious forms of expression. You can reflect, meditate, or simply lose yourself in reverie. They are quiet and often softly lit — ideal settings in which to be alone. Many churches and temples are quite majestic and sweeping in their architecture, inspiring and revitalizing even the most tired spirit. And, except for midnight Mass and Yom Kippur, your chances of finding an empty pew are excellent.

Become a lobbyist

Many hotels, especially some of the older ones, are wonderful buildings that can be a treat to spend time in. You won't be alone here, but chances are you won't be bothered. Although many people are coming and going, don't be surprised if you find a comfortable chair situated in a relatively quiet part of the lobby.

Lose yourself in the shelves

Bookstores, especially the larger ones, can be marvelous places to sit, write, and escape the pressures all around you. I consider my local bookstore my personal library. It's a great place to escape to a quieter mode. The catch? It can be a madhouse on weekends. On good days, however, the unhurried, not crowded floors, lined with wonderful books, become an inviting setting to which you can retreat.

And don't forget the public libraries. Libraries, especially the larger ones, are great places to spend an hour or more in relative solitude. Large tables, vast spaces, and enforced quiet all contribute to an ideal place to work, think, and imagine.

Accentuate the Positive (s)

When you think of reducing your stress, most often you think of ways of eliminating, or at least minimizing the negatives in your life. Get rid of as many of those unpleasant pressures and demands, and your life will be much less stressful. However, creating a lifestyle that is truly stress-resilient means not only eliminating the negatives, it also means finding and building-in positive sources of satisfaction and pleasure that compensate for those negatives that you haven't been able to eliminate. I call these your *stress buffers*. They include a wide range of activities, involvements, and commitments that bring positive feelings to your life.

STRESS QUIZ

Got a life?

Respond to the following statements with "very much," "so-so," or "not really."

✔ I have family I can rely on when I need to.

✔ I have friends I can talk to when problems arise.

✔ I have friends I enjoy spending time with.

✔ I have hobbies and/or interests I enjoy.

✔ I look forward to certain activities during the week.

✔ I get satisfaction from the work I do.

✔ I find my life satisfying and involving.

✔ My spiritual beliefs give me support and comfort.

✔ I enjoy meeting new people.

✔ I like trying new things.

✔ I take a vacation regularly.

✔ I enjoy nature and the outdoors.

✔ I frequently do things that are fun.

✔ I have an adequate income.

✔ I do things for others less fortunate.

Get a life

One of the keys to creating a stress-resilient lifestyle is living more than a one-dimensional life. This means looking at your lifestyle and figuring out what's missing. Complete the checklist in the nearby sidebar to determine whether your lifestyle is providing you with the stress buffers that are important in helping you resist the negative effects of stress.

Connecting with Others

Having people in your life you can talk to, complain to, cry with, and laugh with — not to mention go see a movie with — represent important stress-buffers in your life. Connecting with family members and with friends becomes one of the more important ways you can insulate yourself from stress and strengthen your ability to cope.

Family: The ties that bind

Although, at times, your family may seem like the *source* of much of your stress, for most people, family members can be an important source of caring and emotional support. After all, there are very few other people in your life who know you as well, and are by your side when the chips are down. Being with family, and sharing memories of times past can provide you with a sense of being part of something larger, something that feels warm and comforting. Family events such as birthdays, anniversaries, marriages, christenings, and bar and bas mitzvahs all bring with them a sense of repeated experience and family reunion and provide you with a sense of emotional connectedness that can buffer you from stress.

However, as you well know, maintaining family ties and holding on to those good feelings takes some effort. Make the time to be with those you care about. Work at making these relationships positive and satisfying. It's worth it.

Some research data verifies what seems intuitively true — that being in a good marriage can have stress-reducing benefits. A study conducted by Pamela Jackson, Ph.D., a sociologist at Duke University in Durham, North Carolina, found that, in supportive marriages, the amount of stress experienced by spouses in troubling times was significantly less than that reported by individuals in less supportive relationships. These individuals were less likely to become depressed when their lives became highly stressful. Other research supports these findings. It appears that being in a harmonious marriage results in fewer psychological and biological signs of stress.

You need a Monica, a Rachel, or a Chandler

When you ask people what they value most in life, near the top of that list, right under family, is friends. Most of us regret or will come to regret, that we neglect our friendships at the expense of other, often less rewarding activities. We wish we had spent more time with friends, called them more often, and worked harder to maintain and nurture our friendships.

Your friendships are probably your most important stress buffers. Friends provide company for you, bring you pleasure, and help relieve feelings of loneliness. Good friends listen to your problems, give you guidance, and support you emotionally. They are your therapists.

People with a strong social support system report experiencing less stress and are better able to cope with the stress that they *do* feel. Studies show that friendships can insulate you from the effects of stress in your life.

Having friends can lower your blood pressure, improve your immune system, and even increase your life span. In one research study of some 7,000 women conducted over 17 years, the researchers found that those women who had few friendships had a higher risk of dying from all kinds of cancer. Having good friends, it appeared, was even more protective than being in a marriage.

Another study found that among patients with coronary heart disease, those individuals who were neither married nor had close friends were more likely to die in a five-year period than were those who were married, had a close friend, or both. It seems that having friends and family can reduce the destructive effects of stress on your body.

Do Something, Anything

Finding satisfaction in a hobby or interest is an important way of reducing your stress. Any hobby — whether it's collecting beer cans or stuffed animals, doing some bird-watching, or whatever else suits your fancy — can be absorbing and diverting. The fact is, it really doesn't matter that much what you do. It's a big mistake to reject or abandon a hobby because you think it's unworthy, or less esteemed by others. The fact that you are doing something is what counts. Leave your ego out of it.

I have a friend who collects baseball cards. He can spot a Mickey Mantle rookie card at 30 paces. He visits the card shows, chats with the dealers and other buyers, and generally seems to have a fine old time. He looks forward to arranging his new acquisitions, merging and purging with obvious glee and delight. Though I have little interest myself in collecting these cards, I must admit that I am a little envious of the pleasure and sense of satisfaction my friend feels about these 2x3-inch colored squares of cardboard.

For him, and for countless others, having a hobby or pastime provides an incredibly positive experience that provides joy and interest and acts as a stress buffer, insulating them from much of their daily worries and hassles. When you're engrossed in a hobby or pleasurable pastime, the time seems to fly by, and, often, you're with others who share your interest.

But what about you? Ask yourself how you spend your spare time and if any activities or involvements could add to your life.

Join the group

Every city or town has groups and organizations that can put you together with other like-minded people. By sharing a common interest, you establish a natural bond that can transform your relationship with others in the group from mere acquaintances to good friends. Here are some groups you may want to consider joining:

- Your local church or temple
- Your child's school (attend PTA meetings, be a class parent, organize a fundraiser, serve on safety patrol)

- Your neighborhood association
- A special interest group (a book group, a nature group, a music group, a political group, a singles group, and so on)

Learn a thing or two

You have numerous opportunities to attend classes or join a course on something you find interesting. Can't think of where to go? Here are some suggestions:

- City universities, colleges, and community colleges
- YMCA or YWCA
- Language classes
- Craft schools
- Cooking classes
- Writing classes
- Aerobics classes
- Dancing lessons
- Music lessons

Get in the game

Or, consider getting involved in a sport or a game. Lest you've forgotten, here's a short list of the more popular offerings:

- Bridge
- Tennis
- Golf
- Poker
- Mah-jongg
- Lawn bowling
- Bowling
- Billiards
- Swimming
- Gymnastics

- ✔ Ice skating
- ✔ Baseball
- ✔ Basketball
- ✔ Volleyball
- ✔ Hockey
- ✔ Bingo
- ✔ Scuba diving

Step forward: Serve soup

One of the better stress buffers is becoming a volunteer. You can start small. Help out at your local library, church, or synagogue. You can help those who are house-bound, or be a mentor to a child in the school system. There is no shortage of ways in which you can help others. If you're short on ideas, take a look at the list of volunteering suggestions in Chapter 13.

Get a pet

Having a pet is a marvelous way of combating your stress. Convincing data shows that pets can indeed reduce your stress, and serve as important sources of emotional comfort. The presence of a pet in the room can put you at ease, evoke feelings of caring and tenderness, and provide you with a companion. Pets can lower your blood pressure, make you feel more relaxed, and distract you from your own day-to-day worries and concerns. And because they don't complain, have opinions to disagree with, or know how to operate the television remote, pets trigger less conflict and friction than do the people who live in your house. As a bonus, they can even take care of any roach or rodent problems.

Cultivate calm

How many times have you heard of a gardener going ballistic? In fact, some scientific literature documents the positive, stress-buffering effects of gardening. Gardening is now widely thought of as a form of therapeutic intervention in many medical and psychiatric settings. Author/gardener Linda Yang points out that the word paradise comes from the Greek *paradeisos,* meaning "private park of kings" — where peace and beauty dwelled amid fruit trees and flowers.

Working in a garden can be satisfying. You can find something soothing and peaceful about potting a petunia or tending to a tomato. Why? Because you're in control. The pace is your own, with no one telling you what you're doing wrong or giving you a deadline. It's just you and nature. Your garden doesn't need to be extensive. It can be a small terrace, a shared plot of ground, an indoor herb garden in the winter months, or simply several house-plants that you water and prune. A flower-box works well, too — the effects are the same. A few square yards of paradise can bring a large measure of tranquility to your life.

Cook, bake, broil, fry

I'm not a particularly good cook, but I do enjoy the process. I find it involving, creative, and incredibly relaxing. Maybe it's the kitchen or my love of eating, but I find tinkering with a recipe to be very satisfying. Baking is especially comforting because of the wonderful aromas that emanate from the oven. Eating the end result is great fun too. Of course, this may not be the most exciting idea for you if you already spend hours in the kitchen supplying the rest of your family with sustenance. In that case, making reservations may be your idea of a good way to relieve stress.

Go buy the book

Ah, the joys of a riveting pot-boiler, seething romance, or faithful classic. Reading a good book is one of the more pleasurable ways of reducing your stress. Whether you're lying in bed, lying on the beach, or curling up in your favorite chair, reading can slow your pulse, lower your blood pressure (it's been proven), and distract you from the cares and worries around you. Reading can transport you to another world.

But reading provides more than distraction. It can also stimulate your mind and your imagination. It can enrich your experience, giving you new informa-tion, ideas, and interests. It can even have social benefits. Join a book group, and reading puts you in touch with others who share your interests.

Books are relatively inexpensive, portable, and incredibly convenient. You can read on the train, plane, waiting for a salesperson or your dentist, or any other time you find yourself with some moments to spare.

These days, if you're short of time and can't get to the bookstore, you can use your computer to order a book. You can find virtually (no pun intended) any book online and have it sent to you, often at a greatly reduced price. Turn off your TV set. Read a book.

Sometimes it's the little things

When we think of the things that bring us pleasure in life, we usually come up with the big stuff: getting that job promotion, taking that dream vacation, winning the Nobel Prize. You tend to overlook the smaller satisfactions and enjoyments that happen regularly. For me, having that first cup of coffee in the morning, reading the newspaper, and walking by the park on my way to the subway are very enjoyable. In and of themselves, these events are no big deal, but they add up, and together they contribute to a broader positive picture. Here is a list of some simpler pleasures that can add to the quality of *your* life:

- The smell of newly cut grass
- Writing to a friend
- A spring rain
- New snow on a moonlit street
- The smell of the air after a rain
- The fragrance of someone's perfume
- The warmth of the sun
- Rustling leaves in the fall
- The smell of burning wood
- The sound of children laughing
- The crackling of an open fire
- The smell of freshly baked cookies
- Birds chirping in the morning
- Sunrises and sunsets
- Completing a task

Get out of the house

When was the last time you did one of the following?

- Went out for dinner
- Went to a movie
- Went dancing
- Saw a play
- Heard a concert

✔ People-watched

✔ Went to a nightclub

✔ Strolled in the park

✔ Went shopping just for fun

✔ Explored a new neighborhood

✔ Saw a dance performance

✔ Went to a sports event

✔ Had lunch with friends

✔ Went to a museum

✔ Went to an art gallery

Take the time to find joy in the little things and to explore some new avenues — and reduce your stress while you're at it.

Regrouping and Getting a Grip

Vacations are a wonderful way of regrouping and regaining some perspective on your life. That two-week vacation in the mountains or at the ocean can be glorious. The trouble is, by about 3:00 p.m. on the Monday of your return, you're ready for another vacation, which unfortunately, is now 50 weeks away. Rather than depending on that major vacation to provide you with a timeout, you're better off scheduling some minor or mini-vacations that you can scatter throughout the year.

Try building in more frequent, shorter trips and vacations. These can take the form of half-days away, day trips, sleepovers, weekends, and long week-ends. Think of your time away as a safety valve that needs to be opened from time to time. The trick is to evenly distribute these getaways throughout your year, before the pressure builds.

Pre-schedule time away

The most common reason people give for not getting away is not having enough time. They would *love* to get away, but something always comes up. But if you wait for that perfect time, you may wait forever.

Start by assuming that no perfect time will ever arrive for you to get away. But make a commitment to getting away anyway. Rather than reacting to an imposed schedule, create a time-away schedule early on that insures that you actually follow through with your plans. Build in some getaway time, and make it a higher priority in your life. Sit down with your calendar and block out some major time and some smaller time-periods when you plan to be away. Spread out the dates to cover various times of the year so that you don't have to find the time — it's already scheduled.

Build a getaway file

If you're going to escape, you need to know where to escape to. Isn't it amazing how little you know about getaways even a few hours away from home? Begin collecting information about places you can escape to. Start with the wonderful books on local travel at your bookstore. You can find books describing all kinds of trips, places to stay, and things to do and see. Include in your file favorite places friends have told you about, articles from newspapers and magazines, and brochures. Create two categories: one for shorter, one- or two-day trips, and a second for longer trips. The books, articles, and brochures themselves can encourage greater interest and excitement and give you some new ideas about where to go and what to do.

Take a mini-vacation

For an escape to be short, you have to be able to get there in an hour or less. The plan is to get away from your home for a few hours or a full day and return the same day. Even without a car, you can get out of town. If you live in a major city, you can find day excursions via public transit to places and sites away from where you live. You may be amazed at what there is to see and do — all in a day or less.

One of my favorite short trips out of the city is a visit to a state park and forest about an hour away. In the middle of the park is a lake where you can rent canoes and small sailboats by the hour. I usually bring a picnic. It serves as a wonderful day away.

Here are some other ideas you may want to try:

- ✔ **Check into a hotel or spa.** A night or two in a nice hotel can be energizing. Weekend rates are usually a lot cheaper than week nights, too. Pretend you're a tourist. Or, if you'd rather, you never have to leave the hotel at all. If you want to get out of town, a health spa can be just the thing to revitalize your tired juices.

- ✔ **Take a hike.** Hiking in natural surroundings can have a soothing, calming effect. The views can be spectacular. On a hike, you won't find any elevators, fax machines, or beepers. And you may see animals besides pigeons, squirrels, rats, and roaches. Many routes allow you to park your car and follow a trail that brings you back to your starting point.

Organizations such as the Sierra Club (take a look in your telephone book for the number) are not only a good way of obtaining information about hikes, but also put you into contact with other people if you're short of company.

✔ **Take your bike.** Although I am sure you can bike somewhere in your neighborhood, finding a less congested road or a new vista may have greater appeal. After you get out of town, you'll find many bicycle trails and open roads that offer great scenery and little traffic. If you don't already have one, a bicycle rack for your car is a terrific investment.

✔ **Look for water.** If you live near a body of water — and it doesn't have to be large — a day by the water can be a wonderful escape from the congestion and confusion of your usual day-to-day life. Even if the water is too cold for swimming, strolling on a beach or a promenade above the water can be marvelously relaxing. Many people forget about the shore during off-season, but this is a mistake. In the spring, fall, and winter months, the beaches are beautiful and also wonderfully empty.

✔ **Pick some fruit.** One of my family's favorite outings is to visit one of the many farms about an hour or so away from where we live. Depending on the season, we pick apples, blueberries, strawberries, or raspberries. Then we go home and figure out what to do with them. Pies are the simplest project, but we have recently ventured into the world of jams and jellies. Many of the farms offer other activities, such as horseback-riding and the wonderful taste of freshly pressed cider.

✔ **Stay in a country inn.** Small country inns and out-of-the-way bed-and-breakfasts provide the ideal contrast to the bigness and busyness of the city. You are away from the boring motels and hotels that dot the thruway. Meandering through country roads and byways, you can find that unique, one-of-a-kind hideaway that will not only provide you with a bed but also feed you with home-cooked specialties.

On the other hand, if you live in the country, going into the city and taking in the sights, maybe seeing a show, and people-watching can be a refreshing change of pace.

Other places you may consider visiting include the following:

✔ Botanical gardens

✔ Nature conservatories

✔ Mansions and estates open to the public

✔ Public gardens

✔ Country auctions

✔ Vineyards

✔ County fairs

Fifteen more little things to add to the quality of your life

Sometimes it's the little things you do that transform your day from "just okay" to one that leaves you feeling a sense of pleasure and satisfaction. It may not take much. Some simple encounter, exchange, or involvement that momentarily lifts your spirits and takes you away from your immediate worries and concerns. Here are some suggestions of things you can do to add a dollop of pleasure to your day:

- Find an outdoor cafe and just dawdle for a while.
- Banter with a store clerk.
- Spend a couple of hours at the public library.
- Sit on a park bench and watch people go by.
- Explore a neighborhood that is new to you.
- Cover up and go for a walk in the rain.
- Buy yourself some flowers.
- Buy an ice cream or frozen yogurt.
- Read the newspaper and have a cup of coffee at a coffee bar.
- Strike up a conversation with a stranger.
- Listen to a street musician (and give him/her something).
- Go walking or jogging.
- Browse in a flea market.
- Go to a street fair.
- Have a meal at an outdoor restaurant.

There's No Time Like the Present

When you think about it, much of the stress you experience comes either from upsetting yourself about things that have happened in the past or worrying about what will happen in the future. You worry about what you did or didn't say to a difficult boss or irritating coworker, or agonize about that upcoming meeting or deadline. The present, alas, gets lost in the shuffle.

Too bad, because if you can somehow train yourself to live in the present, focusing on what is happening to you right at this moment, your life can be much less stressful. You may also find that your life slows down and time passes less quickly. This notion even has a name — *mindfulness*. The concept has its origins in Eastern philosophy and religion but clearly has relevance today as we go about our stressful lives.

You may think that focusing only on the present moment should be pretty easy. But it's not. Your mind finds it very difficult to stay in the present. Your past and your future are like magnets, pulling your attention away from what you're doing right now. But if you can overcome the distractions and focus on what is happening in the present moment, you would find that you are less distressed about things going on in your life and that you feel more relaxed and less tense.

It really works

Research shows that mindfulness can result in a significant reduction in stress levels. Dr. Jon Kabat-Zinn, at the Center for Mindfulness in Medicine, Health Care, and Society, in Worcester, Massachusetts, followed a group of more than 6,000 patients presenting a variety of stress-related conditions and disorders. He found that when patients followed an eight-week program of mindfulness training, their stress-related symptoms decreased and their conditions improved. Kabat-Zinn also found that following the mindfulness program helped people reduce their anxiety levels and lessen the severity of depressive episodes. More importantly, these changes were maintained on follow-up visits.

Reinventing your daily grind

Almost every activity in your daily life can become mindful. Much of your day is probably filled with automatic, unconscious behavior that gets the job done but leaves you distressed about some part of your life. By turning these tasks and chores into mindful ones, you can have a very different experience.

There is a wonderful section in Jon Kabat-Zinn's *Wherever You Go, There You Are: Mindfulness Meditation in Everyday Life,* in which he describes how he mindfully cleaned his kitchen stove with the help of a Bobby McFerrin tape. The result was fairly poetic, with the rhythms of cleaning and scrubbing mingling with singing, dancing, and a general total involvement in what is normally seen as a mundane, forgettable task. Any activity can be done mindfully. Doing your laundry, washing the dishes, making the beds, vacuuming the rug, opening a can of soup, even eating — all of these can be done more attentively, with greater awareness of every aspect of the task.

You are how you eat

Many a meal has been missed by racing through the motions of eating. For many of us, the process of eating is simply a matter of getting the food from the plate to the stomach. Try eating more mindfully. Here's what you can do:

✔ Pay particular attention to what your food looks like — the colors, the shapes, the textures. Look at each bite before you put it in your mouth.

✔ Take the time to notice the aromas coming from your food.

✔ Eat much more slowly than you normally do.

✔ Savor each bite. Notice the way the food feels in your mouth.

✔ Chew your food slowly and for much longer than you normally do.

✔ Before taking your next bite, pause for a while. Notice the aftertaste from your last bite and anticipate the taste of your next bite.

Try eating with chopsticks once in a while. If you are not in the habit of eating with chopsticks, it will slow down the eating process for you, and get you to pay more attention to what you're eating and how you eat it. If you're looking at a chunk of meat, cut it up to edible bites first. As a bonus, you'll eat less — and weigh less — if you make this a habit. If chopsticks are not your thing, try eating with your other hand. This trick slows you down equally well.

Taking your fun seriously

Ask yourself when was the last time you did something that was pure fun. When was the last time you just played? Or did nothing? Sometimes, doing nothing or having fun is just what the doctor ordered. It may seem sinful and decadent, and you may feel your guilt level rising just thinking about it, but taking time to do *nothing* really is an important part of your stress management program. Playing or goofing off can distract you from your problems. It can give you time to regroup and regain some equilibrium. You return to your world refreshed, and ready to jump back into the fray.

"That's great," you respond, "I've spent half of my life playing around and goofing off, so I must be well on my way to being totally stress-free." Not quite. I'm not talking about the time you spend avoiding, procrastinating, and otherwise neglecting all those things you would be better off doing. The secret of stress-reducing goofing off and play is goofing off or playing at the right time. It means building in play time and time for yourself with nothing to do.

For example, you can see that a project you've been working on for weeks will be finished later that day. That evening you could do any number of things — paint the house, re-upholster chairs, or clean out all the clutter from your basement. What you'd really like to do is watch the ball-game. Do it. And don't feel guilty.

Be careful not to equate playing and games with having fun. If your golf swing or your backhand is causing you much grief, or if your regular weekly bridge game leaves you feeling homicidal, you may not be having lots of fun. Fun, and goofing-off, means thoroughly enjoying yourself. Remember, your stress level should go down, not up.

Part V
The Part of Tens

In this part . . .

1 present the top ten habits of highly effective stress managers, the top ten stresses, and the ten most stressful jobs.

Chapter 16

The Ten Habits of Highly Effective Stress Managers

• •

The following is a short list of the qualities I consider the most important skills and behaviors for reducing stress and creating stress resilience. See how many of these describe you.

1. They know how to relax.

You need to know how to let go of tension, and be able to relax your body and quiet your mind.

2. They eat right and exercise often.

Be careful about what you put into your mouth. Engage in some form of physical activity regularly during the week.

3. They get enough sleep.

Try not to burn the candle at both ends. Get to sleep at an hour that ensures that you can get enough rest.

4. They don't worry about the unimportant stuff.

Know the difference between what is truly important and what is not. Put things into perspective.

5. They don't get angry often.

Avoid losing your temper, but if you do become angry, try to remain in control of your anger so that it doesn't become destructive.

6. They are organized.

Feel a sense of control over your environment. A cluttered and disorganized life leads to a stressed life.

7. They manage their time efficiently.

Know how to use time effectively. Be in control of your schedule.

8. They have and make use of a strong social support system.

Spend time with your family, friends, and acquaintances. Have people in your life who listen to you and care for you.

9. **They live according to their values.**

   Know what is important and what is not. Make sure your goals are significant and worthwhile.

10. **They have a good sense of humor.**

    Laugh at life's hassles and annoyances. Be able to laugh at yourself, and don't take yourself too seriously.

If you're not able to check off all (or any!) of the above, don't worry — you can change old habits and learn new ones. Managing your stress is not a magical process, but rather one that means mastering new behaviors and finding new ways of looking at yourself and your world.

Chapter 17

The Top Ten Stresses

• •

*S*tress, like beauty, is often in the eye of the beholder. What may be incredibly stressful for you, may be a minor irritation for someone else, and perhaps not stressful at all to a third person. It is largely your perception and interpretation of a situation or event that makes that event or situation stressful. However, certain events tend to be viewed as highly stressful by *most* people, *most* of the time.

What follows is a list of ten events, experiences, and circumstances that people feel are the most stressful. Although this list is taken from my own clinical experience, I don't expect you to agree with most of my choices. You may be surprised however, to see events that you normally think of as positive — getting married, having a child — listed as stress-producers. But they are. Major life changes, even good changes, are usually stressful.

The Loss of a Loved One

Surely nothing can be more devastating than the death of someone you very much care about. The loss of your spouse, your child, a close relative, or very good friend can result in an overwhelming amount of stress. And this stress can last for a very long time. This tragedy comes at the top of just about everyone's list.

Major Illness or Injury

No surprise here, either. I'm not talking about a sprained ankle, the flu, or a case of the measles. The kinds of illnesses and injuries that trigger high levels of stress are the ones that are painful, debilitating, and long-lasting. Life-threatening illnesses and injuries are certainly among the most stressful. Chronic diseases and conditions often lead to chronic stress.

The stress may come from physical pain or from the psychological distress of worrying about the course of the illness or injury — and grieving the loss of what once was, as well as the loss of future hopes and dreams. At times, the stress may come from the more mundane — the difficulties of simply trying to get through the day.

Divorce or Separation

That relationships can and do end is hardly news. Divorce and separation are commonplace. Everyone knows someone who has been affected in some way by a failed relationship. The prevalence of marital break-ups (more than 50 percent of marriages in the United States end in divorce) may make you think, "No big deal. It happens all the time." Unless, of course, yours is the relationship that's ending. Then you realize just how stressful this experience can be. Should there be children in the relationship, the distress is far greater.

Studies show that people who suffer through a divorce report far more stress-related signs and symptoms than to do those who stay married. It can take a very long time to regain your emotional equilibrium, and for your stress level to return to something resembling normal.

Serious Financial Difficulties

Money may or may not be the root of all evil; lack of money, however, is almost always the root of much stress. Your particular financial woes may stem from a salary far too low to meet your needs, a once two-income family becoming a one-income family, or a job change or layoff that results in less money coming in. Or, the stress may be triggered by your expenses. A bigger-than-expected mortgage, that wrap-around sound system, unexpected medical bills, or your kid's college tuition may leave you wondering and worrying about how you're going to pay for all of this. And if you think you can't, you're under stress.

Loss of Job

Losing your job often results in the expected stress of not having enough income to maintain your lifestyle. But the stress can be more complicated. Many people tend to tie up their egos with what they do for a living. Being out of work can seem like a failure, which can leave you feeling less worthwhile as a person. Thrown into the package may be the additional anxiety of whether you can find a comparable job that pays enough and quickly enough to meet your financial obligations. Put all of this together and you have a recipe for stress.

Getting Married

Saying "I do" doesn't seem to be such a distressing process. Yet making that important decision and backing it up with a serious commitment can trigger a great deal of upset and anxiety. It's probably the most important decision you will make in your lifetime. Then, there are the plans you have to make. The details can be overwhelming: deciding when to have it, choosing where to have it, finding a caterer, a florist, the band, a limo . . . the list seems endless.

And then you have the family interactions with not only your own delightful relatives, but also this new set of virtual unknowns. Congratulations!

Moving to a New Place

This winner is deceptive. You may think of moving as a relatively low-level stress, worthy of 35th place on this list. Yet moving can be incredibly stressful. First, you have the practical considerations: looking for a new place, hiring movers, finding the time and energy to pack up everything, only to turn around and unpack it all at the other end.

Then there are the psychological questions: Will I like the new house or apartment? What about my old friends? Will I make new friends? If you have children, you often have the added stress of getting them comfortable with a new school and new friends. Oh, and did I mention the mortgage?

A Serious Falling Out with a Close Friend

A fight or serious disagreement with a good friend that ends the relationship can be highly stressful. The process of fighting or arguing is painful enough in itself, but the residual feelings of anger, upset, and loss can be terribly distressing. You have a void in your life — someone who was a companion, confidant, and sounding board is no longer there. All of this can be very painful.

Birth of a Child

This, you would think, is a blessing, not a stress. And I trust it is a joyful, happy time in your life. But this blessing does not come without other concerns. The birth process itself can be painful. The health of the mother and the new baby can be worrisome. With a new child comes added financial responsibilities, and, often, the birth means one less paycheck. You have concerns about how to parent — will you be able to take care of this brand new person when you get him or her home? And if the new arrival has siblings, you may have concerns about their reactions to their new brother or sister. Not to mention the sleep thing. Sleep? What's that?

Retirement

Retirement is probably the most deceptive source of stress. You think of retirement as a time of prolonged rest and relaxation — a chance to do all those things you've wanted to but couldn't. Stress? Where would the stress come from? Well, finding yourself going from a rather involved, well-defined lifestyle to one of endless options can be stressful. You may find that after a honeymoon period, you begin to get a wee bit bored. You may miss friends and coworkers. You may realize that spending so much time with your spouse is a little harder than you imagined. Away from your job title, and the accepted definition of your duties and responsibilities, you may feel less sure of yourself and have some identity issues.

Be careful what you wish for. I hear even the Garden of Eden had some stress.

Chapter 18

The Ten Most Stressful Jobs

· ·

*W*hat are the most stressful jobs? In this chapter, I present three different perspectives on that question and three different lists of the most stressful jobs. Only one job appears on all three lists — see if you know which one.

The Government's List of Stressful Jobs

You think your job is stressful? You may be surprised to find that there are jobs out there that are, in fact, even *more* stressful. The National Institute for Occupational Safety and Health (NIOSH) reports the ten occupational groups that are the most likely victims of severe stress. The list and ranking were determined by studying hospital records and determining which job groups presented the most stress-related complaints and disorders. Here is their list:

You think your job is stressful? You may be surprised to find that some jobs are, in fact, even *more* stressful than yours. Determining from hospital records which particular job groups present the most stress-related complaints and disorders, NIOSH ranks the ten occupational groups most likely to experience stress. They are:

1. Laborers
2. Secretaries
3. Inspectors
4. Clinical-lab technicians
5. Office managers
6. Foremen (Forepersons?)
7. Managers and administrators
8. Waiters and waitresses
9. Machine operators
10. Farm owners

Not the most exciting careers, you say? What happened to those air traffic controllers, police officers, firefighters, Wall Street traders — the candidates you expect to have high stress? Well, one possible explanation is that there weren't a whole lot of air traffic controllers in the hospital sample selected — not to mention Wall Street traders.

The value of this list is that the occupations on it are more typical of what *most* people really do for a living.

The Institutes' List of Stressful Jobs

Here's the list you were expecting. This high-stress top ten was compiled from information supplied by The National Institute on Workers Compensation and the American Institute of Stress:

1. Inner-city high school teachers
2. Police officers
3. Miners
4. Air-traffic controllers
5. Medical interns
6. Stockbrokers
7. Journalists
8. Customer service/complaint department staffers
9. Waitresses (and waiters?)
10. Secretaries

The Scientific List of Stressful Jobs

For some years now, researcher Robert Karasek and his colleagues at the University of Southern California have been looking at job stress from a scientific perspective. They found two major variables that contribute to the stressfulness of a job. The first is something they call *decision latitude* — the control a worker feels over what he or she does. The second dimension is something they term *psychological demand,* or the demands and pressures of the job. A high-stress, or "high-strain," job (to use their term), is one where the demands of the job are high, but the control the worker has is low.

By determining how members of various job categories scored on both of these measures, the researchers came up with what they felt is a more scientific ranking of most stressful and least stressful jobs. They studied only those occupations that include a relatively large percentage of the population. Thus, some of the more obviously stressful jobs may not be represented. Here's what they found:

Higher stress jobs

People in the following professions experience lots of pressure and have little control:

- Waiters and waitresses
- Assembly line workers
- Nurse's aides
- Garment workers
- Keypunchers
- Telephone operators
- Cashiers
- Typesetters

Waiters and waitresses are the ones who show up on all three lists. The next time you're in a restaurant, be nice to your server. He or she has probably had a very stressful day.

Lower stress jobs

Folks in these professions have fewer demands and more control:

- Repair people
- Natural scientists
- Architects
- Programmers
- Linemen
- Civil engineers
- Health technicians
- Librarians
- Professors

I suspect, somehow, that people whose job appears on this lower stress list may not agree that their jobs are so unstressful. The reality is, no job is without stress. So, use the info and tips throughout this book to help manage your stress.

Appendix

Your Script for Your Personal Relaxation Tape

• •

Making your own relaxation tape can be effective in helping you practice and master many of the relaxation techniques and methods described in this book. This particular script combines many of the relaxation skills I present in Chapters 4 and 5. It includes relaxed breathing, progressive muscle relaxation, imagery, and suggestion.

Preparing Your Script

One good way to make a tape is to have a friend with a relaxing voice record the script for you. The sound of your own voice can be a bit disconcerting. ("Is that what I *really* sound like?!")

The following tips are for whoever ends up recording the instructions:

- Speak in a slow, soothing manner.
- Make your tone stronger for the "tensing" instructions, and softer for the relaxation suggestions.
- Pause for 2 or 3 seconds when the script reads *(pause),* unless a longer pause is indicated.
- Do not record the instructions in parentheses. They're for the speaker's use only.

The Script

This particular script is designed to help you relax in a sitting position. You can, of course, modify the instructions slightly so that they apply when you are lying down.

When you want to listen to your tape, find a quiet, relaxing spot where you won't be disturbed by your phone, your beeper, or anything else. Loosen any tight clothing, and, if you like, take off your shoes. Enjoy your relaxation!

Sit down, and get as comfortable as you can . . . Let your feet rest comfortably on the floor . . . let your arms rest effortlessly on your lap or on the arms of your chair . . . Now, close your eyes . . . Take a few seconds to make yourself even more comfortable (10-second pause). Now, take a deep breath, inhaling through your nostrils . . . filling your lungs . . . Hold that breath . . . hold it (5-second pause). Now *slowly* exhale through your slightly parted lips, emptying your lungs (pause). Continue to breathe in an easy, relaxed manner (15-second pause). Imagine that your body is becoming warmer . . . and heavier . . . Notice feelings of relaxation beginning to spread over your entire body (pause).

Start with your hands and arms . . . Clench both fists, squeezing them fairly tightly and flex both your biceps . . . Hold this tension for about ten seconds or so . . . hold it . . . Feel the tension in your hands, your forearms, and your biceps . . . Focus on these sensations . . . Notice what they feel like (pause). Let go now, slowly releasing *all* the tension in your fingers, your hands, and your arms (pause). Extend your fingers . . . and let your arms fall to your lap or to the arms of the chair. Relax for 10 seconds or so, and feel the warmth and heaviness that comes with relaxation (15-second pause). Let go, becoming even more relaxed (10-second pause).

Take another deep breath, and hold it for several seconds (5-second pause).

Slowly exhale through your slightly parted lips, emptying your lungs . . . Breathe comfortably and easily, letting go of any tension, and notice pleasant feelings of relaxation spreading throughout your body (15-second pause).

Now, relax your hands and arms for a second time . . . Clench both fists, squeezing them tightly, and flex your biceps at the same time . . . Hold this tension for 10 seconds or so . . . hold it . . . Feel the tension in your hands, your forearms, and your biceps (pause). Focus on these sensations (pause). Let go slowly, releasing *all* the tension in your fingers, hands, and arms (pause). Extend your fingers . . . let your arms fall to your lap or to the arms of the chair. Relax for about 10 seconds and feel the warmth and heaviness that comes with relaxation (15-second pause). Let go, becoming ever more relaxed. (15-second pause).

Now, relax your legs and feet. Lift both legs and hold them straight out in front of you, pointing your toes . . . Hold this uncomfortable tension for 10 seconds or so (pause). Notice what this tension feels like (10-second pause). Let your legs fall to the floor, letting go of all tension . . . Release any tension in your toes, your legs, and your feet . . . Notice the difference between the uncomfortable feelings of tension and the wonderful feeling of relaxation. . . .

Take another deep breath and hold it for several seconds (5-second pause).

Slowly exhale through your slightly parted lips, emptying your lungs . . . Continue breathing regularly and slowly . . . breathing comfortably and easily . . . letting go of all tension . . . Notice the feeling of relaxation spreading all over your body (15-second pause).

Stretch your legs again. Lift them, and hold them straight out in front of you . . . point your toes away from you . . . Hold this tension for 10 seconds or so (pause). Notice what this tension feels like (10-second pause). Now, let your legs fall to the floor, and let go of all tension . . . Let go of any tension in your toes, and calves, and legs . . . Your body is becoming more relaxed . . . You can feel your body becoming warmer . . . and heavier . . . (15-second pause).

Now relax your stomach and chest . . . Tense your stomach muscles as if you're preparing for someone to punch you there. . . Tighten those muscles . . . Hold that tension . . . hold it (10-second pause). Now, let go of the tension, letting your stomach and chest muscles relax . . . Notice the difference between tension and relaxation . . . Breathe deeply, slowly, and comfortably . . . Let your feeling of relaxation deepen. . . .

Again, tighten your stomach muscles. Hold that tension for 10 seconds (10-second pause) and relax, letting go of all tension. Continue breathing slowly and easily (15-second pause).

Now relax the muscles of your neck, head, and face . . . Scrunch up your shoulders as if you're trying to get them to touch your ears . . . Close your eyes tightly . . . Clench your jaw tightly . . . Hold that tension for about 10 seconds . . . Notice the uncomfortable feelings that come with tension (10-second pause). Now relax, open your eyes . . . Let go of any tension in your neck, your head, your face . . . Relax the muscles of your forehead . . . let your jaw go slack . . . let your shoulders fall back to a comfortable, relaxed position (15-second pause).

Try it again . . . scrunch up your shoulders, close your eyes tightly, clench your teeth . . . and hold that tension for about 10 seconds . . . hold it . . . hold it (5-second pause). And now let go . . . opening your eyes. . . letting your shoulders relax. . . letting your jaw fall slack . . . letting all the muscles in your face, your head, and your shoulders go limp (10-second pause).

Close your eyes (pause). Take a deep breath. Hold that breath (5-second pause) and exhale, letting go of any left over tension in your body . . . Concentrate on your breathing. . . Breathe comfortably and slowly . . . Notice the way your belly moves slowly in and out as you breathe . . . .

Enjoy the feelings of warmth and heaviness spreading all over your body (pause). Your breathing is slow and regular (pause). You can feel the stress leaving your body . . . You feel relaxed all over . . . You feel very good (pause). You are at peace (pause). Continue to breathe slowly, relaxing your body and mind even further . . . even further (20-second pause).

Continue to relax for as long as you like (pause). When you open your eyes you will feel calm . . . relaxed . . . with your mind at peace and your body free of tension. (End.)

Index

• Y •

• Z •

Notes

Notes

Notes

Notes

Notes

Notes

Notes

Notes

Notes

Notes

Notes

Notes

Notes

Notes

Notes

Notes

Notes

FOR DUMMIES®

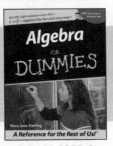
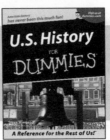

FOR DUMMIES®

Plain-English solutions for everyday challenges

HOME & BUSINESS COMPUTER BASICS

0-7645-0838-5

0-7645-1663-9

0-7645-1548-9

Also available:

Excel 2002 All-in-One Desk Reference For Dummies (0-7645-1794-5)

Office XP 9-in-1 Desk Reference For Dummies (0-7645-0819-9)

PCs All-in-One Desk Reference For Dummies (0-7645-0791-5)

Troubleshooting Your PC For Dummies (0-7645-1669-8)

Upgrading & Fixing PCs For Dummies (0-7645-1665-5)

Windows XP For Dummies (0-7645-0893-8)

Windows XP For Dummies Quick Reference (0-7645-0897-0)

Word 2002 For Dummies (0-7645-0839-3)

INTERNET & DIGITAL MEDIA

0-7645-0894-6

0-7645-1642-6

0-7645-1664-7

Also available:

CD and DVD Recording For Dummies (0-7645-1627-2)

Digital Photography All-in-One Desk Reference For Dummies (0-7645-1800-3)

eBay For Dummies (0-7645-1642-6)

Genealogy Online For Dummies (0-7645-0807-5)

Internet All-in-One Desk Reference For Dummies (0-7645-1659-0)

Internet For Dummies Quick Reference (0-7645-1645-0)

Internet Privacy For Dummies (0-7645-0846-6)

Paint Shop Pro For Dummies (0-7645-2440-2)

Photo Retouching & Restoration For Dummies (0-7645-1662-0)

Photoshop Elements For Dummies (0-7645-1675-2)

Scanners For Dummies (0-7645-0783-4)

Get smart! Visit www.dummies.com

- **Find listings of even more Dummies titles**

- **Browse online articles, excerpts, and how-to's**

- **Sign up for daily or weekly e-mail tips**

- **Check out Dummies fitness videos and other products**

- **Order from our online bookstore**

Available wherever books are sold. Go to www.dummies.com or call 1-877-762-2974 to order direct